LIVING DEEPLY

LIVING DEEPLY

A TRANSFORMATIONAL JOURNEY THROUGH
DEEP PAIN, LOSS AND ABANDONMENT TO
HEALING, SELF-LOVE AND MIRACLES

DEB ACKER

Living Deeply: A Transformational Journey Through Deep Pain, Loss and Abandonment to Healing, Self-Love and Miracles © 2019 by Deb Acker.

Book design: mycustombookcover.com

Printed in the United States of America

First Edition

ISBN: 978-0-578-47590-5 (Paperback)

Disclaimer: Readers are advised to consult their doctors or other health care professionals regarding the treatment of their medical or psychological concerns. Please note that the information in this book is not meant to diagnose, treat, prescribe or substitute consultation with a licensed health care professional.

Table of Contents

I dedicate this book to my family, some of my greatest teachers. I wouldn't be where I am today without your love, leaving and crazy antics. Thank you for being you—ALL OF YOU.

BEGINNING

We must be willing to begin if we want something more.

THIS BOOK IS MY HEART AND SOUL. It's my walk through abandonment, grief and emotional pain to forgiveness, self-love, inner peace, awakening and knowing how to live in joy through it all. It's my adventure from living from the human perspective to living as a soul in a physical body. It's my journey from not knowing or being connected to myself to owning, honoring and speaking my truth at all times. (This is, and I believe, will likely always be, a work in progress!) As I move from fitting in to living life for me from my soul, I share both highs and lows and how these are always serving us, if we let them.

With each story, I uncover something more, meant to help you to think, to reframe and to hopefully motivate you to new action. These stories start out quite intensely, as the first part of my life was just that—intense. As we go, though, and I open to bigger and bigger awarenesses (and some crazy adventures!), the light begins to flood in to take me further within myself and deeper on the journey to more—more richness, more depth and more breadth of life. This craziness I describe is, in part, where the opening occurs, as, after all, we can't expect to grow by doing the same thing over and over.

May you see parts of yourself that you may not be aware of. May you dig deeper than you ever have to look at your life, and its challenges, in a new way. May you know that you are always being guided and that *every single thing* is meant for you, when you let it be.

As we journey together, I'm going to share with you some of my closest and most-defining relationships. Some of these people are still with me in the physical world while others have crossed over. All of them have been crucial in this journey, and I am beyond grateful for the roles they have played, and continue to play, to help me to expand into my biggest vision and version of myself.

As part of this, I would divide this book into three main categories, though stories of each flow throughout. These categories include: Transformation, Magic & Miracles as a Creator Being in a Body and Self-Love, which is one of the first steps to creating the partner love I've been desiring and searching for my whole life. (Hint: It's never been outside of me!)

Guided by this, throughout each chapter, I share my stories, and really, my heart, with you. It's deep. It's raw. It's real. All of it is the work I've done to do whatever it takes to heal myself, to love myself and to never leave myself, my pain or my emotions again. This is the stand I've taken for myself to own my greatness and that every desire I have is meant to be fulfilled, and I am worthy of more than I could ever hope for. *We all are when we choose it.*

As I open to you, I invite you to find your stories within mine. We are all humans on this journey, and many of us forget how similar we truly are, and that we are all just doing the best we can, learning along the way, until we can know, do and be better.

These stories are very close to me, and it is quite vulnerable, even tender at times, for me to share many of them, as some haven't been told to even my closest family members or friends.

But I know a huge part of my journey is to know it's okay to share all pieces of my story, thereby paving the way for others to know this deep truth for themselves. For it's when we can share our truths from the deepest places of ourselves that we can truly connect with each other, and most importantly, when we are set free.

So, what does living deeply mean to me? It's that place where we stop looking for happiness in other things and people and instead we go within. It's that place where we're wiling to go *there*, whether the "there" is painful, scary or unknown. It's the place where we begin living from our soul, which has a very different agenda from our human agenda. Yes, our soul's agenda is rooted in the way we love, the way we forgive and our choice to grow through it all. For it's in this place where we truly find meaning and fulfillment, no matter what's occurring. This is the place where the magic occurs.

As I share with you, it is my intention to give you a fresh perspective and a new way to play in this reality. Life can be hard, and with these hardships, we can shut ourselves down and take life too seriously. It is my intention to show you that light can come from all places, even in the most difficult times, if we choose it, and really, that light is all that there is.

You'll find that in each chapter, I share my story with you, then share the most important lessons and learnings from it. In no way does this encompass all the lessons I learned from each, but it allows me to make these teachings as manageable as possible for you to help you easily cultivate and create permanent change. Sometimes, too, in multiple chapters, I share similar teachings from a slightly different angle. I do so intentionally, to ensure the teaching lands for you and gets fully integrated.

Some of the questions I'm going to ask you are meant to be more reflective and to plant seeds for you to begin thinking in a bigger way, as you move along and grow on your journey. Other questions are ones you're meant to answer and act upon. I'll leave it up to you to decide what this looks like for you and where you want to go, knowing there is no one right way or one right answer to heal any one thing, and the journey is and has always been you identifying and moving toward what feels right for you, modifying as needed. Also know that the more you put into it, the more you will get out of it, and, that if you complete this book having made even one change, you've been successful.

With this, it's important that you take your time reading this. I know in our daily lives we can be conditioned to rush through or force things. Instead, I encourage you to slow down and be as present as possible. Many of these concepts may be new to you, so know it's okay, even expected, if you don't understand everything immediately. You may need to read it several times or pause to process through it before you pick it back up, knowing as you continue on, that my journey will enlighten yours.

Also, if you find yourself triggered at all, while that was not my intention as I was writing this, the nature of everything I do is to help you to identify what's true for you, taking you deeper within yourself, and dare I say, making you a bit uncomfortable. With that said, I encourage you to stay with it and look at this, as our triggers hold valuable insight and growth for us, if we are willing to go within and ask why we are being triggered, holding the thought that if you are willing to stay with it to shift and heal it that you may not have to experience that exact trigger again in this life or the next, if that is part of your beliefs.

Moreover, I use the words "Source," "God" and "Universe" interchangeably, so please feel free to replace this with what feels true for you. This is more about the strong force that's always guiding us as we are moving throughout this world.

Of course, too, there are so many nuances with energy and transformation and there are subconscious parts of ourselves that we can be blind to, so if you're struggling with any of these lessons, teachings or tools and looking for further support at any point in this book or on your journey, please don't hesitate to reach out.

All that said, I invite you to sit back, relax and enjoy the ride! Quite the ride it has been!

May you finish this book transformed from where you started, rooted in a fresh perspective on life (and death) and closer than you've ever been to your soul.

Much love,
Deb

CHAPTER 1

Love comes in all kinds of packages, including mirror reflections.

MY JOURNEY INTO THIS TIME AND SPACE PARADIGM WAS QUITE UNIQUE. I was born into this world as an identical twin, weighing four pounds, five ounces. I came out second, as a breech baby, and while I always joke that I stole all of my sister's food (she was only three pounds when she was born) and then kicked her out of the womb, there has always been some truth to this, as I have always been the dominant one in our relationship. Well, that, and the fact that even my entrance into this world was about making a big entrance and doing it differently, which in this case meant coming out feet first.

Coming into the world as an identical twin was a special way to come in. I believe we choose and create everything, and as I look back, I realize this relationship provided a way to learn separation, oneness and differentiation all in one beautiful package. Separation in the sense that we are all in our own physical body, which inherently creates the illusion of being separate, different and unique, except, in this case, with the big distinction that this person looks like you. Oneness in the sense that we are all one and we are all connected, even if we don't always get along with this person. Then, add differentiating, and really, figuring out who you are, and that while you may look alike, you are quite different, to these dynamics. It can be quite challenging!

Now knowing the adventures that we would take on together, though, I'm glad I had someone to walk side by side with, who could relate to many of my childhood experiences, as she was having her own equally enduring challenges.

These challenges would begin before the age of two with my dad leaving. While I don't have a memory of this in the physical sense, there's a part of me, energetically and emotionally, that remembers it all. I remember the feeling of heartbreak. I remember the feeling that I had done something wrong to make him leave. I remember the feeling that I never wanted to experience this pain again.

It was in this moment that I subconsciously decided that I would do anything in my power to make sure this didn't happen again, and this would be the backdrop from which I would begin living my life.

My childhood was very traditional in some senses and completely untraditional in others. I grew up in a northern suburb of Chicago, under the backdrop that to have a good life, you get married, have children and get a good job. I went to good schools, and we always had food on the table and a roof over our heads. While my sister and I rarely asked for anything, we had everything we needed and more. On the outside, it appeared we had a pretty normal childhood. This was the traditional part of it.

Inside, though, even growing up with an identical twin, I often felt so isolated and alone. I felt misunderstood. I felt scared to be myself. And, yet, with this, I felt like I had to do everything by myself.

Even as a young girl, I was constantly creating a reality where I couldn't rely on anyone else and where it wasn't safe to get close to anyone.

As part of this, the experience of my dad leaving at such a young age left such a big imprint on me. I was always scared of being left, so, over and over, I left myself and tried to become the person that people wanted me to be, so this wouldn't happen again.

This manifested as my saying yes or agreeing even when I didn't, mainly relating through compliments. I remember my mom always asking me how she looked, and for me there was only one right answer: "Pretty." Yes, this was true, but of course there was also the part of me that didn't want to ever hurt her feelings because, deeply wired within me, though my mom would never have done this, was the fear that if I did, I might be abandoned again.

I became a total people pleaser, and I always tried to be "the good girl." Now, don't get me wrong. Being good isn't bad, but in this identity, there was a way I wasn't in my full truth and this truth for me was about being able to express *all* of myself.

Most of the time I didn't know what I was feeling, and there was only one volume in my household, and that volume was set to everything is okay, and if it isn't, we'll pretend it is. This wasn't because there wasn't the space to cry or feel my feelings. It was more that, when I had subconsciously left myself at the age of two, I had completely disconnected from my feelings.

There was a lot of comedy and making jokes in our house, and this was a huge part of how I learned to avoid my feelings. This was coupled with the fact that my mother had to raise two children on her own, which was really hard on her, so she chose to offset it by subconsciously not always living in reality.

In part, this was good, as at an early age, it became deeply embedded in me that anything was possible. In contrast, though, I subconsciously learned to deal with reality by not truly dealing with it. I learned to put a smile on my face no matter what was occurring. I learned to avoid my pain and to live in a fantasy world.

To add to this, my dad's family avoided reality by avoiding confrontation and pretending everything was okay, even when it wasn't. As a result, no matter what, my dad could never do anything wrong. This translated to a subconscious belief that men had all of the answers and to be seen and loved, I should be like them. It also translated to the unconscious conclusion that if he hadn't done something wrong, then I must have done something wrong that made him leave.

All in all, it was the perfect mix for learning what owning my reality and truth *didn't* look like, so I could move into what was really true for me. During that time, though, it was hard. *Really, really hard.*

A huge part of my loneliness, too, was that my mom was constantly working to put food on our table, and when she wasn't working, she was exercising. While I was grateful for her and everything she was doing to make sure I was taken care of, it meant she wasn't home a lot.

With this, I felt like I was in a constant state of anxiety. I would anxiously await her return home with the subconscious fear that something might happen to her and she might not make it home that day. Later, a version of this reality would be realized, when she passed away from cancer when I was just seventeen years old.

This fear would be coupled with an indescribable feeling of emptiness. I now know that this is the same feeling I felt when I would be left in a love relationship, and really, this is because during these formative years, when I perceived that my dad's leaving was my fault and had subsequently left myself, I had never returned, not to mention the fact that I had never been taught how to love myself.

Now, of course, at the time, there was no way to know this or to not leave myself, without recognizing it, so I spent many years living inside myself, mainly in fear or denial, making myself as small as possible. For my mom, this meant that I was doing everything I could to not make her life any harder than it already was, and for my dad, it was to ensure he wouldn't leave me again.

On the flip side, even in doing this, I always felt like I was too much—too emotional with too many needs. Heck, having a need, even a basic one like food, to me, subconsciously meant being too much and that I was in the way.

On the other hand, one of the biggest ways I did feel seen, valued and rewarded, though, was in getting good grades, doing and overachieving. This was highly valued in my family, and especially with my dad's family, this was one of the best ways to be seen and to ensure I wouldn't be left.

This was coupled with being the dominant twin, which meant I was always the leader of the two of us, holding the masculine to my sister's feminine nature and speaking on our behalf. (You may notice throughout this book, that I use "we" and "our" a lot. This is because for my first eighteen years, this was my main identity.)

Growing up this way, while I wasn't conscious of it, I think I was always searching for individuality. I always had to share everything with my sister, and half of the time, people wouldn't get to know our names, and instead would just refer to us as "twins" or "twin," if they wanted to get my individual attention. It was a weird dichotomy. In some ways, I felt more seen being a twin; in some ways, I felt less.

I also felt like I was in a constant competition with her. While this wasn't consciously fostered in my childhood, I was always trying to find ways to feel seen and loved in an environment where I felt like I was constantly fighting for limited time, attention and love.

Deep down, this wiring embedded deep scarcity, competitiveness and an abandonment pattern that would take close to forty years to heal, but looking back, I know that this was a huge part of my journey, and I love this part of my story, and really, this part of me.

Also, it's important to note that I did have a loving childhood, and my parents were doing the best that they could in that moment. It was just hard not being connected to myself and not having the tools I needed to know that this was even missing, and really, to change this.

I also share these pieces with you, not to make anyone wrong, but to give you a better understanding of my wiring and that I lived in a pretty isolating, and at times, extremely painful space. This is so you can know that you're not alone, and, most importantly, that if I can clear the pain and deeply embedded childhood patterns I grew up in, so can you.

LIFE LESSONS AND LEARNINGS

CHILDHOOD PATTERNS

Looking back, I see how much my childhood environment served me. First, I know it can seem like a radical idea to some, but I believe we choose our parents and immediate family members.

When you really look at it, there are two main ways we could end up with our parents: 1) We are just at the mercy of how parents get assigned, which means we are a victim of our reality or 2) We choose our parents, thereby owning the role of powerful creator, which is what I believe us to be. For me, the latter means that I made a conscious choice in setting the stage for the lessons I would learn in this lifetime. I think this is much more powerful. It means I'm actually in control of my reality, so when it comes to my own life, this is what I believe.

Don't get me wrong. At one time, I thought I had gotten the short end of the stick, but the more I studied consciousness and the laws of the Universe, the more I knew this wasn't true. The sense I get is that I looked at a bunch of different possibilities, and decided that this family would be the best way for me to learn the lessons I came here to learn and to clear certain patterns, some of which I have lived with for many lifetimes. These lessons included clearing my abandonment pattern, which I had experienced in many past lives, and moving into living a life of truth—really, a life that was true for me.

As part of this, the awareness that came to me several years ago was that our childhood patterns are really our "inherited truths" (i.e., the truths we took on from our parents and loved ones), and while it may feel like we we're wearing a sheer body suit, our patterns are really like a 300-pound sumo-wrestling costume. As you peel layer by layer of these patterns, though, you'll begin to feel lighter and lighter and the weight you've been carrying around, living from someone else's truth, will begin to lift.

QUESTIONS:

- If you choose to believe that you create your reality and thus chose your parents and family, why do you think you chose them? How are (or were) they here to help you learn, grow and be your true self? (A part of this may be that you had to buy into their reality in order to learn who you really are. For example, if you grew up in a family of doctors, and then decided to become a doctor, this may or may not be your truth, and really, your true desire. This is a simple example, but I invite you to look at how all the ways who they were/ are and who you became as a result served you and how all the identities you took on from them aren't necessarily true for you.)

- How did your childhood, and really the way your parents showed up and treated you, serve you? (On the outside, this may not be obvious, but try to look at it from the perspective of how their actions and behaviors, both good and bad, were helping you to grow into the best, most authentic version of yourself.)

- What patterns, stories and beliefs have you learned from your parents, that you may have adopted unconsciously, that may not actually be fully working for you? (One example of this may be saying yes to everything, because subconsciously you believe you're not a good person if you say no.)

TOOLS:

Write these patterns down, and throughout this book, I'll be giving you tools to work with and shift these. (You don't have to use every tool every time. I encourage you to "feel into" what tool(s) is/are right for each pattern.)

Important to note: While I know our "negative" childhood patterns many times are referred to as our shadow, I choose not to use this term, as I think it makes this part of us seem separate, wrong and even like something we should hide or be ashamed of. I think all parts of us, including the things that we define as "bad," are lovable, and if we're truly working on integrating these parts into our wholeness, it's important that we love them and not label them in a negative way. That being said, if this term works for you, feel free to use it interchangeably anytime I talk about childhood patterns.

SEPARATION AND ONENESS

In addition to the above, growing up with a twin sister was one of my first consciousness lessons. While I didn't know this at the time, looking back, and now knowing the person I was meant to become and the lessons I was meant to teach in this lifetime, if I opted to remember why I chose this, I could see that this was a beautiful way to set this up.

If you're not familiar with the concepts of separation and oneness, here's more on how I define them:

Separation

We are all in our own physical body. Inherently, this creates the illusion of being separate, different and unique. Now, imagine this idea and belief system, but you have someone in your life who looks quite similar to you. This is separation at its best.

Oneness

On the opposite end, there's oneness. This is the idea that we're all the same, and really, that we're all connected. It can take lifetimes for us to learn and remember this, and most importantly, to act from it in our everyday lives. Again, being in separate physical bodies doesn't help with this. Owning this with someone who looks very similar to you, but is constantly pushing your buttons, is a true opportunity to own the oneness that is our truth.

QUESTIONS:

- Where do you use separation to push a loved one, friend, coworker or even a stranger away? Why? Notice if it makes you feel right or superior. What's one way you can see yourself in them and them in you?

- As part of this, where are you not owning that we're all connected? What's the benefit of this? How does this serve you?

TOOLS:

See yourself in another.

Every single day there is an opportunity for us to see ourselves in another. When you're around someone you don't know or like or someone who pushes your buttons, can you find one thing about them that you can relate to or connect with? Maybe it's a similarity, or you can relate to their passion in their belief, even if it's on the opposite end of yours, or maybe it's just compassion for the way they are showing up. With this, it can help to see the little boy or girl that lives within them that learned when he or she was a child that this was the "right" way to do it, or at a minimum, this was the way you get love.

CHAPTER 2

Our relationships are the biggest opportunity we have to learn, love and grow with another—and ourselves.

GROWING UP AS THE DOMINANT TWIN, I BECAME THE NATURAL LEADER OF THE TWO OF US, TAKING RESPONSIBILITY FOR BOTH OF US AND ALWAYS SPEAKING ON "OUR" BEHALF. Taken one step further, at times, I was the one put in charge of the two of us, which when you think of it, is funny and ridiculous, as we are technically the same age.

I remember one such time when we were at my grandma's house. We were probably eleven or twelve years old, and my dad had to step out for a few minutes. He put me in charge. While I don't think my sister appreciated this very much, I felt a sense of pride and importance with this responsibility.

Also, as I look back on our childhood, it didn't appear that we had separate personalities. Knowing what I know now, she had taken on my personality, mostly because I was the one doing all of the talking and her submissiveness was one "natural" piece of her. Later, when she went to college, she would separate from this, but up until that point, the only things that separated us were our grades (I was always more motivated, which is one of the reasons why I think my parents always saw me as more responsible) and our sizes. (I was always bigger than her, which I'm sure was another subconscious reason why I "appeared" older.)

Now knowing what I know, while we appear to be the same age in this lifetime, the energy reads that I am actually an older soul, so it does make sense that my parents would subconsciously view me that way. And, it was all perfect, as part of my sister's lessons in this lifetime include her choosing and taking responsibility for herself. (This is likely one of the reasons why she chose me.)

So, as my sister and I went off to college, we chose different schools in the same state. I chose The University of Florida, and she chose Florida State University. As part of this, she finally started to differentiate from me. This differentiation came in the form of big partying for her. Initially, when we got to school, our family didn't hear from her for a good month or six weeks. We were worried, but my sister was finding herself and coming out of the identity of being the "good girl," which was really my identity and wasn't hers to begin with.

As this happened, we moved farther and farther away from each other emotionally, with my mom's death being the one thing that kept us connected. This was hard for me, as I subconsciously wanted her to stay the same. I was resisting her changing. *Couldn't she just continue to be like me?*

With my mom's passing, while being in my first year of college was fun, it was difficult at the same time. I was going through my own journey of loss, and I didn't have any directions for it. My sister was too.

When we did see each other, she would mainly come up to see me, mostly because Tallahassee was harder to get around and I had more room for her to stay.

This initial separation we experienced at college continued

post-college, as we stopped seeing ourselves in each other. My sister was still partying and marching to the beat of her own drum, and I was busy standing in my success, and some superiority, acting like she was wrong in her choices. My sister easily fell in line with this, as she was so used to my taking responsibility for her. She naturally played the victim in our relationship. Either way, it was not a strong recipe for love.

Of course, there would be bouts of love, but the love we felt would be overshadowed by knockdown, drag-out fights.

Deep down we knew we loved each other, and each of us still held our childhood, and really, the death of our mom, in our hearts, but this wasn't enough for us to stop fighting, even with my mom's voice in my head, beckoning, *"You're all each other has. Remember that."* My mom had said this to us our entire lives, almost like she knew she needed to prepare us for a time when she wouldn't be there to remind us of this.

It would take nearly two decades for us to start to come back to each other, and it would be a slow and imperfect process. For my part, I started to realize I had *chosen* to partner with her in this lifetime. I started to realize that she was my biggest test in love. This included loving her, and really, as she was just a reflection of me, loving myself. I started to realize that if I couldn't find the place in me that could love her unconditionally in this lifetime, then no matter how much I studied, learned or even taught this to others, I would have failed miserably.

So I made a new choice.

I started to see the little girl within her that was struggling and just doing the best she could, until she could know, do and be better. I started to see her innocence. Really, I started to see her heart. Some times were harder than others, as my need to be right would take over. At other times, I could see her as the lovable girl I grew up with.

It was one of our recent experiences where we started to get along again. We were at my cousin's bar mitzvah, and we stayed together. For the first time in a long time, we really didn't fight. The one time we almost started to fight, it was like we both remembered that this vicious cycle didn't get us anywhere, and we just stopped. She had more respect for my boundaries and requests, and I had more respect for the person who she is, which isn't always mindful, but isn't intentionally trying to hurt me.

While, after this, we still weren't talking as much as I'd like, and when we did, we could still fall into our old patterns of behavior, we were *finally* finding respect and love for each other. I could feel my mom smiling from heaven.

LIFE LESSONS AND LEARNINGS

DIFFICULT RELATIONSHIPS AND VICIOUS CYCLES

I regret not always getting along with my sister. While I know that everything that happened served me (and her) perfectly, it hurts that it took us close to two decades to find a way to connect with each other in a real and easy way. We lost a lot of valuable time, time that we could have enjoyed together and used to have gotten closer.

As part of this, so many times, when we were in our twenties, we would fall into vicious cycles. What are these? These are when you keep falling into old patterns of behavior. One person says one thing that triggers a common response from the other, and before you know it, you're in a screaming match.

Questions:

- Are there any relationships in your life that you struggle with, or maybe are even estranged from? Will you have any regrets if you don't make up with this person and let your walls, defenses and maybe even your righteousness go?

- Which of your relationships, if any, fall into vicious cycles? Do you want to change this?

Tools:

I see it all the time. Families that are broken apart, many times by something that's not even important or significant, and they don't talk for ten or twenty years, and sometimes even a lifetime. If this is you, I encourage you to take a long, hard look at this. What's truly important to you? Is being right or holding a grudge more important than having a relationship with this person? Will you have regrets later in life for letting this grudge, whether big or small, dictate the course of your relationship? Only you can determine that. Either way, it's important to make a decision you won't feel remorseful about later.

If this decision is to *choose* to have a relationship with this person, reach out to them and let them know your intention and that having a relationship with them is important to you. Then, take small steps towards showing them love and reconnecting with them. While they may or may not be open to it, I think the biggest piece is choosing it, many times, over and over, until things shift or you feel like nothing is ever going to change, no matter what you do, and it doesn't feel like you'll hold any regrets if you let it go. (If this second part never comes, continue reaching out to them, even if it's just with small gestures like remembering them on their birthday and the holidays.

When it comes down to it, we are all love, and, while nothing is guaranteed, the love you show toward them can melt the boundary they learned that keeps them from reaching back. If nothing else, at least you are putting love out into the world, which is always helpful.)

With this, if you find yourself in a vicious cycle, before it goes too far, stop, take some deep breaths and even walk away, if you need to. Then, once you've cooled off, return to the conversation, with the intention of being kind to them and working out a resolution, or at a minimum, not fighting with them.

Self-Love

Many times, when my sister and I would get together and then get in a fight, many of the things I didn't like about her were also in me. At the time, I didn't have the consciousness to realize the reflection she was providing or to look at why this was in my field, including where it lived in me. Instead, I pointed fingers and didn't really take ownership of my role in these dynamics, and even at times thought I wasn't doing anything wrong, or really, anything to cause this. The only thing that this ended up doing, though, was to push her further away and to create further separation between the two of us and more pain within myself. My journey to self-love hasn't been an easy one, and this was one of the primary relationships that helped me to really know how to love all parts of myself.

Questions:

- What parts of yourself don't you love? Where do you see those reflected in your relationships and the people around you, especially your family relationships? What do you do about it when you notice this? (A good way to identify these is to look at the things that frustrate you in all of your relationships and then, being *extremely* honest with yourself, ask yourself what version of their behavior lives in you. Sometimes it's the exact same thing, while other times, it's the same vibration, but the opposite thing. One example of this is, say you have a lot of relationship dynamics with people who want their way and end up pushing you around. You may also do this in your relationships or, on the opposite end, you may always get pushed around. This is the same vibration, feeling or energy, just on opposite ends of the spectrum.)

- Also, what does love equal for you? (For instance, while it's counterintuitive, if you grew up in a household where there was a lot of fighting, love may subconsciously equal fighting for you. With this, you may have chosen a partner/friends that reflect this.)

- When you see something in another that you don't like, can you ask where that lives in you?

- How can you use your difficult relationships to love yourself more?

Tools:

Everything is a chance for us to love ourselves more—*every single thing*. When you have a difficult experience with a family member, friend, loved one or stranger, especially when you don't like something that person has said, done or just how they are and/or when you feel triggered, it's important to take note of where that lives within you. From there, in addition to shifting it, which I share how to do throughout this book, it's important to start to love that within yourself to resonate it back into wholeness, so that your inner child is not ruling your present-day reality.

Here's how:

1. Begin to talk with the little boy or girl who lives within you. If you're new to this work, at first, it may be hard to see or connect with them, as you've likely let them down and broken their trust. But, I encourage you to stay with it, and really, *them,* letting them know, if this is true for you, that you're not going anywhere and you want to have a relationship with them. You'll find that soon enough you'll start to be able to connect with them.

2. Then, from there, ask the little boy or girl who lives within you what they don't like about the quality you identified. Why don't they like it? Maybe someone from their childhood hurt them because of it or maybe they were shamed for having that trait. On the opposite end, maybe that's how they were subconsciously taught to love. (For me, an example of this in my family was that criticism equaled love. As I've understood that this was one of the patterns that I had learned in my childhood, though, I've been able to let go of how this plays out in my everyday reality.) Whatever it is, it's important to take note and give your little one that voice to share this. As you're doing this, I recommend saying this out loud, in the first person, from their voice, staying connected to, and really feeling, what you're saying. For example, from the voice of your inner child, this might sound like, "When they do whatever they want without considering me, I don't feel seen." With this, as much as possible, allow yourself to feel the pain of not being seen.

3. Then, from there, open your heart to have compassion for the person you're feeling challenged with and also have compassion for you. Can you see where they learned what

they learned and where you learned your own version of this? Can you see the little child that lives within both you and them who's just doing the best that they can? (Also, important to note: Sometimes, if someone's being a victim, for instance, one reflection can be that you're also being a victim, but another reflection of this can be that you're the victimizer—i.e., it's not always true that it's always a direct reflection.)

4. From there, bring this quality back into your heart. You're just human, and you are enough, just as you are. Feel the love you have for it, for you and if possible, for the other person, and see the little child that lives within you coming back into your body and integrating as one.

Important to note: While yoga, meditation, mindfulness and energy and breath work can create an opening and are all very helpful to living a full, calm and present life, working with your inner child is a very important key to wholeness, and many times, the thing that's missing if you've tried everything and yet are still struggling. Also, there are many nuances to working with your inner child, so if you find yourself struggling with this, please don't hesitate to reach out. (I talk more about this in Chapter 10, but if you typically feel like you need to do everything yourself, all the more reason to reach out for support.)

CHAPTER 3

Kindness is always the right choice—always.

Growing up, my relationship with my dad was never great. With him leaving before I was two, from a young age I was subconsciously conditioned to think my mom was right, and even an angel, which she wasn't, though my innocent eyes could only see the perfection of the parent who was my primary support system. Inherently with this, my dad was wrong.

I spent a huge part of my childhood not wanting to be around him and subconsciously withholding from him when I was around him. I just wanted to be as small as possible when I was in his presence. Looking back, I think I was subconsciously feeling like if I didn't exist, then he couldn't have left me and the pain wouldn't be so great.

When he would come to pick us up, I would barely hug him. In stark contrast, when we would leave or return home, we would tackle my mom with hugs and kisses. He saw it. I saw it. And, there was no denying the difference.

Even at that young age, I had taken in the pain that he had caused my mom, albeit subconsciously, so I didn't want to be close to him. I now know that this was a cover-up for the pain he had caused me. Of course, as a kid, I wasn't fully conscious of why I didn't want to be near him; I just knew I didn't.

It didn't help that I had heard stories from my mom's mom, whom my father "lovingly" called "Battle-axe," that my mom had to have a conversation with my dad's father to "convince" him to be in our lives. All in all, it was a recipe for disaster.

I remember one fight my mom's mom had with my dad. I was only three at the time, and they were fighting and screaming. My grandma was so mad at my father for leaving my mom, and my dad, while I'm sure he did what he thought was best at the time, like he had so many times before and he would many times after, had not truly factored in his impact on his family. *He had not factored his impact on me.*

We were still in our apartment with the dark brown carpeting on Sheridan Road, and I had to cover my ears, it was so loud. It was scary seeing two people that were supposed to be responsible for me and my well-being, and really two people that were supposed to love me, fighting like that. *I wanted it to stop*, and while I didn't realize it until decades later, I thought the fight was my fault. I would spend many more years, trying to make myself invisible and trying not to be "in the way," blaming myself anytime my dad didn't show up for me.

And, this would not be the first or last time that I would want to disappear.

Over the years, we would see my dad once a week. Many times, he would take us over to his mom and dad's house and we would play gin rummy with my grandparents.

Sometimes, my dad would take us out with the girl he was dating at the time. Many times, I enjoyed these times the most, mainly because we would do something fun, and, as harsh as it sounds, it helped having someone to lessen the burden of spending time with him. You see, I felt like he didn't really want to be there, and truth be told, many times, neither did I.

LIFE LESSONS AND LEARNINGS

KINDNESS

My biggest lesson with my dad at this time, though I wouldn't realize it until decades later, was around kindness. Looking back, I wish I could have been kinder and more compassionate toward him. I wish I hadn't made him wrong all the time. I wish I hadn't held a grudge around the choice he had made. While, of course, I was only a child, I think we get so conditioned to holding onto someone's actions when they hurt us, never letting them off of the hook, that we can miss the joy that's right in front of us.

QUESTIONS:

- Where have you held onto a grudge, maybe longer than you should have?

- Where have you made someone wrong to make yourself feel better? Where has this been at the expense of your relationship with this person? Has it really made you feel better?

TOOLS:

We don't know until we know, but now that I know, I always try to choose kindness and compassion.

How do you do this?

1. See the little child that lives within the person you're struggling with that learned what they learned and is just doing the best they can, until they know better.

2. Open your heart. To do this, simply relax your body, including relaxing into your heart space.

3. Send them love and light by seeing light and the feeling of love filling their body.

4. Choose it over and over, whether you're in their presence or just talking (or not talking) to them, especially when you are feeling angry with them, you find yourself wanting to make them wrong for their choices or something they did in the past that hurt you comes up.

CHAPTER 4

Our grandparents are the unopened treasures of our time with stories of gold.

It was in this backdrop that I became solely reliant on my mom. She could never do anything wrong, and she always wanted the best for my sister and me. This included the fact that she would have done anything for the two of us.

Now, granted, this meant a boundaryless household, where I began to associate boundaries, people saying no and being disciplined, which not so coincidentally my dad would try to do, as the opposite of love.

But, in this space with my mom, especially being around her, this was the only place I felt truly safe, loved and cared for.

I remember being around eight years old, standing by our big front window, eagerly waiting for her to come home. When her car would pull up, I would feel my whole body relax, with the subconscious feeling that I was okay, that my time with my mom, and with this, my being, had been preserved for another day.

When she wasn't home, her parents, my grandparents, would take care of us.

Given that my mom worked a lot, growing up my grandparents were constant fixtures in my life. My grandpa Dan, my mother's father, was always quite the character. Observing him growing up, he was one of the strongest male figures in my childhood, which may or may not have been good, as he was a goof.

My best memories of him are of his crazy stories; one never knew whether they were true or not. He would share with us everything from having to wear a dress as a little boy, because he was the youngest of eight children, with several girls before him, to the story about how two women had fought over him, and my grandma lost. He even invented an imaginary granddaughter, Matilda, when my sister and I were misbehaving. I also remember anytime he had to go to the bathroom in a public place, he said he had to go see a man about a dog.

As you can imagine, growing up with him as a primary influence, things were always interesting and fun. I inherited a lot of his personality, humor and quick wit. My grandma Roz, his wife, echoed this sentiment.

In stark contrast, Grandma Roz couldn't have been more on the opposite end of the spectrum. She was always very serious; she didn't know how to fully let go and have fun. Part of this was because she had not had an easy life. The other part was her drive to excel in school, so much so that she finished high school a year or two early. I would imagine, though, that in doing so, she didn't have too many friends or felt like she fit in and always felt like an outsider.

Either way, my grandparents definitely pushed each others' buttons and were quite the comedy team, I mean, pair.

I remember the two of them coming over to my house often when I was young, when my mother was out working or exercising. My grandpa would be in the den, watching TV (he loved wrestling, *Columbo* and *Perry Mason*), while she would be cooking one of her outrageously amazing meals, which included steak, lamb chops, salmon or chicken, always to perfection.

When we would go on a vacation, Grandma Roz would pack our suitcases for us, using tissue paper between each garment. We would arrive at our destination without a single wrinkle in our clothes, which I'm guessing is a skill she picked up from her father, an expert tailor. This skill was only one of the ways she learned to show love to the people around her. Either way, it was impressive and is a skill I haven't been able to replicate since, nor do I try.

Then, of course, there was her OCD. She washed her hands—a lot. I remember my mother saying to her, "You're going to make my kids neurotic." She succeeded (a little bit) with me, as I sought to have control in an environment where I had little.

My grandpa Dan passed away when I was 16, and a little over six months later, my mom passed away too. It was a hard year for my grandma, but after years of holding it all together, and really, holding it all in, she finally opened. Death has a way of doing that to you.

After I graduated college, I moved in with her for a year. It was a difficult year for both of us. She wanted more time with me, and I was finding my way as a post-grad moving into adulthood.

When I was in my late twenties, she put me in charge of her affairs. This time of packing up her house, which had nearly 30 years, if not more, of her stuff, mixed with finding the next home for her, which needed to be a nursing home that accepted public aid, yet wasn't a complete dump, was one of the most challenging of my life. Instead of going out with my friends or on dates, I spent much of my time figuring out how to file for public aid, which is an absolute nightmare, and shopping for a nursing home. I was glad to do it, though, and thankfully, I was able to find a good home that would take care of her.

It wasn't long after this that she began to soften. For years she'd had a chip on her shoulder about all the things she felt people owed her, and really, all the regrets she had for desires unpursued.

Toward the end of her life, though, she began to let go of past hurts and be grateful for everything she had. As we would sit, her eating her hot dog with all of the fixings that I would break into pieces to make chewable for her, me with my cheeseburger, filled with lettuce, tomato, mayo and ketchup, she would reminisce about her life. It would be a mix of good times and regrets, sometimes clear and sometimes not so clear. Many times, she would repeat the same stories or ask the same questions over and over. It would take years, long after she passed, for me to learn patience around this. Through these stories, though, I learned of my grandma as a person with dreams, successes and hurts.

When she was a little girl, she had won a car at the Chicago World's Fair. She had lost her brother before the age of 20 and her mom not too long after. There was another man before my grandpa whom she had wanted to marry. I learned of all of these things and more in our time together.

When I was 32, she passed away when I was on a business trip. I had known it was coming and had intended to see her one last time when I got back to say goodbye and give her permission to pass. (She always looked to others for guidance on what to do with everything from what to eat to where to go.) So, instead, one of the nurses gave her permission. She was 92 years old.

LIFE LESSONS AND LEARNINGS

HAVING BOUNDARIES OR A LACK THEREOF

Growing up with my mom, there was a lot of enmeshment, which is where there are very blurred lines and poor boundaries and you lose yourself. With this, she almost never disciplined us. I think, in part, this was because she knew we had already had a rough child-hood and didn't want to make it any harder for us. Growing up in this environment, though, I subconsciously took on that love meant having no boundaries, never being disciplined or having a difference of opinion, and with this, never saying no.

It took decades to shift this, and at times, I'm still not fully comfortable with boundaries.

QUESTIONS:

- Did you experience enmeshment in your childhood? How did it feel growing up in this kind of household and how has growing up in this environment impacted you, and even served you?

- As part of this, did you have boundaries growing up? Why or why not?

- What do boundaries, being disciplined, having a difference of opinion and saying no mean to you? (For example, for me, for a long time, having no boundaries equaled feeling loved.)

- Are you comfortable with having boundaries? If not, why not?

TOOLS:

If you are uncomfortable having boundaries and saying no, and grew up in an enmeshed household and you're desiring to change this, it's important to tune in when you're saying yes to something you don't want to be and get a sense of why this is. Maybe it's because you're scared they will leave you. Maybe it's because you've equated enmeshment and/or a lack of boundaries with being loved. Whatever it is, start tuning into this, and then, take small steps to start to say no when it's true for you. This can be anything from saying no to getting together with someone to leaving earlier than you initially planned because you're feeling tired or it's not feeling right, to not *always* doing something for someone just because you've done it in the past.

DON'T TAKE LIFE TOO SERIOUSLY

When it came to my grandpa Dan, the thing about him that stuck with me the most, to this day, was his approach to life. He never took anything too seriously. So many times, we make life too serious, like we're going to get an award if we work harder or achieve more. The truth is, though, that the Universe wants us to have fun, and you don't win any award by having a hard life or being so serious. For me, this has been a very helpful tool to take into my everyday world.

QUESTIONS:

- Where do you take your life too seriously? Do you work too hard? Is your only persona your professional one (i.e., do you take your professional persona into your personal life or do you allow yourself to let go)? If you don't allow yourself to have a lot of fun, where can you add more play into your life?

- As part of this, are you scared to let go? If so, where in your life does this apply? Why?

TOOLS:

I remember not too long ago, I was in a session, and I got guided to tell a client to "let her girls out." This was a channeled message, but the truth is, sometimes we are just too serious and too focused. Many times, it's when we can let go and play that the best ideas come and the energy can flow to create miracles. If this describes you, make a conscious choice every week (or day!) to do something fun for yourself. This can include working out, taking walks, going to dinner with a friend or seeing a movie.

Using Humor to Mask Feelings

On the flip side, though, especially watching my grandpa Dan, I learned to mask my feelings with humor. I spent most of my life not at all connected to what I was feeling, and comedy was just one more layer to subconsciously protect me from the truth of my life, which was pretty painful at times.

Questions:

- Are there any places in your life where you mask your feelings? Do you use comedy or another tool to block yourself from this? If so, what do you use to mask your feelings? Why do you do this? What are you scared of?

Tools:

If you do use humor to mask your feelings, it's important to start noticing when you're doing this. Many times, for me, I was using humor to mask fear—fear of putting myself out there, fear of new situations and fear of not being good enough in whatever it was I was doing.

Once you start to notice this, choose if you want to make a new decision or not. Of course, humor is always an option, or you can make the choice to be vulnerable and express your fear. There's a time and place for both, and the most important piece of this is to notice what you're doing and why you're doing it, and then make a conscious choice either way.

HAVING PATIENCE AND COMPASSION

With my grandma Roz, the biggest things I learned from her were patience and compassion. Patience for when she would get angry, and in her later years, forget and ask about the same thing over and over; compassion for the woman who had had a hard life with some regrets and, really, the moments when I would receive the impact of those choices.

I regret that I didn't know then what I know now, and really, that I didn't have the patience and compassion then that I have now. But, many times, you go through difficult moments and show up in ways you're not always proud of so you can do better the next time around. I can definitely say, with my dad's parents, I was able to do better.

QUESTIONS:

- In what relationships have you struggled with patience and compassion? Where can you add (more) patience and compassion in your life and relationships?

TOOLS:

When you find yourself struggling with being patient and compassionate, especially in your relationships, it's important to slow down. Take some deep breaths and refocus on what's important to you. Is this how you want to show up in this relationship? If not, choose again. If, at some point, you find yourself feeling impatient or not as compassionate as you'd like to be, don't beat up on yourself. Simply take a few breaths and start again.

CHAPTER 5

At any moment in time, life can change in a second. It's in these moments when you have a choice—to let it propel you forward or take you down.

I REMEMBER IT LIKE IT WAS YESTERDAY. My mom had decided it was best to tell me on a walk. It was mid-June, and relatively warm, though it wasn't sunny that day and I was about to find out the symbolism behind this.

This walk began like any other walk, except for the fact that my sister wasn't with us. Usually, when we did anything, including going on a walk, it was the three of us. But that day it was only my mom and me.

We were on Pratt Avenue, the street I grew up on. It's kind of a main street through the town of Lincolnwood, Illinois. While you didn't find many people walking on it, you did find a fair amount of cars. In days past, when my sister and I would walk home from school, we'd hear cat calls out the pickup windows of men driving home from a hard day's labor.

Today, though, in contrast, it was quite quiet, as we walked down the cement sidewalks, houses to our left, cars to our right.

I don't remember a lot about that day, but for some reason, I can picture what my mom was wearing like it was yesterday—a sleeveless red-and-white-striped sweater with red shorts, at least that's what she's wearing in my mind.

I'm not sure at what point on our walk she said it, and if she led up to it or just blurted it out, but at some point, the life-changing words, "I have cancer," came out.

I remember being scared in that moment, maybe even frozen in my tracks. I know my body crawled back inside itself, and my heart sank, though I'm not sure I was connected to any of that to show it.

Despite my shock in that moment, the one thing I do remember is what she said next. They were words she would echo several times in the next few years. "But I'm going to be there for you. I'm going to be there for your graduation. I'm going to be there to see you get married. I'm going to be there for you."

While I wouldn't realize this until decades later, inherently in those words was the implication that she might not be there. In that initial moment, a deep part of me knew this. I think she knew it too. Neither of us was ready to accept it yet, though.

Over the course of those next few years, many things would happen and there would be many challenges. My friend's brother would be killed in a drunk driving crash. I can still feel the impact of that news. While I didn't know him well, the thought that something, and really someone that I loved so much, could be taken from me like this, in an instant, petrified me.

I started sleeping more, too. I remember many times, on the weekends, sleeping until 1 or 2 in the afternoon, which wasn't normal, and I remember this huge heaviness that took over my body. I now know I was depressed, though I don't think this was ever defined for me at the time, and of course, I was too young to recognize what this was for myself.

It was also around this time that I became anorexic. My anorexia actually started even before my mom had been fully diagnosed, some time around when she first started to have pain.

I remember my mom being in bed, unable to eat for over a month. She had been in and out of doctors' offices, but no one knew what was wrong with her.

So, unconsciously, I chose to stop eating too, and so did my sister. I was scared. Seeing my mom, the one person I knew I could count on, unravel, unraveled me.

As I'm sure it does for many people, my anorexia started out quite innocently. I remember one day, during my freshman year of high school, sitting outside on the grass with a group of friends, *sharing* a ham and Lorraine Swiss cheese sandwich with my twin sister. This was only the beginning.

By the time I was in my sophomore year, my anorexia was full blown. Initially, people, especially my family, would compliment the two of us on losing weight. But when we lost our periods—that's when they realized something was terribly wrong. Of course, at that age, we didn't realize the consequences of our actions or the impact of eating only 700 calories a day. For me, I equated being thin with being pretty. Subconsciously, deep down, though, it was to have control, as I felt myself losing the one person I loved more than anything.

After being diagnosed with anorexia, my sister and I both began seeing a nutritionist and therapist together. Initially, the therapy was especially helpful. For me, looking back, I realize that this consistency was comforting, something I could rely on in the chaos. It was during this time that our relationship with our therapist took on a whole different form. I remember when we'd go to see her, many times we would order a pizza. While this may not have been a great tactic for making emotional progress in our sessions, it did help with our eating disorder. For me, it was one of the bright spots in a dark time.

Over the next year, my mom would take herself back and forth to chemo. She didn't lose her hair, though I remember her often coming home exhausted. There were many nights when she fell asleep in front of the TV. I felt powerless to change anything or to help. I also felt like a burden. It was during this time that, again, I subconsciously shut down my needs and tried to make myself as small as possible, as I thought this would make it easier for my mom to focus on getting better. I remember feeling like it didn't feel right to want anything. After all, I was healthy, and my mom wasn't.

Things seemed to go into a normal routine. I was going to school and mainly working out after school. Working out was a way for me to bond with my mom. It was a way for me to get time with her, and it was a way to be like her. My whole life I had emulated her. This was how I got love, and really, subconsciously, how I reassured myself I wouldn't be abandoned, though my mom would never have dreamed of leaving me.

I remember during those times, too, feeling like an adult. Feeling this way when you're a teenage girl is very gratifying; I felt so important, and in many ways, like I was living a secret life—normal teenager by day, adult by night.

I remember, too, one day being over at my dad's house. He asked my sister and me where we wanted to live when my mom passed away. While he knew she had terminal cancer, in an effort to protect us, my mom had only told us that she had cancer, not that it was terminal. When he asked this, we burst into tears. *She wasn't going to die.*

It was at the beginning of our junior year, nearly one and a half years after her first diagnosis, when my mom was diagnosed as cancer-free. While I should have been happy (and I was), I remember the gut feeling I had at hearing the news. *That's not true. Something isn't right here.*

I can't tell you how I knew it. I just knew she wasn't healed. Of course, my teenage self didn't pay attention to the voice coming through, let alone distinguish if it was my intuition or fear talking. Later I would look back and realize that even as a teenager my intuition was strong.

LIFE LESSONS AND LEARNINGS

DISCONNECTING FROM MYSELF AND MY EMOTIONS

So much of what happened during this time, everything from my anorexia to pretending I didn't have needs or that everything was going to be okay, involved my disconnecting from and leaving myself. Even now as I write this, I feel my whole body contracting, but this was the only way for me to survive the pain and hardship that was going on with my mom.

Looking back, I was living in a very disconnected household. It's not that feelings were unwelcome. My mom definitely gave us space for our emotions. I just don't think she was very connected to her own, at least not enough to know what she was truly feeling, let alone be able to express it or help guide me in connecting to or expressing myself. Instead, the way that I learned how to cope was to mask everything, put on a happy face and pretend it was okay, even when it wasn't. I spent most of my childhood, including my teenage years, like this, in a high state of denial.

QUESTIONS:

- Where have you disconnected from yourself and your emotions?

- How was this modeled when you were growing up?

- How does disconnecting from yourself and your emotions serve you?

TOOLS:

To start to reconnect to yourself and your emotions, regularly ask yourself:

1. What do I want right now?

2. What am I feeling right now?

3. What's going on for me right now? Am I disconnecting because there's something I'm scared of or something that I'm uncomfortable with? If so, what is it?

IDENTIFYING AND LISTENING TO YOUR INTUITION

It's oftentimes the words we don't say, not the words we say, that carry the most weight. What I realized so many years later was that a piece of me knew my mom wasn't telling me the full story when she initially told me she had cancer, and a piece of me knew that something wasn't right when the doctor said she was healthy. Of course, neither was intentionally lying, but even at that age, I could tell when something was off. At the time, though, I wasn't tuned in enough to myself or to my own knowing to notice either of these. (By the way, I believe we all have this inner ability to know when something is off, but many of us aren't tuned into it or have shut it down to protect ourselves.)

QUESTIONS:

• How does your intuition come through? (I explain a bit about this in the Tools section below, and for more information, you can head to: bit.ly/intuitionvideo, a video I did for my Living in Your Truth Facebook Community on how our intuition comes through.)

- Is there something you know about a situation that you're not paying attention to? Maybe you have a gut feeling about something or you know someone isn't telling the full truth. Whatever it is, start to practice paying attention to it and reading between the lines.

TOOLS:

It's important to begin to listen to your intuition. Our intuition comes in many forms including seeing (clairvoyance), knowing (claircognizance), feeling (clairsentience) hearing (clairaudience) and smell (clairsalience/clairolfaction). Most of us have one or two dominant forms.

When I started this journey, my most dominant "clairs" were feeling and knowing. Because I wasn't tuned in to what this looked like, though, which included gut feelings and just knowing certain things, yet not knowing how I knew them, I didn't pay attention to these for a long time. I also remember, in the early days of learning how to work with these tools, having a session with a coach of mine who connected to my Guides and Angels. During that session, many of the things she was saying gave me chills. It was then that I started to realize that this was one of my body's ways of sharing that something was part of my soul truth, which helped me to feel more guided in this world as well as to tune into this during my sessions with my clients to help them identify their soul truths.

With this, I recommend starting to notice when you get a sense about something that's not in the physical world. At first, this might take a lot of practice, but the more you pay attention, and as part of this, notice the ways you are being communicated with, the easier it will become.

Another way to start to tune into these is to close your eyes. Now think of a person. They could be alive or dead. As you think of this person, notice what you are experiencing. Do you see them? Hear them? Feel them? Does a color pop up? Or, do you just know that they are here or even something about them, but don't know how? Notice these, as this is a very strong way to begin to identify how your intuition is coming through.

With this, too, know that each person is different, and you are being communicated with in the way that's best for you, and really, in the way that you can receive and understand the messages coming through. Also, while this is an amazing tool we have, it takes consistent practice to be able to fully recognize and connect to our intuition at all times. (I believe this is a constant work in progress!)

Also, it is possible to clear the parts of our intuition that are blocked, so you can have access to all of them. I had to work to open my clairvoyance (seeing) and clairaudience (hearing), as I shut these down as a child, because I saw and heard things I shouldn't or didn't want to, but I now have access to these as well. I've helped many clients to open theirs, too, so know that this is also possible for you. (It's important to note, while seeing and hearing are a bit more tangible, many times these come through the mind's eye and our own voices.) Of course, if you're looking for further support around this, don't hesitate to reach out.

CHAPTER 6

The only things that are impossible are those we believe to be.

DURING THIS TIME, ONE OF THE BIGGEST THINGS THAT WAS
WORKING FOR ME WAS MY CAREER. It's funny to think of a fifteen-
year-old having a career, but I was.

It all started when my mom suggested I get a job the summer
before I turned sixteen. Being the ambitious, hard-working and loyal
child I was, I took her suggestion. There was a McDonald's just
up the street from my house, so I started there. Unfortunately (or
fortunately), they told me I had to be sixteen to work there. While
I remember being disappointed, as it appeared that it would have
been easy to work there, I asked myself what I'd want to do instead.
Advertising came up, as for a few years already I'd had a desire to
work in that field. (I had even done my eighth grade project on what
the most effective advertising technique was!)

So I took the phone book and started cold calling ad agencies.
At the time, I don't remember having any ideas about cold calling
being hard or uncomfortable. This really served me, as I found two
internships in the area. That summer, every Monday, Wednesday

and Friday, I would head to Skokie, which meant walking a good mile and then taking the bus to Old Orchard, a mall in the north suburbs of Chicago, and then walking another two blocks to the office. At that office, I began learning the creative side of advertising, working on Simmons bedding. On Tuesdays and Thursdays, I would head to Niles, another north suburb of Chicago. This was a little less involved, yet still included a bus ride and long walks. In that internship, I learned about promotions and the account side of the industry, working on Coca-Cola's Fruitopia.

This time in my life taught me tenacity, independence and going after what I wanted. It got me comfortable with cold calling, and I began learning advertising and marketing skills that I still use to this day.

Even though I wasn't conscious of it at the time, looking back, I realize my soul knew we had a mission here, and we weren't wasting any time! It was time to get started.

LIFE LESSONS AND LEARNINGS

PURSUING YOUR DESIRES AND DREAMS

You're never too young (or too old!) to start something. If I can cold call when I'm fifteen, you can do anything you set your mind to. It's important to note, too, that if I had listened to the naysayers who told me advertising was hard to break into or that I was too young, I wouldn't be where I am now. Everyone always has an opinion, but yours is the only one that matters, unless you believe otherwise.

QUESTIONS:

- What's something you've desired but haven't moved toward (yet!)? What's one thing you can do to move toward it immediately?

- What are people telling you about your dreams and desires or about how hard something that you need to do to achieve your dreams and desires is? Do you believe them? Are these serving you? If not, if you're believing them, why is this? Does listening to them serve you in some way, maybe even keeping you safe or small?

TOOLS:

Moving Toward Your Dreams and Desires
When something seems out of reach, the easiest way to bring it in reach is to break it down into manageable tasks. For me, one of my most recent examples of this is writing my book. Initially, I set a goal to write a certain amount of words a day. This made it manageable, instead of just setting the goal to write a book, which, from that standpoint, can seem overwhelming.

Shifting Naysayers' Beliefs About Your Dreams and Desires
If you are believing other people's beliefs about your dreams and desires, first know that many times what people express to us is just a reflection of an inner belief.

To release this, identify why and then see your inner child in front of you (or feel them in your heart) and talk to them about their fears or concerns around their dreams and why they are believing what others are saying. It could include everything from being scared to fail to being scared to move forward because of a fear of success. (While this may seem counterintuitive, many people are scared of success, because they are comfortable where they are and can be scared of losing their friends and old life if they change.) Once you've identified these reasons, say this out loud, until it no longer holds its charge. This can seem counterproductive, but many times, it's the voices that we don't acknowledge in our head from our childhood that keeps the belief present. Once you give voice to them, you give them space to release.

Once you've done this, replace it with something in the positive/affirmative. So, for example, you might start off by saying, "I'm scared I'm going to fail. I'm scared I'm going to fail. I'm scared I'm going to fail…" and then once it feels like it doesn't carry any weight or is no longer heavy for you, replace it by saying out loud something like, "I am successful. I am successful. I am successful…"

Also, note if there's something you specifically need to say this naysayer. If so, visualize them in front of you and say it multiple times, until again, you don't feel like you need to say it anymore. This might look like, "You don't get to say this to me anymore," or "What you're saying me is not okay and it needs to stop."

Important to note: The feeling may release and then could come back not as strong. If so, repeat the above process until the feeling is no longer relevant for you. Also, if you're still finding the feeling is relevant after going through this process multiple times, it's likely there's a nuance to the feeling that you're missing. I would try different statements to see if anything helps it to release. Alternatively, this is a big part of the work I do with my clients (releasing childhood patterns and beliefs that are no longer serving them), so don't hesitate to reach out.

Along with this, if you have taken on a negative belief about a task that needs to be done, think of some ways you can reframe the task to make it more fun. For me, more recently, I've experienced resistance around cold calling, so one way I'm now choosing to reframe cold calls is by calling them "connection calls" instead.

CHAPTER 7

Challenges don't card you.

As I was venturing into a new career, over that next year, my mom began to make a slow decline. At this point, she was no longer on chemo, and while at first she seemed to be doing pretty well, the cancer was returning with a vengeance. In truth, it likely had never left.

I remember the summer before my senior year. I had just gotten my license, and my mom was at the University of Chicago Hospital, where she was being treated. My sister didn't have her license yet, so there were many days and nights where I ended up driving the three of us back and forth to the hospital, a good hour from my house. (My grandma was there too.) It was *heart-wrenching*. I still wanted to be a kid, but I felt like an adult. I spent a lot of time exhausted and depressed.

Eventually, toward the end of the summer, my mom came back home and started working again. For nearly two decades, she had worked as a second-grade teacher at Williams School, a Southside school in Chicago, and not too long before, had recently been promoted to head of the math department.

With her going back to work, I felt the relief of some normalcy, though it wouldn't last very long. My mom ended up putting in for leave just a few months later, right before the Thanksgiving holiday. She was getting sicker, and while I didn't realize at the time the significance of this, she was declining and we were reaching the end.

It was early in 1996 when I awoke to loud screams.

"God, God, please take me. Pleeeaase take me."

When I woke up, I didn't know what was happening. It was disorienting and terrifying at the same time. I had never heard screams like that before. Were they coming from my mom's room? *I knew they were.*

I went in to see what was wrong and, really, what I could do. *But I didn't know what to do. How could I know what to do? I was only 17.*

She was lying there in agony.

I rubbed her back to try to help soothe her and to help make her more comfortable, though I don't know that it really helped. I sat with her a while, feeling scared and powerless, and if I'm honest, the kid in me wanted to go back to sleep. *My adult self knew this was important.*

She would pass less than a month later.

LIFE LESSONS AND LEARNINGS

FACING REGRET

As I look back on this moment, I realize that this was a moment in time just for me. While it was one of the hardest moments of my life, it was also one of the most defining and this, coupled with my mom's passing, would be an impetus to a desire to throw myself into every aspect of life, to want to taste every experience, to relish every adventure, to dive into every fear and to live my life to the fullest.

Questions:

- Where can you dive into more in your life—more fear, more experiences, more everything?

- Where can you relish more that this life has for you?

- Where do you hold yourself back?

- Where you do let fear determine your experiences?

- What will you regret if you don't choose it in this lifetime?

Tools:

1. Facing regret.

Close your eyes and see yourself at the end of your time here, lying on your deathbed. If your life continues down the current path you're on, are you satisfied with it? Are there any chances you regret not taking? Are there any relationships you regret not healing? Is there anything you regret not doing? If there is, take note of it, and if you choose, course correct now.

2. Overcoming fear.

I mention many tools for overcoming fear in the next chapter, but there's one more thing I want to mention around this. One of the biggest keys to overcoming fear is recognizing what this feels like in your body. For example, one thing I notice for me is that every time I do something heights-oriented, I know I'm going to be scared. I know my body is going to start shaking. I know, at some point, I'm likely going to scream or start making weird noises.

As this has happened over and over, though, I've become conditioned to this fear. I *know* what to expect, which allows me to lean in to it, and to even, dare I say, enjoy it.

This is something you can condition yourself to, too. The more you're willing to put yourself in situations that scare you, the more comfortable you will get with this fear. It doesn't take it away, but it does help to build up your capacity for it.

CHAPTER 8

Death feels so final, until you realize it opens the door to other worlds.

I WAS 17, AND IT WAS A WEEK AFTER MY MOM HAD PASSED. I hadn't gone back to school yet, and I was lying in bed, sleeping and feeling this intense heaviness in my body. It felt utterly unbearable and like it would never stop. I felt like I had climbed into a dark abyss, one I might never climb out of. It felt like it could take me down forever.

Growing up, my mom was my world. With my dad leaving before I was two, while I saw him weekly, I had come to rely solely on the love and unending support that poured from every inch of my mom's body. Whether it was the way she'd put me to bed, playing the tickle game, or the way she'd come into my room in the morning to wake me up, singing, "Rise and Shine and Give God Your Glory, Glory..." mixed with "You gotta get up, you gotta get up, you gotta get up in the morning," a song I still hear in my head each morning when I wake up, there was a way I always knew my mom was there for me—until she wasn't.

The night she passed had been different. It was February 14, coincidentally (or not- so-coincidentally) Valentine's Day, and my twin sister and I had made the fateful decision to go to the gym.

Now on any other day, it would have been no big deal that we were doing this. On that day, though, it was. This was coupled with the fact that I'd lost an evening with my mom just a few days earlier to go to traffic school because of a speeding ticket. I deeply resented and regretted this for many years, as this was precious time with her I'd lost. *Either way, on this night, didn't I know I was running out of time with her??*

While we were there, I remember going through our typical routine—getting ready in the locker room, heading to the chlorine-drenched swimming pool, flirting with the cute, blonde, sun-kissed, Californian-looking lifeguard and getting in the pool.

I also distinctly remember the feeling that time had slowed down.

I wouldn't realize the importance of this until quite some time later, or even that my sense about this was true and it was possible. But, looking back, and knowing what I now know, which in part, includes that time and space are an illusion, I realize that time can be manipulated, when it's important. I'm not sure who decides when that's the case, and while I know it doesn't happen often, I do know this is possible because it's happened twice in my life. (The second time was at a retreat I was on where we were opening a portal to new levels of consciousness.)

So, we finished up what normally took us hours in what felt like half the time, and we headed home, arriving to an ambulance in our driveway and my grandma panicking. As we pulled up, I felt this fear rush through my body. *What was happening? Why was there an ambulance in my driveway?* I can't remember what happened next. Maybe I used the confusion to cover my sheer fear.

Whatever the case, I remember racing to the hospital in my friend's black sports car, and I remember a few pieces of a conversation I had with my mom in the hospital somewhere in the chaos.

This was the conversation you have with someone who is single-handedly the most important person in your life, the conversation you have when you don't fully understand the implication of what's happening, and really, that your world is going to be ripped away from you in just a few short hours and you subconsciously realize that your time with them is coming to a close. *Damn, I needed more time.*

Somehow, in some way, though, I had the presence of mind to know I needed to have this conversation. I knew I needed to ask for a sign that, when she did decide to go, that she was okay. Of course, I didn't want her to leave, but there was something deep within me that knew this part of our relationship was completing, and I was using this conversation to cope with this hard-hitting reality.

Looking back, I can't tell you what gave me the presence of mind to say this. After all, I was only seventeen. But now, in hindsight, I believe this was my soul remembering. *You've been here before. Don't let this opportunity to say what you need to say and ask for what you need for closure to pass you by. If you do nothing else at all tonight, this is important.*

Even with this conversation, though, I was latching onto every thread of hope. With this, there was a part of me that didn't think my mom was going to die. She had always looked healthy, and even though she had colon cancer, and had gone through chemo, she had never lost her hair. For two and a half years, I had lived in a state of hard-core denial or maybe just the innocence of teenage youth. I'm sure it was a bit of both.

But, as we sat in her hospital room and watched her vitals and her ability to answer the hospital staff's simple questions about herself disappear, I saw her fading. In this moment, I instinctively took over, answering everything from her date of birth to questions about her cancer. Heck, if I could have breathed for her, I would have. Yet, there was nothing I, and really my will, could do to change what was happening. *She was leaving.*

It was close to 3 a.m. when we left the hospital. I didn't want to leave—every inch of me was begging to stay. Had I been a little older or more connected to myself, I wouldn't have left, but my grandma guided us to go, perhaps with her own knowing that my mom was getting ready to pass, so we left. Right before saying our final good-bye, we talked about seeing her the following day. We wouldn't go to school. We would come there first thing in the morning. Maybe we knew it would never happen and maybe we didn't. Either way, morning couldn't come fast enough.

We arrived home about thirty minutes later. I felt disoriented, defeated and devastated. I don't know that I was fully in my body at the time, but of course, I wasn't aware of this. Either way, it was all too much for me to take in.

Begrudgingly, I began getting ready for bed, and it was then that the phone rang. Alarm bells went off inside of my head.

This could not be good. The phone ringing at 3 a.m. is never good.

My grandma came into our room, tears in her eyes. I don't remember the exact thing she said. All I remember is the gut-wrenching news hitting my body, dropping me to the floor, tears rolling from my eyes.

In that moment, I remember it hitting me how final it really was. She was not coming back, and there was nothing I, nor any of my loved ones, could do about it.

This was mixed in with a tiny bit of relief. *It had been a hard haul.*

Later, too, I would realize that she had made a conscious choice to pass when we weren't there. *She would not pass in front of her children.*

Either way, it was over.

Being a kid, it's hard to fully understand the definitiveness of death or that your last time with a parent is really your last time. No more hugs. No more laughs or fun adventures. No more them. My heart was broken and every ounce of me wanted to believe it wasn't true or to will her back to life. I remember feeling like it would be an eternity until I would see her again. My whole body sank at the thought of this—and how I was going to live without her in this lifetime.

It hurt—really bad.

So, I did the only thing I knew that might potentially comfort me, and I began praying to my mom. Looking back, in this moment, I had decided to replace God, and really, my belief in God, with my mom.

This was because shortly after my mom had gotten sick, I'd started praying to God. We all become believers when there's something we want or need. And I needed my mom to live.

When she passed, though, I had perceived that God had let me down, and so I started to talk with my mom like she was God. This felt like a good way to stay connected to her while gaining some control over my life because, of course, my mom wouldn't let anything bad happen to me.

The next week would be filled with her funeral and lots of "I'm sorry's." While well-meaning, every time I heard them, it reminded me of the depth of my loss and that my mom really wasn't coming home. I remember the day we went to go view her body. It was pouring outside, which at the time felt reflective of what I was feeling on the inside.

When we got to the hospital area where they were keeping her, I remember the distinct feeling of how cold it was in there. *Creepily, eerily cold.*

We walked into the room, and they pulled out the casket. I'd heard stories of olden times where they would take pictures of the body. *Would that be weird?* I thought. *Would it be weird to jump in the casket with her? Would it be weird to never leave?*

My family was there with me, and I was feeling rushed, self-conscious and maybe even a little disloyal. I knew I didn't want to let go of my mom, and I also knew that the only person I had now was my dad. I felt crushed and all alone. He was not my mom, nor could he take her place. Yet, wasn't I supposed to love him as much as I loved her? Was it wrong that I would rather join her than face this new reality? So many thoughts were going through my mind. Was there some way I could preserve her, be with her, go back in time?

What I wish I had realized the gravity of on February 14 had finally sunk in. *It was final. She was not coming back.*

I don't remember a lot about her funeral, except for the big yelp that came out of my mouth when I turned around and saw everyone who was there. I wanted to drop to the floor and curl up in a ball. Instead, I sat down until it was time for me to say goodbye and honor her memory.

My sister and I read this piece titled "Please," written by Rita Moran, though I'm not sure how much of it was audible through our tears. Either way, the rabbi had given it to us, or maybe he had given it to my grandma, in an effort to comfort her, and we had latched onto it like it was our last drop of water. While it's about losing a child, so much of the words echoed my devastation at the time. I've seen a few versions of this poem, but here's a piece of what we shared:

PLEASE – don't ask me if I'm over it yet. I'll never be "over it."

PLEASE – don't tell me she's in a better place. She isn't here.

PLEASE – don't say "at least she isn't suffering." I haven't come to terms with why she had to suffer at all.

. . . .

PLEASE – don't tell me "at least you had her for 28 years." (Or in our case, 17 years.) What year would you choose for your daughter (parent) to die?

. . . .

PLEASE – just say you are sorry.

PLEASE – just say you remember her if you do.

PLEASE – just let me talk if I want to.

PLEASE – let me cry when I must. (1-3, 8, 10-13)

The next several days were a whirlwind. I remember lots of family coming to pay their condolences. I remember lots of food. While I didn't realize it at the time, looking back, while it was nice to have them around, I think all of this was really uncomfortable for me, as I felt the need to put on a happy face and pretend I was okay. It felt like I was holding everything in and myself together all week.

The following week, I remember lying in my new bed at my grandma's house, dreaming, a lot of fear running through me about what was going to happen to me and my life now that my mom was gone.

With this, I remember the feeling of the dream like it was yesterday.

In it, we were at my grandma's house, in her living room, which was always filled with figurines, her best china and the golden couches.

My grandma's there. My aunt, my mom's sister, is there. And I'm there, though it feels like I'm watching from the outside looking in. My grandma and aunt are fighting, and I'm wishing my mom were there to break it up. She was always the peacemaker.

It's then that I hear these words. "She's here. She's here." I'm not sure who's saying them, but it's clear as day. And, while I'm hearing this in my dream, in real life, as I'm lying on my bed, I feel something physically going through my body. The feeling is pronounced and distinct; there is no mistaking it.

As I wake up, I realize that this is the sign I had asked her for.

It would be the first of many.

LIFE LESSONS AND LEARNINGS

LIVING LIFE TO THE FULLEST

My mom's passing was one of the biggest defining moments of my life. It taught me many things about how I wanted to live my life and treat people. From that point forward, I began living my life to the fullest. What did this mean to me? It meant living a life with no regret. It meant diving into every adventure. It meant not taking life, or anyone in it, for granted. This was such a huge gift, as, at age seventeen, I grabbed life by the horns and went after it. I pursued the career I desired with unmatched fury. I went traveling around the world to places most people only dream about visiting. And, I truly valued all of my relationships. I always made an effort when it mattered, and it gave me the ability to be able to see things from another's perspective with real compassion.

I remember years later a colleague asking me what the worst thing that could happen to me was. My reply: "Losing my mom." His response was memorable: "The worst is over."

QUESTIONS:

- What do you value most in your life? Is what you take action toward in full alignment with these values?

- How can you live life to the fullest every single day? What's on your bucket list, and what will you regret if you don't move toward or choose it?

- Is there something you've desired in your life, big or small, that you haven't moved toward? What's stopping you? What's one step you can take to move forward?

TOOLS:

If you don't know what you want, you can't move toward it. With that said, I highly recommend making a list of what you desire in this lifetime. Lay it out in one-year, five-year and ten-year brackets, and put as much detail into it as possible. As part of this, make a bucket list of things you want to accomplish in this lifetime. Make them unreasonable, and then move toward them. (One of my "soft" goals is to hit every country before I leave this physical body. Yes, it's unreasonable, but that's what makes it more fun! I call it a "soft" goal, too, because I'm not going to beat up on myself if it doesn't happen, and if I'm not called to go somewhere because it doesn't excite me, I'm not going to go there just to say I went there.) An important piece to doing this is making this exclusively about you. This isn't about what someone else will think about you if you do this or even what someone else wants you to do. This is about you and what you desire.

OVERCOMING FEAR

I believe this experience was a key to how I met fear, too. Yes, we all feel fear, but it's what we do with it that matters. For me, there was nothing that could stop me. I jumped in headfirst, sometimes literally! I'm terrified of heights, but this didn't stop me from doing everything from skydiving to zip lining, to hang gliding, screaming all the way. It was scary to do improv in front of 700 people, but several years ago now, I did exactly that. Also, one of my biggest (subconscious) fears was around being seen, so, as I began putting myself out there for my business, it was truly intimidating. But, I knew that if I didn't move forward, I would always regret it, so I chose through the fear. Most of my life has been centered around the below thought:

You have to determine if your excuse now is more important than your regret later.

QUESTIONS:

- What are you most scared of? What's one way you can lean into the fear?

TOOLS:

1. Breathe.
This might seem simple, but so often we get pulled in by overwhelm that we end up forgetting this one helpful tool. I personally love the Fifteen-Second Breath to help with this. Breathe in seven seconds, hold for one second at the top and then exhale for seven seconds. Yes. It. Can. Be. That. Easy.

2. Just do it (anyway).

This isn't a major slogan in the athletic arena for nothing. So many times, we make the challenge feel wrong because of fear and use it as a reason (i.e., excuse!) to stop ourselves. But fear can be a major opportunity for strength and empowerment. You know when you gave your first presentation, and started off, palms sweaty, knees weak, your whole body shaking like the Loch Ness Monster was in front of you? How did you feel after, when your boss came up and told you that you killed it? (Figuratively, of course.) It felt good, right? With this, I recommend internalizing how good it feels when you overcome your fear. This is an important key to beginning to enjoy and own the fear.

3. Get support.

Hey, we all need help sometimes. Whether it's reaching out to a friend or hiring a coach, therapist or another expert, one of the biggest ways to shift fear is by working with someone. I remember the first (and only!) time I jumped out of an airplane, I had several friends with me, and you know what? It helped. Now maybe it was the peer pressure, but in all seriousness, there was something about having a common goal and doing it together that made it more fun.

ASKING FOR SIGNS FROM THE OTHER SIDE

The other piece of my mom's death was the beginning of asking for signs and help from the other side. For me, this was a way to stay connected with her. Yes, in part, there was some denial about the pain of her not being there, but there was something inside that called to me where I knew she would answer. As I went off to college, I remember asking for signs and help from her. *She never let me down.*

I remember one such time going to my marketing teacher, who had literally met me once and never saw me again in his class. (I had a scheduling conflict at the time, so I'd watch his class on video replay. Yes, we had video replay at the University of Florida!)

I remember going there to ask for a better grade, even though he had sent out an email to his 1,500-plus students specifically saying not to do this. (I was always a determined kid.) On my way over, I asked my mom for some help. After a few minutes of making a case for myself in his office, and him picking up an imaginary violin to represent the sob song I was singing, he relented, and I got my A. *Thanks, Mom!*

QUESTIONS:

- Do you believe you can get help from your loved ones on the other side? If not, why not? Would you open to it, if you knew it could make your life easier?

TOOLS:

Asking for help and signs from the Universe and your Guides and Angels is such an important, fun and useful tool! It's easy, too! All you need to do is ask, simply saying, "Hey Guides and Angels/Universe, I'd like some help with this!" or "Please give me a sign that _____," inserting whatever it is you're needing. This might look like "Please give me a sign that you're still here," or "Please give me a sign that I'm going in the right direction." Then, pay attention! Signs and help don't always come in the forms we expect them to.

Also, important to note: What you think will help you and what the Universe thinks will help can be two totally different things. For instance, when I am doing energy clearings, we clear the next layer of energy that's in the way of my clients having what they're desiring. Sometimes that means that what they're desiring appears, and sometimes it means that the original thing shows up, with the Universe asking if they're ready to make a new choice. Both are signs of progress to know you're always supported. It just might not look the way you thought it would.

ENMESHMENT

While I've already touched on enmeshment in Chapter 4, I do want to point out a few of the examples of the enmeshment that was occurring during this time, to help you see your own versions of these, if this is true for you. For me, this included me wanting to join my mom in the casket and wanting to breathe for her and wanting to take her pain away in the hospital by taking it myself.

QUESTIONS:

- If you grew up in an enmeshed household, what does it mean about you if you chose to buy into this? (For me, it meant I was a good person.) As part of this, how does showing up in this way serve you?

- Do you often get your worth and feel good about yourself by what you do and how you show up for others? While it's important to have self-worth regardless of what you're doing for another, doing nice things for others isn't necessarily a bad thing unless it begins to overtake your life, where you are suffering because of this.

TOOLS:

The first step to changing this is determining if this was in the household you grew up in, including if there was a lot of enmeshment and poor boundaries when you were growing up. Then, from there, if you are ready to change this, when you find yourself with poor boundaries or doing what doesn't feel right to feel loved or worthy, identify why. Is it because this is how you feel seen or where you get your worth? Whatever the case, I recommend identifying where the hole is for you that you're desiring to fill from this action and to start filling it yourself. Mirror affirmations can be good for this. So, for example, if you're doing this to feel seen, I'd recommend saying to yourself, while looking in a mirror, something like "I see you. No matter what you do or don't do, I see you, and I love you as you are." (If this doesn't feel true for you as you say it, many times this is because you need to honor the negative belief first. While many teachers don't recommend this, I've seen that honoring this piece of you shifts this so that when you do say, "I see you," it feels true. In other areas of this book, I address how to work with your inner child to shift these negative beliefs.)

In conjunction with the mirror affirmations, when you find yourself being asked or doing something that doesn't feel right for you, start to check in with yourself to see if you really want to be doing what you're doing or agreeing to do, and start to say no more when this isn't true for you.

CHAPTER 9

The best kind of family is the one that chooses to be your family.

I__T WAS DURING THIS TUMULTUOUS TIME THAT MY STEPMOM,
P__ATTY, ENTERED MY LIFE__. Truthfully, I hate using the word stepmom, though I haven't figured out a better title to call her, and
given that I was so close to my mom, it hasn't felt right to call
her this either. This is by no means a statement, though, about the
wonderful woman with the generous heart that she is.

I was first introduced to Patty, when I was fifteen, amidst my
mom's battle with cancer. It didn't help that one of the first times
my dad came to pick us up with her, my mom had made a comment
about her, as she observed her from the big window over the garage
of our two-flat.

Needless to say, our beginning didn't start off so great. I struggled
with how to welcome and love her while staying loyal to my mom.

It would take some time for me to realize that she had my back.
It would take some time to realize that having her in my life was a
good thing and that she made my dad a better person. It would take
some time to realize that it was okay to love her, that really, my mom
would have wanted this.

My dad married her just shortly after my mom's passing, and we moved into their condo not too long after we graduated high school. This transitional time was hard, as we were both just finding our way in this new relationship. It didn't help, too, that my dad was disciplining us, and for the first time, we had to listen. (Historically anytime he tried to lay down the law, my mom had cushioned the blow.)

Over time, though, my relationship with her grew. She was becoming family, and while we didn't always understand each other, there was genuine love there.

She was always up for anything, which helped open my dad up to things he may have said no to if she hadn't been in the picture. And, when he wasn't up for it, we went, just the two of us.

I remember one time going roller-skating with her. Here's this 60-year-old woman skating backward. I was holding onto her! To put it mildly, her spirit has always been contagious!

Our trip to Australia was really special, too. When I travel, I can be quite intense, as I love to see *everything* when I'm visiting a new place. It didn't help that we were on an extremely limited travel schedule. So, even though she was officially working on her trip, she was quite the sport to my "let's go here, let's go there" travel requests. I was truly grateful for our time and the opportunity to travel alone together.

It was a couple of years ago when I got a panicked call from my dad. "Patty's had a stroke, and she's at a hospital in Denver."

My heart sank. Even without knowing the full depth of her stroke, I knew this was going to have a big impact on our family. Patty was always the strong, fun one, and it was hard for me to hear that her body had failed her.

It wasn't too long after that I went and visited her and my dad. Seeing her, it was difficult to see someone who had so much life left in them struggling.

During this time, I struggled with how to support both of them fully. On my dad's part, he wouldn't accept help most of the time, and with Patty, she was understandably having a hard time communicating what was going on with her or what she needed during that time.

It's been over two years since then, and while she's not fully recovered yet, she improves each time I see her. While she still has some physical limitations at the moment, her spirit that I opened my heart to so many years ago is still the same.

LIFE LESSONS AND LEARNINGS

OPENING TO MORE LOVE

My relationship with Patty has been an opportunity to open to more love. I started our relationship with the parameter that there was only so much love to go around, and if I fully, truly loved her, I was being disloyal to my mom.

Over the years, though, I've seen the truth—that there is an abundance of love in this world, and that my mom would want me to love and accept her fully, just as Patty has accepted me. Even deeper, my mom would be grateful for the support she has given me over the years.

QUESTIONS:

- What tough/challenging relationships do you have? Do you withhold love from them in any way? Why? Is there something you don't like about them or some way you feel better by making them wrong? Are you being loyal to someone?

TOOLS:

The first step to changing any challenging relationship is the desire to change it. If you don't want to change it, no matter what I say or do, it won't work. So, make a choice—to change it or not—and then stand by that choice, until if/when something changes for you.

If you decide to make a choice to change your relationship, the biggest piece with changing it is opening your heart. When we can see others from compassion and their heart and human side, the side that's doing the best they can that's also seeking love and acceptance, that's when we can start to connect and love them for who they are.

Here's how to begin to do this:

1. Simply place your hand on your heart, breathing into your heart space.

2. Once you feel connected to your own heart, see them in front of you and imagine your heart connecting with theirs. You can see this as rays being sent from you to them and back or simply feel their love coming towards you and your love going towards them, opening your body and heart to this. (If this shows up for you in a different way, I definitely encourage you to follow that.)

3. The third key here is practicing this in person and any time you talk to them. Set the intention before you see them (or talk with them) that you will keep an open heart, and if you find yourself struggling when you are connecting with them, relax, surrender and return to your heart. This one takes practice, but over time, you will definitely see your relationship shift.

CHAPTER 10

We don't have to take on someone else's story to keep their memory alive.

It was shortly after Patty entered my life when I went off to college. I had this big hole in my heart from just having lost my mom a few months earlier, and I remember feeling so lost when I got there.

My dad and Patty, along with my sister, dropped me off. Then, Patty made my bed, and they left. That was that. I remember that first day not knowing what to do with myself and feeling quite overwhelmed. I had just met my roommate, who was an African American girl starting her junior year. As I walked into my room (we were sharing a suite, with our own private rooms), there was loud music playing and she was there with many of her friends and her boyfriend. I'm sure I wondered what I had gotten myself into, but immediately, she started to help me with where to get school supplies and food, and she even let me share her refrigerator with her and would often help me get groceries.

While most freshmen wanted to have a freshman roommate and live in the freshmen dorms, as time went on, I began to realize how lucky I was to have someone who was older and more responsible and mature who could guide me. And while she, too, had had her own challenges, making her thick shell hard to crack, over time we became friends.

I do also remember that first day alone, making three trips to Eckerd's, the local drugstore. Every time I would get back to my dorm room, I would realize that I had forgotten something else, and then I would go back out again. Truth be told, I think I was just looking to fill the space, as I didn't know what to do with myself, and I felt all alone with my family leaving to help my sister get situated too.

Eventually, though, I did settle in, and most of the time, I was pretty self-sufficient, making new friends and going to all of my classes, even making the early morning ones, despite the warning I had received from a high school teacher not to take these.

It was when the grief would wash over me, though, that all of the normalcy I had tried to create to keep it all together would come crashing down. Death has a way of doing that to you. It invites you into your true essence, and like an old friend, it sits down and summons you into your own depths, asking you to really get to know yourself, calling you to more—more pain, more emotion and more truth.

I remember lying in my bed at times sobbing, the overwhelming heartache overtaking me, hoping that my roommate didn't hear. I was eighteen years old and getting a crash course in grief, and I didn't have a road map for it. It wasn't fair that I even needed one.

What I did really need, though, was my mom. I needed her to guide me through all of my firsts—first dates, first exams, first presentations, first kisses, first heartbreaks.

But instead I was taking on my mom's modeling of doing it all herself, which in my first seventeen years I witnessed daily, and I began doing it all myself. While at the time, I thought it was a good thing, and in part, it was, as during this time and after it helped me to survive and with this, to become self-sufficient and hyper-successful in all areas that would make it appear I was a highly functioning human being, I also put up a lot of subconscious walls and defenses just to get by and to make sure I didn't get hurt, and really, abandoned, again.

It was an unsteady time, especially in the beginning, but I was getting my footing and excelling as a college student, as I started to deal with the grief that had come knocking on my door, ready to take me into its intense embrace.

LIFE LESSONS AND LEARNINGS

TAKING ON OUR LOVED ONES' STORIES

Growing up with my mom as my primary support system, I adored her. She was definitely my favorite person in this world, and I always wanted to be like her.

Of course, with this, I took on many of her stories. In part, in addition to the above, this was to be loved, and at a deep subconscious level, for survival.

When she passed, though, I didn't realize that I had also subconsciously taken on many stories that weren't working for me. These stories included possibly getting cancer and ending up alone. Even as I write this now, it feels a bit scary to put in writing, as there's a fear of creating it by putting it out there. Also, the closer I get to the age when my mom passed, even with knowing all the good things that are meant for me, the more real it becomes. Oddly enough, during that time of my life, in some ways, I was closer to these stories, and in some ways, as I get older, I'm closer to these stories now.

Either way, though, taking on these stories was how I learned to create my life and to keep her memory alive.

As I started to do more and more work, though, I started to realize that I didn't have to take on my mom's reality and that I could create my reality, my way. While it took years to really heal and undo the stories that I thought would just be how it was, and occasionally these still creep in, I found out it is possible to let go of these without letting go of her memory.

QUESTIONS:

- Where have you taken on parents' or loved ones' stories that aren't working for you? Why? Does it make you feel like a good person? Are you scared of losing a piece of them if you don't keep these memories and stories, even if they're not working for you, alive?

TOOLS:

To let go of your loved ones' stories:

1. Talk to the little one that lives inside of you and ask them why they are keeping this person's memory alive this way. What are they scared of? One reason may be that they might be scared to lose them or to let them go.

2. Whatever the reason, say this out loud until it holds no weight for you. In the above example, this may look like, "I'm scared to lose them. I'm scared to let them go. I'm scared to lose them. I'm scared to let them go…"

3. Then, notice, if there are any other reasons why you're

keeping their memory alive and repeat the first two steps until it feels like there are no other reasons.

4. Once this holds no weight, start to visualize your life looking differently. If, for instance, you're scared you're going to end up alone, and that's why you've held onto their stories, see yourself in a new story with a partner that loves, cares about and supports you.

If You Feel Like You Have to Do Everything Yourself

Feeling like you have to do everything yourself is definitely a more masculine energy. I talk more about moving into the feminine later in this book, but, if you're ready to receive more support in your life, here's how to get started.

Questions:

- Do you have to do everything yourself? Where did you learn this from? How has it served you (i.e., I feel safe. I know it will get done right., etc.)?

Tools:

1. Notice how many times you are offered help but don't accept it.

2. While this may seem like a novel idea (and ingenious!), start to accept it, even when you think you could do it or even you could just do it better yourself.

3. Then, take in the help you received, noticing how good it feels.

CHAPTER 11

People show up how we need them to so we can heal ourselves. Even if it appears differently, it is always love in disguise.

As I entered adulthood, especially with the passing of my mom, I found myself reaching out to my father more and more. I so desperately wanted him to show up for me fully just one time. I wanted his support, and really, I wanted his love. In those earlier days, though, when I did reach out, I would find myself disappointed.

It was one of these times, in my early twenties, when I called him after a breakup with a man I had dated for a year. I had gone over to my ex's house, and we had slept together one more time. I remember talking to my dad about the situation, seeking comfort, guidance and some hope that this man and I might get back together, or at a minimum, that I wouldn't be alone for the rest of my life. As I reached out to him, asking for his advice, it only made me feel worse. I remember the sense of feeling shamed and ashamed for making this choice. I was so hurt. It was in that moment that I semi-subconsciously made a decision that this would be the last time I would reach out to him for help in my relationships. After all, this was the only way my twenty-something self knew how to protect herself.

It was also around this time that I started seeing a therapist regularly. As a teenager, when my mom got sick, I was in and out of therapy. There was one therapist, in particular, whom I had taken to during this time. Knowing, too, that she had known my mom made me feel safe with her, so I decided to start seeing her again regularly.

During our sessions together, we would talk about many things, including my father and his impact on my dating relationships. It was during these beginning sessions that I would realize that my attracting men that couldn't show up for me fully, and would eventually leave me, was primarily rooted in my relationship with my dad.

It was after this initial relationship post-college that I began dating more and more. I was looking for love, which always felt like it was at arm's length, and, really, seeking love from others that I didn't feel for myself and wasn't giving myself. I was looking for someone to save me. I was looking for a happy life. I was looking for someone to take the place of my dad, though I wasn't consciously aware of any of this. Whatever the case, I was looking for it in all of the wrong places.

To put it mildly, it was a disaster.

Many times, I would get into these dating relationships. Usually, they would last for only one to three months, occasionally six months, and even rarer, a year or longer. Each time, I was hoping I wouldn't be left. This hope, and really this focus, created the exact thing I was trying to avoid.

It was gut-wrenching.

What I realize now is that each time I would be left, it would be a re-wounding of when my dad had left. This was a moment that I couldn't remember, but viscerally lived in my cells. My two-year-old self was desperately crying out for her daddy to stay, and I thought, and really hoped, I could create a new result with my partners.

It would take close to fifteen years of having this experience over and over, though, for me to make a new choice. Yet, this pain would be the impetus for my change, and really, my awakening, and for that, I could not be more grateful to my father for playing this role for me.

LIFE LESSONS AND LEARNINGS

THE ROLES PEOPLE PLAY

I believe that people show up in our lives exactly how we need them to. While they may not be conscious of this, their higher self knows exactly how they need to show up for us, to help us to learn and grow to be the best version of ourselves.

If you doubt this is true, all you need to do is look at how your parent treats you compared to your sibling. If you think this is biology, another good way to look at this is with a boss or at a job. Why do some people get passed over while others get promoted, even though their work is sometimes even better? While again, you could chalk this up to favoritism or nepotism or even sexism, I would ask you to look at the belief systems of the two individuals. I guarantee you that the one who got promoted had a different belief system about themselves and the outcome than the one who didn't.

QUESTIONS:

- Looking back, what's one situation where even though in the physical world it may not have appeared so and their decision may have even hurt you, where this person's decision or response was in your highest good, and even, where their decision or response was helping you to grow? Maybe it was around a time when you got rejected or you didn't get the response or support you were hoping for. How did this help you on your path? How did you grow from this? While you may not have recognized this at the time, looking back, what did this show you that still lived with you that needed to be healed? For example, when I reached out to my dad and felt rejected by him, while I wasn't aware of it until decades later, this showed me the part of myself that wasn't fully loving myself or okay with my choices. This also showed me the part of myself that was still seeking love from outside of myself. If I had been aware of it at the time, and most importantly, understood its impact, I would have started doing more self-love work. As part of this, notice where this rejection may have even redirected you to something better.

Tools:

As I began my inner journey, I began to use every situation as an opportunity to show me more of myself to help me to learn and grow. I began to see that *every single thing* was for me. (I know I've said this a few times throughout this book, but that's because it's important!)

With this, every time something would happen, especially when I didn't like it, I would ask:

- What is this here for?

- How is this helping me to learn and grow?

- Why is this person showing up for me this way?

One example of this for me, that happened several years ago, was around a car accident I was in. While the accident was not my fault (he had not yielded right away), on the spot he started bullying me and verbally abusing me. When I got home, after I had calmed down, I started to feel all of it. This included the part of me that had always thought men were right and I was wrong. This included the part of me that was so angry. This included the part of me that was scared to use her voice. I did a lot of punching the air around this, seeing him in front of me and screaming, even though I live in a high-rise building, but it was important for me to feel how mad and upset I was. After the accident, I felt very unseen, unacknowledged and diminished. So I used the feelings that came up to feel them. After all, the accident had already happened, so there was no going back, but I might as well use it for all it was worth to help me clear what was coming up, with the idea that if I went there, that I might not have to experience this specific feeling of diminishment and not feeling seen again.

Also, a side note to this story: It's important to notice how you're treating another and, really, what energy you're putting on them. Most of us, especially when we're getting irrationally angry with someone, like this man was with me (and I've been there too), are energetically vomiting on them. Then, most of the time, the person who received this is carrying around that energy unbeknownst to them, and while they don't always know why, they don't feel good. So when you find yourself showing up in a way that you wouldn't be proud of, it's important to be mindful of this and ask yourself if this is who you want to be. If not, if it's possible in the moment, take some deep breaths and make a decision to be kind, or at least, not to be mean, even if you're mad. Whether you are able to be kind in real time or not, when you're out of their presence, I recommend using one of the many tools found in this book to feel the anger or whatever was coming up for you in that moment, as it's important to feel it without putting it on another person. Also, if you were mean to them and regret showing up in this way, see or feel them in front of you and verbally apologize to them for your actions.

Also, if you find yourself on the receiving end of this, when you are out of their presence, see the energy they put on you as a physical thing, like fire, a storm or a cloud, for example, and pull it out of your body, filling your body with light. (Also, if you have something you need to say to them, use one of the practices in this book to communicate it.)

USING OUR PAIN

One of the biggest lessons I learned from my dad, which is at the root of the work I do today, is that we can use our pain to create great things. I believe we choose our parents, and I believe, after lifetimes of abandonment in various forms, I chose my dad in the hopes that I could heal this pattern once and for all.

I get that this may be a stretch for you. You don't have to believe this, but I will say, for me, this is my truth. In believing this, I've moved myself out of one of the biggest ways we can believe life is just happening to us and into believing that we can take control of our lives and become a conscious creator. To me, this is so much more powerful than believing I had no control over my childhood, how I was treated or what occurred.

As part of this, what happened to me at age two, and then was recreated with the loss of my mom at age seventeen, were the two biggest drivers for me to truly change. After all, sometimes our wiring as humans means it has to get *that* bad for us to do anything about it. For me, if these things hadn't happened, my abandonment pattern wouldn't have been such a dominant factor, which maybe would have meant that I might have been comfortable settling into a relationship that was less than I truly desired, and really, settling for something that didn't set my heart on fire.

Instead, though, I believe I set it up to experience major pain early, as I knew this could be a powerful impetus to creating an amazing life. It's important to note, we live in a world of infinite possibilities. So, while it was highly likely that my dad was going to leave physically, and even more likely that he was going to leave emotionally, this was not guaranteed before I came into my physical body. Also, my mom's passing was one of her own creation, with me as the role of co-creator.

QUESTIONS:

- What have been your biggest life challenges? How can and have you used these to change? How can and have you turned these into opportunities to create great things in your life? It's important to note these so you can start to, if you haven't already, have gratitude for these experiences while conditioning yourself to always use your challenges to grow, as that's one of the biggest reasons why we're here.

- With this, how can you see these as the Universe supporting you and always having your back? (Everything, especially the hard stuff, is helping us to heal ourselves and return us to our truth, when we can see it that way.)

TOOLS:

With this, it's important to start using your pain to rewire you to greatness. We can either allow our pain to take us down or rise us up. Don't be a victim of your circumstances. Instead, allow it to take you higher. As part of this, it's important to first heal and make peace with your pain. One strong way to do this is by noticing how your pain has served you and taken you farther than you would have been able to go without it. This is an important step in healing yourself.

One of the biggest keys to this is forgiveness and gratitude for the experiences that occurred and the roles that each person has played for you. (I walk you through a forgiveness process below. It's important to do this work first, feeling your feelings and pain, before being grateful, as gratitude without this tends to just be covering up the pain that's still there and can be a spiritual bypass to doing the work, which is why you're here in the first place.)

Also, I remember years ago, a teacher of mine commenting that we are all light beings and our true nature is love, so if someone does something that's truly dark or hurtful, think of how much they have to contract, diminish and really darken themselves to show up that way (i.e., their higher selves would never do anything to hurt you). So, to think, they did this so that you could heal, grow and expand as a being—now that's a true gift. While this isn't the only perspective, this is a pretty powerful way to begin to look at your loved ones hurting you and to start to open to forgiveness.

FORGIVENESS

For me, my dad has been my biggest teacher of forgiveness. I spent my entire teenage years subconsciously making him wrong for when he had left when I was two. When it came time to finally let go, though, I didn't want to because I thought in some way, in doing this, I was saying what he had done was okay. I had to get to the point where I realized that forgiving him was for me. There's an old saying by Max Lucado, "Forgiveness is unlocking the door to set someone free and realizing you were the prisoner." It's so true. Our hate, anger and resentment only hurts us, and the process of forgiving my father, which took years and many layers, set me free from my own pain. I was no longer carrying this chip on my shoulder, which was more like a thousand-pound bag of hurt. I felt relieved. I felt open. I felt free. I felt love.

QUESTIONS:

- Whom do you need to forgive, if you haven't already? What's holding you back from doing this, if anything?

TOOLS:

The process I'm going to share with you below is one process you can use to begin to forgive your loved one or perpetrator. Important to note: when I do this work with my clients, it looks a bit different, as I just focus on the energies that need to be cleared to quickly and powerfully bring my clients to full healing, love and forgiveness. That being said, if you're struggling with the below, please reach out to me or another professional for help.

Also, important to note: Forgiveness isn't just something you say; it's something you feel. And it's more than just neutrality; it's love. Most people give up on forgiveness work before they've fully forgiven someone. Personally, I've heard everything from "I've forgiven him, but I'm not going to condone his behavior or what he did" to "I just can't let him off the hook for what he did (to me, my sibling, my other parent, etc.)." If there is any feeling of heaviness or holding onto making the other person wrong, know there's still more work to do. Of course, you don't have to do it in this lifetime. That's your decision. Just know that, while in your human form, you couldn't imagine choosing the lesson again, your soul has a different perspective and may choose another forgiveness lesson to learn the full depth of forgiveness, if it's something you don't choose in this lifetime. Also, it's important not to lie to yourself. Instead, just own that this is as far as you want to go right now and have compassion for this part of you.

Either way, know that one of the biggest keys to true forgiveness is choosing it and that when you let go of this, again, you are set free, and there is so much lightness and joy that comes along with this—FOR YOU, and the work is and has always been about you.

Step One

To your perpetrator/the person you need to forgive, write or state out loud all of the ways they have hurt and impacted you. Much of what keeps us stuck is the energy that certain moments hold, and many times, we have to be the victim in our life before we can be the hero. Thus, when we are given an opportunity to give voice to these moments, whether written or spoken, it gives the opportunity for the energy to release. With this, it's important to go really deep, and you may need to do this several times (and even use your body to act out the anger or any other emotion that's present) to get at the full impact and energy that's there.

When I do this, much of it involves using the voice and the body, as many times, we have lifetimes worth of blocks in our cells and chakras, including our throat chakra, heart chakra and our solar plexus, which is our power center and underneath our chest. That being said, it's important to follow where you feel called to go. If writing feels like the right direction in this moment, go there. If speaking it feels better to you, go there. When I initially started doing this work, I wrote letters to my loved ones. Then, I used my body to express my anger, and really, rage. (It's important to note: the first time I expressed my anger and rage, while I have no clue how much time it was, as I was on a retreat when I was doing this, I likely spent hours expressing this. As I worked on this more and more, though, and the rage dissipated, I started feeling called to speak out what I needed to say that I didn't have a chance to say when I was a little girl.) Do what feels best, as there is no one right way to heal, knowing that you may need to try many different practices to fully shift it.

Step Two

See where the person you need to forgive learned what they learned. Maybe they learned it from a parent, teacher or someone else. The important piece is beginning to bring in compassion for your loved one or perpetrator. Also, if you don't know where they learned it because your loved one or perpetrator was someone who you didn't know or you just don't know a lot about your parents, you can imagine where they learned it from. It's important, as you're doing this, to see them as the innocent child they were when they likely learned this in some form and that this may have been how love was represented to them. With this, feel that they were doing the best that they could, until they could know, do and be better.

Step Three

The third key, which some miss, is being able to see the higher perspective of how the pattern, pain or trauma/abuse has really served you. For me, as I describe the above and I realize this was the impetus for all of the work that I do now, it genuinely brings tears to my eyes when I think of my dad's role. Once you can see it this way without any resentment or holding onto it to make them wrong, and with this, once you can have gratitude for how it has shaped you for the better, this is when most can really let go and move forward.

Please note: It took me years of doing forgiveness work, tackling it from many different angles, to fully feel and heal this. It's important to stay with this work, following your guidance and working with many different practices until it is completely cleared and no longer holds a charge for you.

CHAPTER 12

Signs are like kisses from our loved ones on the other side.

It was amidst this backdrop that I was always looking for signs and support from my mom on the other side. It is hard to lose a parent at any age, but it's completely disorienting to lose them before you've even had a chance to get your footing as an adult and before you've even had a chance to know who you are and what's important to you in this world.

So, as I was in my twenties, working as a copywriter for a large promotions agency, I found myself thinking of her. It was right around the anniversary of her death, and I had had a rough week. It was the kind of week where I needed my mom. Oh, did I need her.

I had decided to visit her. I wouldn't go to visit her often, but when I did, I would sit by her grave and talk to her. Usually, I would ask her for help, and I would never leave without giving her at least 100 "air" kisses and leaving rocks on her and my grandpa's grave. (My mom always got more.) This time, as I often did, I also asked her for a sign. Upon asking this, needing to go to work, I reluctantly left.

Even though I knew this wasn't the only place I could connect with her, for me, it was always so hard to leave. I was always reassured being graveside, as I knew, in some way, she was there.

After my morning chat, I went to work, pretending everything was normal and forgetting that I had even made this request.

It wasn't more than a couple of days later that I was sitting with my friend, Patti, which coincidentally (or not so much), is my mom's name, spelled the same way. (Yes, it is also my stepmom's name, though she spells it with a "y!")

We were at a coffee cup reading at a Greek restaurant in Greek Town in Chicago. One of the things I always loved about hanging out with Patti was that she liked the weird stuff like me.

So, that Thursday night, we found ourselves at a coffee cup reading. In case you're not familiar with coffee cup readings, they serve you a cup of Greek coffee. Then, you pour out the grinds, and they read the markings the grinds make on the inside of the cup to provide guidance and talk to you about your future. Yes, it's weird, and that's why I like it.

So, we ate dinner, and finally, the "coffee cup reader," who in my mind is dressed like a belly dancer, though I'm not sure she really was, came up to us.

She read me first, and the first thing that came out of her mouth had me hooked.

"There's a name on the inside of this cup. Does Pat or Pam mean anything to you?" I looked at her with a mix of glee and stun.

"Pat is my mom's name," I said. (She did go by Pat, too.)

That's when it hit me. I remembered I had asked my mom for a sign earlier that week. Here it was, too, hand-delivered on a silver platter, or cup, so to speak.

During the rest of the reading, she could have told me I was going to be the first human to physically take flight, and I would have believed her.

Either way, though, I had gotten my sign.

LIFE LESSONS AND LEARNINGS

WORKING WITH YOUR GUIDES AND ANGELS

While at the time, I didn't call them my Guides and Angels, I was starting to realize that my Guides and Angels, whom at the time I was defining as my loved ones from the other side, were always around me. I just had to ask, and they would support me. As part of this, the reinforcement I was getting was that once I reached out, nothing was impossible when my Guides and Angels wanted me to get a message.

I now know that a huge key to this is believing in it. If I hadn't believed it was possible to hear from my Guides when I reached out, I wouldn't have heard from them. If I did, I would have dismissed it as coincidence. (By the way, there are no coincidences. The Universe is always supporting you—*always*.) As part of this, we create what we believe is possible, so if you're willing to stay open and know anything is possible, it will be. Then, it's important to pay attention to what comes your way.

Another important piece that has been a part of every sign I've received, though it wasn't conscious at the time was, after I asked for the sign, not getting attached to it showing up or how it would show up. In the above story, I asked for a sign, and then I let it go. Many times when we don't let something go, we only prolong the experience we are resisting, squashing the energy and many of the possibilities of if and how it will show up. Even if it does show up, we aren't able to see it. Then, we wonder why "nothing" has happened. So, if you ask for something, ask for it, and let it go—simple as that. (For more on attaching to outcomes, head to Chapter 20.)

Also, part of noticing signs is "tuning" to them. For me, the biggest ways I've been able to "tune" to these messages is clearing my subconscious and unconscious blocks, which is done by recognizing and healing many of the childhood patterns and beliefs I took on. As I do this, I raise my vibration and start to be able to tune into the messages that are always coming through, but that I'm not always connected to.

QUESTIONS:

- Do you need a sign? If so, are you willing to ask for it and then to believe it's possible you'll receive it? Then, will you pay attention when it's delivered? (Many times, if you don't notice it the first time, your Guides will deliver it several more times. It's especially important during these times to pay attention. If you hear about a book or teacher several times, again, *this is not coincidence*. It's synchronicity, and it's important to notice this, as we are always being supported.)

TOOLS:

The biggest key to working with your Guides and Angels is to simply start a conversation with them. Again, you can do this by literally saying your request, question or desire out loud, though it doesn't have to be said out loud. You can say it in your head too. Know they are always around, but they will not interfere without permission. In the above example, I asked for a sign. That's why I received one.

The more I communicate with my Guides, and the more intuitive I get, the more they find different and unique ways to communicate with me, and the more I recognize their presence in my life. It really is that easy.

For more information on asking for signs, see Chapter 8.

CHAPTER 13

When we are truly ready to change, there is no mountain we won't climb.

IT WAS SEVERAL YEARS AGO NOW, AFTER HAVING RE-CREATED THE SAME PATTERN OVER AND OVER AGAIN IN DATING, WHEN IT FINAL-LY HAPPENED. I had met a guy I was truly excited about, and we were starting to date.

This time was going to be different.

I remember the night we met. I felt butterflies. He seemed to check off all of the boxes, and I remember even looking to ensure he was available, like he was wearing a sign or something. *It appeared he was perfect.*

In my mind, at least, this time, I was making a *different choice.* Plus, I had all of the awarenesses around the type of guy I had previously attracted (with years of therapy to prove it), and it was finally going to happen.

We went out on this great first date. Dinner. Check. Movies. Check. And electricity. Oh, was there electricity. And, this wasn't any kind of electricity. This was the kind of electricity that we all live for. *At least, in this moment, I thought so.*

Then, nothing. No call. No text. Nothing.

I tried to wait, but I ended up succumbing to the temptation and reached out.

Big mistake.

While he may have been into me, he was into me for only one thing. *I'll give you a hint. It wasn't for my intelligence, drive or quick wit.*

To make matters worse, he was using me to get over his ex-girl-friend. *Oh shit, he's unavailable.* I still don't think it had fully hit me at the time that this was happening, though.

So, this went on for a few more weeks. The waiting for him to call. The nervous knots in my stomach when I'd hear from him and when I wouldn't. The overanalyzing with my friends and making excuses for him.

Do you think I'll hear from him again? Does he like me? Oh, I'm sure he's just not calling because he's busy. I'm sure I'll hear from him soon.

It was within one month, and I finally had had enough. (On the bright side, these types of trysts weren't lasting as long now.)

We finished our fling, like I always did, on the phone, cornering him, wanting to know why he was leaving. (Surprisingly, he had no clue, nor did he care to know.)

Either way, it was the perfect ending *and beginning.*

That weekend, I ended up at the house of a family friend, who was a therapist, crying, irrationally devastated.

That's when she suggested trying something different, *and I was finally ready to listen.*

You see for years I had had family members and friends try to gently suggest seeing a different therapist or doing something different to change my life. While I said I wanted to change, and inside of me, I believed I did, for all of my twenties and the first few years of my thirties, my actions spoke louder than my words.

But now I was finally ready.

There was a retreat in California that had received rave reviews. They were all about creating change and working with family patterns, and I was really ready to see my life look different.

It would be single-handedly the biggest investment I had ever made in myself. Heck, up until that point, it would be the only true investment (that I can remember) that I had made in myself to really change.

In the weeks leading up to the retreat, I could feel the anticipation in the air.

I just knew something was going to change—thank God.

LIFE LESSONS AND LEARNINGS

CHOOSING IT TO CREATE CHANGE IN YOUR LIFE

The biggest learning I had from this, and I wouldn't have it until quite some time later, was that our choice dictates so much. So many times I had said I wanted to change, and yet I stayed in therapy, working with the same therapist, telling the same story over and over. What I was finally realizing was that wanting to change and taking new action to create it are two totally different things.

A piece of this, too, was maybe for the first time ever, having skin (i.e., a financial investment) in the game. When I was in therapy, my therapist had generously agreed to only bill my insurance. I am confident this didn't help with my commitment to myself and getting results from my time. Instead, my therapist took on the role of just being someone nice to talk to. Yes, it felt good, as she was comforting and had known my mom, yet it was not an ideal recipe for change.

QUESTIONS:

- What in your life are you saying you want to change, but haven't done anything different to get a new result? Why is this? Notice what your reason is and if there's something you're scared of. For me, with my therapist, I had developed a codependent relationship with her, and letting go of her felt like letting go of a piece of my mom, given that they had known each other and a part of me felt that my therapist was committed to watching over me for my mom.

- On the opposite end, where have you chosen money over yourself? Yes, you have to have money to live, but so many times, I see people choosing money and "stuff," including vacations, new appliances or gadgets, over themselves, changing and really, their little boy or girl. I get that, in this culture, we've been trained to value things over ourselves, but as you know, we can't be buried with it, and choosing to do this kind of work is likely one of the real reasons why you're here anyway (i.e., your soul came here to learn, expand and grow, not to acquire more stuff). Also, important to note: Every time you put yourself second and choose money over you, you tell the Universe to do this too. And, if your reason for not moving forward is related to money or time, I want you to notice, when you have *truly* wanted something, did you make it happen in your life? This is good information. Lastly, notice, too, if time or money is just an excuse because you're scared to change.

TOOLS:

For all of these, energy clearing is a great option. Energy clearing clears out old childhood patterns and beliefs that stop us from having what we want in our lives. Through energy clearing, I've seen self-sabotaging behaviors eliminated and more money and time created. (In addition to shifting our blocks, including money and love blocks, energy clearing can help to clear out your anxiety, so you can feel more calm, peace and ease.)

To start experiencing energy clearing, you can head to my website for workshops and audios as well as downloading my free Clearing Childhood Patterns video at bit.ly/childhoodpatternsvideo.

In addition to this, I recommend:

1. If you're choosing money over yourself and it's because you're scared to change:
Sit in a quiet place and get present with yourself, taking some nice deep breaths. Then, I would start by asking why this is. What are you scared is going to happen if you choose you and, with this, if you choose to change?

Then, connect with your inner child and give voice to the fear and what you're feeling scared of. Say this out loud until it doesn't feel true for you. Then, replace it with a positive that's true for you. So, for example, you might start off saying, "I'm scared to change. I'm scared to change. I'm scared to change..." and then once you feel like the charge is off of that, you can replace it with, "I'm excited to change. I'm excited to change. I'm excited to change..." The most important thing here is that what you're saying is actually true for you and that you're not beating up on yourself in any way. (Important to note: This can take multiple times and sayings for this to really be true.)

2. If money is really the issue:
If there is something that's truly important to you that you're really wanting to do, and you're struggling financially, I would ask what you can add to your life to make additional income. So many times, when we look to have extra income, we look to take things out of our lives. This can be a scarcity mindset. Instead, come from an abundance perspective and look at what you can add, whether it's another part-time job, selling items you're no longer using, or, if it's a possi-

bility, doing an exchange of services with the person you're seeking help from. Alternatively, see if the organization offers a scholarship or discount. Most importantly, if you're truly desiring it, keep your options open for how it can happen and ask the Universe for help.

3. If time is really the issue:

Ask yourself what's really important to you. This is an important question in understanding what you're choosing to prioritize and why. Then, if this is really important to you, shift your priorities to include it. If it isn't, that's okay too. It's more important just to get the clarity you need and to let go of beating up on yourself if this isn't a priority for you right now.

Also, one of the analogies my Guides and Angels gave me around time, and really there always being enough time (i.e., that time is infinite), is to think of our soul's life like an infinite roll of film. While your life in this physical body is captured on one part of that film and does end, your next journey will pick up where that film (and your growth) left off, and because we are always changing forms (i.e., from spirit to human back to spirit), the film continues on forever.

CHAPTER 14

Our decision to change is what changes everything.

THE TIME WAS FINALLY HERE. I was finally heading off on my retreat. I was like a kid on Christmas morning, though it was the middle of July over my 34th birthday. It would be the perfect birthday present to myself.

Before going, they had us fill out close to thirty pages of prep work. Most of the work was related to identifying our parents' patterns, and while at the time, I knew I had an abandonment pattern that was attracting unavailable partners, if you asked me about any of the other patterns I had gotten from my parents and family, I couldn't have told you what these were.

I got to the retreat late that night, so I didn't get a chance to meet any of the participants, outside of my roommate, who was in bed when I got there, but lovingly told me to make myself at home.

The next morning, as I sat in the room with the other forty participants, I found myself smiling a lot and using humor to block what I was feeling, which was actually subtle nervousness about what was about to happen. I didn't notice it then, but this would be pattern number one.

I remember, too, my assigned teacher talking to me about how the work might reveal that my mom wasn't perfect and that her patterns had played a role in her cancer. I remember feeling defensive, and really protective, as she said this to me.

How could she say this? This couldn't be true, could it?

So, as we started working on our parents, I found working on my mom was easier, or really harder, than my dad. My whole life, to me, she could never do anything wrong, so as I started to peel back the pieces of her that were holding me back, it was hard to see these. It didn't help, too, that she had passed away from cancer, in essence making her a "victim."

On the other hand, when I began working on my dad, I was very connected to the pain I had experienced from the choices he had made. I remember the epiphany I had when I realized why I had had such trouble exiting negative relationships—it was because I had perceived that he had vacated so easily.

And, the thing I remember being most connected to was my anger. Actually, it was more like rage, and it seemed to be endless. I was so furious at him for leaving.

How could he do that to me? HOW COULD HE DO THAT TO ME?

The hurt I had experienced from this in all of my relationships was unbearable. So even though there were forty other people in that room, you could hear my screams over it all. I couldn't tell you how long they went on for; it seemed like it would never stop, so much so that I remember at one point one of the other teachers going up to my assigned teacher. I didn't hear what he asked her, but my sense was he was asking her what had happened to me.

I also remember, at one point in this process, I stopped screaming and looked up. It was then that I saw it—I saw the other participants' pain, and I felt more connected to them, not less. My entire life I had subconsciously thought I needed to be perfect to be loved, but it was in this moment that I realized the connection occurred outside of the perfection and in the pain, and really, the vulnerability—not outside of it.

That day, though, at the end of it all, I felt different. I felt tender. I felt good. I felt more open and vulnerable. I didn't know why at the time, but I now realize it was because I was letting go of all of the anger, rage and hurt I had been, literally, carrying around my entire life. All of the stories where I wondered why I had gotten the short end of the stick. All of the pain that I thought would define me forever. All of the hurt that had weighed me down for so long. For the first time ever, I was making myself matter, and I had taken the first step to forgiving my father.

It was mid-way through the retreat when I realized it, though I remember it like it was yesterday. I was getting into bed and preparing to tell myself, "I love you," like I had said every night since the night my mom had passed away to replace her loving words, when it hit me. *I knew it from the inside out.* I felt an indescribable wholeness. I felt love. Really, I felt full.

I left the retreat, likely for the first time ever, clear-headed and in a euphoric state, so much so that when I went to go rent a car later that afternoon, I started to drive off of the lot with the driver's side front door *open*.

No matter what, though, I was awake, and there was no going back.

LIFE LESSONS AND LEARNINGS

BEING AWAKE

Waking up isn't as easy as it may appear to be. I had spent the first 34 years of my life asleep, which had many benefits.

I could be the victim. (This meant pretending that life was just happening to me and I had little to no control over my circumstances or choices.)

I could pretend I didn't know when someone was lying to me. (Do you know how many times people, including myself, have lied because lying is easier than telling the truth? It's a way of life in our society, and while it may be easier, it hurts not to mention that when we lie, we are subconsciously saying it's okay for others to lie to us. Plus, when we do this, we give mixed messages to the Universe, as we are not being clear around who we are and what we want and don't want.)

Even deeper than that, though, I could pretend I wasn't living a lie. This meant I could pretend I was happy.

When I woke up, though, everything started to change. I felt happy amidst a sea of general unhappiness. You don't realize how much comfort there is in struggle and fitting in, until it's no longer there. For me, I had been comfortable in that place for so long, until I wasn't. And, while I never fit in, I was now keenly aware that I didn't. I saw everything clearly, including the excuses I had been making and the lies I had been telling, and I could no longer pretend I didn't know better, because I did.

As part of this, I was beginning to realize I was creating everything. This meant I had control over *every single thing* that was occurring in my life. This also meant, though, I couldn't pretend otherwise. The in-between, the bad, the good—I was responsible for it all.

Also, I was now living from my soul's mission, and she had a completely different agenda than the one my human self did. Her mission, if I chose to accept it, was of love, forgiveness and growth. *It was "better," but it wouldn't be easy.*

Fun fact—as part of my awakening, I had a newfound inner peace. I also thought it would be a good idea to share this with my medical sales' clients. (I didn't get any weird looks.)

QUESTIONS:

- What patterns do you have in your life that you learned growing up that aren't serving you? Are you critical or a perfectionist? Are you a know-it-all or on the opposite end, do you diminish what you know?

- Where do you feel like you're not enough? In your relationships? Career? Body image/health? Income?

- Where do you play the victim in your life? As part of this, where are you not taking responsibility? Why? How does this work for you?

- Where do you lie to yourself? Why? Where do you lie to others? Why?

- Where do you try to fit in? Is this true for you or did you come here to be different?

TOOLS:

To move out of your patterns and being a victim and into being a powerful creator:

Step One

While I share similar questions in starting to identify the roles our loved ones play, the following questions are also key to owning the powerful creator we each are. As part of this, keep asking these at all times, especially when you don't want to own that you played a role in creating what you created:

Why is this in my field? What is this here to show me? What thoughts, beliefs and feelings created this and how did they create this?

Also, important to note, from whom did you learn this?

As you do this, you'll start to notice how you're always co-creating your environment with Spirit, God and your Guides and Angels, and you'll notice most of the things you're doing, creating and even believe in and about your life are from your childhood.

Step Two

Notice how these thoughts, feelings and beliefs serve you. Even if they're not creating what you want, in some way they keep you safe, small and in control of your life.

Step Three

If you let go of these, what are you scared will happen? Sit with this fear as long as you can, until you can feel it dissipate. As you do this, you may even need to give it a voice, saying out loud, "I'm scared that _____." Examples include "I'm scared that I may get what I want," "I'm scared that I won't fit in" and "I'm scared that I won't be able to play small in my life anymore." As you are saying these, see these beliefs leaving your body.

You'll notice as you give voice to these, the feelings will start to lessen. As this happens, you may notice yourself making different choices in your life that are more from your truth and less from your patterns.

(Do this as many times as it takes to completely undo the pattern.) Most importantly, it's key not to leave yourself or your emotions, no matter how difficult or challenging feeling this is. If this gets too intense, it's okay to take a break, as long as you come back to it, and really, to you, when it feels right. This could mean that day, later that week or in a couple of weeks. There's no rush, just as long as you stay committed to it (and you!), and you come back to it when the timing feels right.

These steps are the first steps to becoming a powerful creator. You'll find many other tools in this book to support you with this as well.

Step Four

Once you feel like what you're wanting to shift has dissipated, replace it with what you're wanting to create in your life. With the above examples, this may look like "I'm playing big in my life," "I'm making choices/choosing life for me" or "I love getting what I truly want." Important to note: This should be in the affirmative and not the negative (i.e., "I'm choosing big in my life," NOT "I'm no longer scared I won't fit in"). Again, the important piece is not just saying these to say them, but actually believing and feeling them in your body. This might mean that you'll need to do Step Three multiple times.

FITTING IN

For fitting in, do the steps above, specifically related to your fears around not fitting in and then ask yourself:

Step Five

If I wasn't trying to fit in, what would I do?

Whatever that is, do it and continue to keep choosing it until it becomes part of who you are.

CREATING CONNECTION THROUGH VULNERABILITY AND LETTING GO OF PERFECTIONISM

In addition to waking up, one of my biggest aha's on this retreat was realizing other people (often enormously successful) had significant pain in their lives, too, and with this, seeing my response to seeing their pain, imperfections and vulnerability, which was to love them more, not less. I remember the feeling of wanting to be closer to them and really, to reach out and hug them. Of course, in this setting, I didn't, but recognizing and feeling this alone was huge, and really, life-changing. In part, I think this is because we get so conditioned to comparing our insides to everyone else's outsides, so it can be easy to think we are the only ones who are suffering and we don't realize that everyone is going through their own challenges and struggles. Also, I think sometimes the people who have had the most pain in their lives, also have the most success (i.e., pain can be a great driver for big success, if we let it be).

QUESTIONS:

- When you share your imperfections and are vulnerable, how does this feel? How do you feel when someone shares these with you? In both cases, how can you use these to create deeper connection with another?

- As part of this, do you believe you have to be perfect to be loved? Are you ready to let go of this to create deeper connection?

TOOLS:

If you're ready to begin creating more vulnerability in all of your relationships:

Start practicing being vulnerable. Prior to doing this, you'll want to tune in to connect with what relationships you want to create this in. (Not every relationship may be appropriate for this.) With the ones that do feel right, you can simply start practicing, by connecting to what's going on inside of you and sharing that or alternatively, you can talk to them about your intention and see if they're onboard with creating this too. Then, it's important to keep choosing it and noticing what happens as you share with them, and them with you (i.e., do you feel closer to them? how does your relationship evolve?).

For more on letting go of perfectionism, see Chapter 32. With this, I recommend adding:

If I didn't need to be perfect here, what would I do? Then, do it!

CHAPTER 15

Your only way out is in.

THE RETREAT I TOOK FINALLY HELPED ME TO BEGIN TO GET CONNECTED TO MYSELF AND MY EMOTIONS. With all of the challenges on my journey, as you can imagine, tears have made up a fair amount of my life. From the time I was a young girl, I remember the numerous times I would be at my family's house and something would inevitably happen. I would start crying, and I would get told I was "too emotional" or "too sensitive." Then, I would make myself wrong, and I would try to hold back my tears. Of course, this didn't help, as it would mean holding back my natural feeling, which was to let out the pain, emotions and sensitivity I was feeling in that moment. Instead, the pain would get stored in my body, and I would pretend nothing had happened. I would end up feeling like I was too much, which meant more holding myself back from my true nature. To put it mildly, the pain of these moments was unbearable, and during these times, I wanted to shut every piece of myself down while simultaneously crying out loud at the loudest volume I could. Of course, I never did the latter. Either way, though, I never felt more alone, and at many times, crazy.

Why did no one else feel this way? There must be something wrong with me.

Even deeper, what I didn't realize until much later was, I really loved my emotions—all of them. I had been so conditioned that emotions were bad that I hadn't connected to my inner truth, which was that I loved feeling it all! This was simply the way I felt, though for a long time, I just wasn't connected enough to myself to realize this.

As part of this, looking back, I wish I had known that my tears and emotions would be the key to healing. I wish I had known that there was nothing wrong with my tears. Most importantly, I wish I had known that providing a safe space for tears and emotions was part of what I was meant to bring to the world.

If you consider yourself an Empath, which means being sensitive to all emotions, including your own, or have been labeled any of the above, know your emotions have a purpose. Know your emotions are your guidance system. Know your emotions are the key to feeling, dealing and healing.

Allow yourself to really take this in.

LIFE LESSONS AND LEARNINGS

FEELING OUR FEELINGS

As humans, we have to learn how to embrace *all* of our feelings. For me, my journey to truth was realizing that I loved all of my emotions, and really, that *I loved feeling.*

As part of this, when I feel, I know that I'm alive. When I was a kid, one of the subconscious and unconscious messages throughout my childhood was that feeling my feelings was bad, wrong, or even deeper, that it could kill me. It took quite some time to realize that the deeper I dove into my emotions and allowed myself to feel it all, even the hard pieces, the better I felt. Many times, when a difficult moment or emotion presents itself, I get excited to feel what's up for me, and while I still have moments where I can avoid something that's painful, when I do go "there," I'm always grateful that I did, and I feel better and lighter because of it.

Taken one step further, what I've learned is that our pain, emotions and suffering are all joy in disguise. When something hard is occurring, most, if not all of us, are conditioned to try to avoid or leave it. What I found, though, is if I stayed with it (i.e., feeling whatever was coming up for me in that moment, whether it was fear, hurt, shame, control or something else), what's lying underneath that is joy. It may be several layers down, but for me, and I believe this is true for all of us if we take the journey, it's always been there, waiting to be revealed. The more work I do on myself, and really, the more clearing I do of my childhood patterns, the quicker this occurs and the lighter and more positive I feel. What I'm describing is always our truth, but is usually buried under our familial patterns and many times, our pain.

I've also seen the impact that feeling my feelings has on the way others honor my feelings, everything from when someone sees that I'm upset, their stopping and checking on me to their standing up for me. Recently, someone was trying to bully me on an airplane, and while I knew I wasn't going to listen to him or his request, I found the lady across from me standing up for me, without my saying a word. This was humbling and beautiful, and all of this started as I started to honor and love all of me, including my feelings.

QUESTIONS:

- When you were growing up, what messages did you receive around your emotions? This might have included things like "Toughen up," "Get over it," "Crying is for babies," or, even better, "Crying about it won't get you anywhere." It's important to notice what these are, as these might block you from allowing yourself to feel what is occurring for you.

- Are you connected to your feelings? A good way to notice if you are (or aren't) is to ask yourself what you are feeling in this moment. Another thing you can do is to notice (and look back on the times) when you're going (or have gone) through something rough, what do you do with your emotions? Do you feel them or do you stuff them down, push them away or escape from them with alcohol, drugs or even doing? (One good way to connect to this is to notice how you respond to the chapters in this book that touch you.)

- If you find yourself scared to feel your feelings, I would ask, "What am I scared of?" As part of this, you may want to check in with the little girl or boy who lives within you and give them the voice they may have never had around what's scary for them with this.

- Do you consider yourself "sensitive" or have you been told you're "too emotional"? It's important to notice this. You may be an Empath, and if you are, this is an important piece to understand about yourself to move out of feeling like you're too much and making yourself wrong for feeling what you've been feeling. After all, this can be used as an asset, once you understand it. (For me, as I've learned how to embrace this, honoring, loving and feeling all of my feelings, this has taken me higher than I would have been able to go without doing so.)

Tools:

1. Begin to practice connecting to your feelings. One good way to do this is to periodically, during your day, check in with yourself and ask what you are feeling.

2. Once you notice what you're feeling, when it's something that's hard or hurtful, notice what you do with it.

3. If you don't already, begin to practice staying with and feeling your emotions. With this, start to notice when a "negative" emotion comes up and give yourself the time to actually feel it, ideally, in that moment, but if not, set aside time later that day or on the weekend to sit with it. Even if nothing comes up, the more you do this practice, the more you'll start to open yourself to and begin to release these emotions. With this, the more you focus on these, the more you tell the Universe, my feelings matter, and no matter what, I'm not leaving me during these difficult times. Then, the more others will reflect this.

4. If you do find yourself feeling like your emotions are too much or making your emotions wrong, notice why. Is this something you learned or were you told you were wrong for having strong emotions when you were a child? It's important to use one of the inner child processes in this book to work with your inner child on this, allowing them to express their feelings to you. Also, if you find yourself feeling overwhelmed or suppressing your emotions, I want to plant the seed that, my personal experience with this is that, in doing and focusing on this, it actually feels worse than just feeling what you're feeling and giving yourself the space to be with it.

CHAPTER 16

When we trust, we give the Universe the opportunity to show us a miracle.

It was shortly after I got home from my awakening retreat that a group of my friends had organized a paddleboarding expedition on Lake Michigan on the north side of Chicago. Coming home from my retreat, I have to say that I was excited to share this experience with anyone who would listen, especially my friends.

As I met up with this group, I felt alive, open and in full trust. In my mind, nothing could go wrong!

The day started like any other. As I got there and saw my friends, I was eager to get started and to talk with them about my most recent adventure. As we walked out on the sand, though, I might as well have been chasing them, as it appeared that they couldn't have cared less. It didn't matter, though. Everything was going my way!

When we got to where the paddleboards were, the paddleboard company proceeded to walk us through some instructions, though in the state I was in, they might as well have been speaking Swahili. I was completely unbothered that I had missed all of the instructions, though. I was in flow, and I had this. ("Flow" being the operative word here.)

So, I picked up the paddleboard. It was heavy, *really heavy*, but if you can't tell already, nothing was going to get me down! I had the secret to life, and I was flying high, with or without a 30-pound paddleboard on my shoulders.

I put the paddleboard in the water, and I was on my way. As I started going, I found myself being pulled by the wind away from my friends. No matter what I did, whether it was paddling forward or backward, sitting still or standing up, I was getting farther and farther away from them and farther away from help.

As you guessed it, though, I was not concerned. *"You don't have anything to worry about,"* the Universe echoed. I believed it in every ounce of my body too.

It was an hour or two later, and I started to see my friends from the distance heading in. *I should probably start to head back in, too,* I thought. *But, how the heck am I going to get there?*

That's when this couple saw me, and unsolicited, asked me if I wanted help.

"I would love help," I exclaimed.

The man grabbed my board, and they proceeded to help me out of the water.

"Where do you need to take this?" the man asked me.

"Over there," I motioned.

"Oh, well we should probably get the car then."

Should I be worried? I thought. They looked perfectly fine, though, and, of course, I was in flow. It would be fine.

So, we headed to their car, and while initially I started out in the front passenger seat, I was too short to hold onto the board, so he told me to drive his car while he held onto the board from the front seat and his wife held onto the board in the back seat.

When we got to the spot, he carried the board to where I needed to drop it off.

"Thank you so much," I said, feeling super grateful to them, smiling at the feeling in my body that knew it would be okay.

When I got over to my friends, who had been placing bets on how long I would be, they couldn't believe what had happened.

I could, though. That's what happens when you're in flow.

LIFE LESSONS AND LEARNINGS

FLOW

I've spent most of my life worrying, many times about things I couldn't control and things that would never take place. After I got home from my first retreat, though, all of this had changed. I felt more calm, peace and ease from my insides. All of a sudden it was quiet inside, and I felt free.

When I went paddleboarding that day, it was the chance for me to see this big change reflected in my outer world. As I had started that excursion, every ounce of my being knew I was going to be fine. No matter how far I drifted from my friends, I felt calm, peaceful and open. Years earlier, I cannot say that this would have been my experience, but it was powerful to feel this inside, and then to see how this got reflected on the outside and really, how everything worked out at the end of the day. This was my favorite part of this day. And, while I didn't realize it at the time, this was one of my first steps toward owning the powerful creator that I was, and really, that we all are, if we choose to own this piece of ourselves and project this into our reality.

QUESTIONS:

- How would you have responded to the above situation? If you would have gone into worry or panic, this is important to note.

- How do you respond to similar situations where you lose control or have no control to begin with? Take note of this as well.

Tools:

Through our thoughts, words, beliefs, feelings and actions, we are always creating our reality, good or bad. It's important to recognize whether what you are thinking, saying, feeling and believing is what you actually want to create. This was one of the most important pieces to creating the ease I created in the above story—the firm belief, and really, the feeling, that everything was going to be okay.

So, if your thoughts, beliefs, feelings and actions aren't matching your desires, what do you do? *Simply put, you pivot.*

Here's how:

1. Notice what you're thinking and feeling. If it's not desirable, ask yourself why you're stuck to this. Many times, it's because our inner child is scared of something or has something to say about this. (For more on how to work with your inner child, refer to one of the many exercises found in this book.)

2. Once you've shifted the internal belief or feeling, start putting out what you're wanting to create. For me, my internal dialogue throughout that entire day was *everything is going to work out for me.* No matter how far I got from my friends, or how hopeless it could have felt, I kept putting this out there, and most importantly, felt this in every ounce of my being. With this belief and feeling, of course it did.

CHAPTER 17

There is no end point on the journey to change. It's the journey itself that is, and has always been, our real reason to take the adventure.

MY PADDLEBOARD EXPERIENCE WAS ONE OF MY FIRST EXPERIENC-ES COMING BACK FROM MY RETREAT. I remember leaving the retreat, in a total state of bliss. This felt so good that I spent the next six months trying to maintain this, not fully realizing what I was doing.

Yes, part of it was real for me. I'd go outside and notice the beauty in everything. I took a meditation class and started meditating fairly regularly. Oh, and I smiled a lot—at strangers and friends and family, on walks, at work and even inside my apartment. While I enjoyed it, trying to maintain this state was also quite stressful and exhausting.

And, while I didn't realize it at the time, holding onto happiness like this was actually blocking the flow of energy, and really, true happiness. And, let me tell you, the one way to ensure you aren't happy is to try to hold onto it indefinitely and not allow for the full ride.

I remember, toward the end of these six months, when it happened—I finally popped. My wacky neighbor had invited someone to stay at her place who had brought in bed bugs. While I live in a fairly clean building, trying to stay in inner peace with that looming in the background was a definitive buzzkill. I remember, during that time, too, being totally stressed out.

Were they going to come out one night when I was sitting on the sofa or lying in bed and get me? I didn't know, and I didn't want to find out.

Thankfully, I never did find out, but it was definitely enough stress to bring me back down to earth.

Looking back, though, I realize that it was just enough of a kick to pull me out of my high, so I could start living fully and stop worrying about trying to maintain a state that wasn't always serving me.

LIFE LESSONS AND LEARNINGS

HOLDING ONTO HAPPINESS

When I look back, I know that holding onto happiness the way that I had been was a rookie mistake, as I wasn't allowing for the flow of energy. Part of what we come to experience in this physical form, as human beings, is the full ride, and really, the flow of life. This allows for the highs and lows and the ups and downs. After all, if we wanted it to be "all good," we wouldn't have come down here.

To understand this further, think about anyone who has described a near-death experience. They describe the other side as feeling really good and all "love and light." That's because, when we're in that state, it is all love and light there (i.e., while there are different kinds of lessons there, and the reviewing of our life choices in the physical body, if we choose it, there is no contrast, unless we choose to create this; there it's mainly one volume, so to speak: the volume of "great").

But here, we came for the contrast and really, the full ride. With this, it's when we can learn how to lean into this ride and everything that comes with it, that we begin to have full control over our life. No more avoiding the bad. No more resisting the bad when it does occur. Even deeper, no more seeing the bad as bad. With this, we can begin to experience true happiness, no matter what's happening, as even when we are experiencing something difficult, our higher self knows it is taking us higher.

QUESTIONS:

- Where are you trying to "hold onto" happiness or keep it all together? Why? What are you scared of? Does this desire stem from a perfectionist pattern and thinking you're supposed to have the perfect life?

- What can you do to get comfortable with the ride of life versus trying to achieve an end goal? With this, I love the analogy of the roller coaster of life. You can either hold on tightly or put your arms up. It's the same ride, but which one do you think is more fun?

TOOLS:

If you find yourself trying to hold onto happiness, it's important to stop and get present. Take some deep breaths and as I've recommended in previous chapters, ask yourself, and really the little girl or boy who lives within you, about these fears. "What am I scared will happen if I let go?" Maybe you're scared that this is a sign of failure or that your life will fall apart. Take note of this as well as whom you learned this from, likely your mom or dad. Then, I recommend stating the fear out loud, until it doesn't feel relevant for you anymore (i.e., "I'm scared this means I've failed. I'm scared my life is going to fall apart..."). After this, see your body filling with light and love.

CHAPTER 18

Our decision to love ourselves creates a ripple effect of love that lifts us higher than we ever dreamed we could go.

WHEN I GOT HOME FROM THE RETREAT, ONE OF THE OTHER THINGS I STARTED TO PUT TOGETHER WAS HOW I HAD BEEN IN MY RELATIONSHIPS UP UNTIL THAT POINT. After all, my initial purpose for going on the retreat was to heal my abandonment pattern, so that I could finally meet my love partner, but when I got home, while I had some awareness of this prior to going, what I started to see clear as day was how most of my relationships consisted of trying to fit a square peg into a round hole.

Prior to leaving, I was desperately looking for a person to fill the hole I had within myself. It hurt to be alone, and at the same time, it seemed to hurt less, or at least, I perceived it as such, to be around someone else, even if they weren't the right fit for me.

Growing up, I had been trained that the way to happiness was getting married and having kids. There was very minimal mindfulness in who that partner was as a person, or even if he was a good match. The closest to this that existed was if he looked good on paper and if there was some attraction, as if that held the key to anything.

So, as I stepped out into the dating world, post-college, with my abandonment pattern in tact, I found myself dating whoever was in front of me that I felt attracted to. At times, this meant verbally or emotionally abusive men, though I didn't realize this at the time. At other times, it was men who weren't that interested in me or who were only interested in me for one thing.

It was truly painful to keep going through this revolving door of men, and I felt powerless to change the outcome.

As part of this, who I was in these relationships was definitely not my best self, and even more importantly, who I was, wasn't rooted in self-love or self-worth.

What did this look like?

I was extremely defended. I had a ton of walls up, and the only place from which it felt safe to let someone in was a neediness and desperation to no longer be single, which of course, didn't yield good results.

Many times, too, I would subconsciously try to tell a guy how to date me, which included hinting, or even telling him, when to call or when we should go out again. Later, I would realize that this was one way I was in my masculine, but either way, as you may have guessed, this did not go over well.

Most importantly, I was scared to be truly, fully, completely, all of myself. I was constantly modifying myself and just trying to be what someone else wanted. This was exhausting. *After all, it is exhausting not to be ourselves!* With this, I held back things I thought I shouldn't say and did things, looking back, that make me cringe.

By the time I got to my breaking point, after many years of painful relationships where I was left over and over, I felt a lot of despair, worthlessness, and the sense of being unlovable. [I'm not sure how much I even liked myself, which had been wedged in further and further with each relationship, though I'm sure if you had asked me at the time if I loved (and liked) myself, I would have said yes.]

Truth be told, I didn't have a lot of hope that anything would or could change. How could it when, in each relationship, no matter what

I did, no matter how much I tried to protect myself or avoid "bad" guys, it always came back to my abandonment pattern, and really, it always came back to me?

But, of course, many times, it's this breaking point that motivates us toward something more, and after my awakening, I was finally ready to start treating myself with some respect and to start becoming mindful about who I was allowing in my field. I was ready to take a true stand for myself, and really, for what I wanted out of my partnerships.

This first stand came just days after my retreat. The guy who had been the final impetus for signing up for the retreat texted me.

"Hey Debra," (He didn't even know how to spell my name.) *"You want to come on a boat with me and some friends today."*

The Universe was giving me a good test, equipped with a boat! This time, though, I was filled with enough self-love to say no. Maybe I didn't even respond. The details weren't important. What was important was that I had a taste of self-love, and I was not going back.

After this test, I ended up in one more short-term relationship that ended not too differently from before I had started this journey. (Even though I loved myself more, there was definitely more work to be done.)

After this, though, I finally decided I would take a true break. I came to a complete stop in dating and started toward a full, conscious self-love journey.

LIFE LESSONS AND LEARNINGS

Unconscious Coupling and Settling for Less Than We Desire and Deserve

For years, I had been doing what most of us are taught—what I lovingly call unconscious coupling. You know, where two people meet, maybe in a bar or online, find each other attractive and get together based mainly on this, without much mindfulness of whether this is really a good long-term partner. For me, much of this partnering was based on attraction, and an idea I'd learned in childhood, rooted in scarcity, that I was running out of time to find a man and have children.

As I started this work, though, I became invested in something more. I became invested in being true to myself. I became invested in loving myself, and with this, I became invested in deep love and intimacy, which meant that I was determined that I wouldn't fall into the trap of the "It's time to have children, so you'll do" attitude.

Truth be told, as I got to know myself more and more, I started to realize that my desire for children was more rooted in what I had learned than in what I truly wanted.

The other piece that came with this self-love was that I was starting to know myself better. I knew I deserved more than just trying to fill the space with the wrong person and just checking a box on a list just so I could say I was married. I knew this wouldn't make me happy. As this was happening, and I was loving myself more and more, I knew I'd wait forever for the right person, if that's how long it took.

QUESTIONS:

- Where in your life have you settled for less than you've desired and deserved? (While the above is around relationship, there may be another area where this feels true for you.)

- What stand are you willing to take in your life for what you want?

- Do you "unconsciously couple"? How does it feel to partner in this way? Is this something you want to change? If so, what choice will you make to begin to change this?

- Do you love yourself? (I mean, truly love yourself.) Part of this includes taking a stand for what you want and setting healthy boundaries in your relationships. Many of us think we love ourselves, but there's a part of us that has accepted less than we've desired and deserved, has said yes, even when we meant no, and has allowed others to treat us disrespectfully for love. This can include not communicating when something bothers you. I know I can relate to this, and I bet you can too, if you're really honest with yourself.

Tools:

If you're looking to change this, here are some steps to help. Important to note: I identify this for dating, but if you've identified this pattern in some other area of your life, feel free to modify these steps accordingly.

Step One

When taking a stand for something you're desiring in your life, you first need to ask if you're truly willing to do it differently. If not, that's perfectly okay. Just be honest with yourself. If you are, though, move on to Step Two.

Step Two

Determine what you're willing to do differently. Will you stop dating for a while? If you do decide to stop, will you stop accepting invitations for things that don't feel good? Will you say no when you mean no? Will you get rid of the things that are holding you down? And, are you willing to be alone (or to not fill the space with whatever you identified, which can include any form of doing) and work on self-love, even if it means feeling lonely or scared at times? Only you can determine this. (By the way, the more you love yourself, the less lonely you feel. It doesn't mean you never feel the desire to have a partner around you, there's just a certain wholeness that comes with true self-love.)

Step Three

Start acting on the above. What will you do to move toward more self-love? Will you read a book or take a course? How will you move toward what you want and tell the Universe that you want more in your life? Will you turn down a date on a Saturday night, even if it means being alone? Will you go without sex for a while, even if they're cute or it's been months or years? Will you take the time to get clear on what you want and clean out the pieces of your life that are holding you back? On the opposite end, if you do choose to date, will you make sure you are being treated with the love and respect you deserve and setting healthy boundaries around what feels right for you? Whatever the case, start to move toward it.

Important to note: Don't beat yourself up if you slip. Just make a new choice to do it differently the next time.

Also, important to note: None of these are the magic formula for calling in your partner, but the journey has always been to self-love anyway, so if you're loving yourself, you're on the right path.

CHAPTER 19

Death and loss provide a great opportunity for us to heal ourselves, if we let it.

IT WASN'T TOO LONG AFTER COMING DOWN FROM MY HIGH, TOO, AS I WAS STARTING TO COMMIT MORE AND MORE TO MYSELF, WHEN THE UNIVERSE GAVE ME ANOTHER PIECE AROUND SELF-LOVE. This piece was all about healing a piece of me and closing a relationship I'd had, which had caused me a fair amount of pain.

For ten years, like a couple of high school kids, this man, with whom I worked, and I had played a never-ending game of cat and mouse, and a month prior, he had taken his life.

In truth, our relationship is hard to describe. We weren't close, but there was a way that, for me, we felt extremely close. I always had his back, even when I shouldn't have, even at the expense of other relationships. On some level, I felt the same from him.

Either way, it just felt like we had known each other before, and from day one, he couldn't take his eyes off me, and for someone who hadn't felt seen by the opposite sex her whole life, it was a drink that I couldn't get enough of.

It was the kind of feeling that had me doing outrageous things. I would leave my post as a waitress at the high-end restaurant where

I worked to "accidentally" run into him. I would hope to run into him in the parking lot (and sometimes I would stall just to create this). Oh, and there was the time that I saw his car at the Blockbuster, and I stopped in just to "bump" into him.

Not to mention the obsessing and fixating.

Anything to be seen by him.

On the opposite end, he reflected his own version of this, complimenting me on everything under the sun, often staring at me when I would leave wherever we were together, not to mention the time I was away for a couple of weeks, and when I was back and he first saw me, not knowing that I had been on vacation, he told me he was worried that I had left for good. You could tell it had freaked him out.

Either way, with him, no boundaries existed. Mine, that is, though he matched this. There was one time, though, when he asked for an exclusively sexual relationship and I said no. Looking back, I can't believe I said no to him, not because I never said no, but because my love addiction was so strong and I completely lost myself anytime I was around him. But even I had my limits.

I still remember the day I received the text from my friend and old coworker. It was the summer of 2013, and I was sitting at a cheap Chinese restaurant with a friend I hadn't seen in ages.

"Did you hear?" my friend texted, referring to my love addiction.

I felt my heart sink. This couldn't be good. This could not be good.

"He passed away."

When I asked what happened, that's when my friend told me he had killed himself. The gravity of the news paralyzed me, taking my breath away. I don't know if I finished my lunch or what my friend said in response to the news; I was in a complete blur, and I felt my body filled with fear, the same kind of fear I felt in high school when I heard my friend's brother had been killed in the drunk driving crash. *He was gone, and there was nothing I could do about it.*

I know my friend sat with me a while, as I started to process what had happened.

As I sat with the news, I did what most people do when a loved one passes. Amid the shock, I remembered our last moment together. *It really had only been a moment.*

It had been nearly two months earlier, and as my memory flashed back to that day, I remembered the overwhelming feeling I had that I was never going to see him again.

I was leaving where we had worked together, and I was sitting on my black leather seats in my blue Nissan Altima. I was having trouble moving.

"Go back, go back," my soul was screaming.

The voice in my head dismissed it. *But, I always want more time with him.*

This time was different, though, or was it? It just wasn't feeling right. Something unexplainable was telling me to go back.

As I sat in my car after our most recent rendezvous, which consisted of a five-minute conversation with polite exchanges, I felt my heart thumping through my chest, the way it always did when I saw him. *Him.* The guy whose smile could paint the town. The guy who I would race up to. The guy who had noticed my feet, a compliment I fed on for days.

But, I knew we felt off. Correction, he felt off, but, like so many times before, I had lost the identity of where I ended and where he began.

I was sitting in my car, having a conversation with myself. It was silly, really. I had wanted to show him my bio from the Improv Show I had just been in. See, I told you it was silly. But for the girl who many times felt like if he didn't see it, it didn't really happen, it felt important.

It felt especially important with the overwhelming feeling I was getting.

"If I don't show it to him now, I may never get a chance to," my gut whispered.

It would turn out that my gut was right. It always was, but it would take many more gut feelings to listen.

When it came to him, it was just one of the many times my intuition would speak to me.

You see, the week of his passing, I had been getting "hits" to call him. It was many years after our games on the "playground," so getting these kinds of messages was definitely not normal. At the time, though, I wasn't fully tuned in yet to my own knowings.

The day he died, too, had been weird. I was still in medical sales at the time, and I remember distinctly being out in the Rockford area of Illinois with a day full of client meetings. Around the time I believe he passed, I had been driving on a country back road, and a cat jumped out in front of my car and I hit it. From an energetic perspective, it felt like, as he was transitioning, his spirit had jumped in the cat's body, and that's when the cat had run out in front of my car. I don't know that that actually happened, but I know the cat getting hit was reflective of his death.

So, fast-forward to after his death, and I had to begin to unwind myself from the merging I had done when he was still in physical form. This was a merging I had learned from my mother from years of watching her date and how she would relate to men, where she was playing out her own version of trying to get a man to stay.

Through this unwinding, though, I had to unwind myself from the natural response of guilt and powerlessness I felt that I didn't know he was struggling and hadn't helped him. *Maybe, if I had known, things would have been different.* (It didn't help, either, that it was a year to the day of my awakening, which was eerily "coincidental.")

With this, I had to unwind myself from the entanglement I had felt, thinking he would always be there and I would also always be able to "be seen" by him. I also had to unwind myself from the merging that had begun, as I started to wonder what it was like to commit suicide and if this was something that was right for me too.

I had always had an obsession and curiosity with death and what happens when we cross over. Of course, this was understandable, given losing my mom at such a young age. This was then magnified by the loss of loved one after loved one in my twenties and into my early thirties.

Needless to say, it was a dark time, and it was right around that time I was working on my love addiction, which had just been formally diagnosed by my therapist and was resurfacing with this devastating loss.

It was finally time to heal from it.

It was then that my therapist suggested a love addiction program at The Meadows. In case you're not familiar with The Meadows, it's an Addiction-Treatment Center in Arizona.

I have to say, even though I realized I had a problem, it felt weird to go to an addiction-treatment center. I had never thought of myself as an addict. I would imagine most addicts say that, though. This time, though, I was ready to do whatever it took to let go of the relationship patterns that were causing me so much pain, so that I didn't show up that way again. So, I took the advice of my therapist, and I signed up for their love addiction class.

Then something weird happened; they lost my reservation and the class was sold out. Normally, when things like this happen, it ends up getting resolved in my favor, but this time, even though it was their mistake, they said there was nothing they could do about it. I was really disappointed. I'd thought this class would save, err, I mean help, me. It was no longer an option, though, and I was already committed to the date with my work, and truthfully, excited for my "vacation," so, I ended up agreeing to take their "Survivors One" class.

While I didn't think about it at the time, looking back, I have to believe it was synchronistic that I ended up in this class, which works on all kinds of trauma and codependency. It was only a few months earlier that I had realized I was codependent, another piece that I got from my enmeshment with my mom.

This codependency, though, is a bit different from how we

typically define codependency. This codependency was how Pia Mellody defines it, and if you grew up in a traumatic, pain-filled or addiction-based environment, have struggled with boundaries and/ or you've ever felt crazy for no reason, which many times is the result of living in an environment with poor boundaries and a parent(s) who is struggling in their life, I highly recommend her book, *Facing Codependency.*

So, I ended up in a women-only class with one other outside participant and several Meadows's inpatients. Many of these women appeared to be successful on the outside, and from the looks of them, I would never have guessed they were struggling.

Yet, each day, one by one, they would share their stories of abuse, addiction and hardship.

Day after day, I remember leaving the room (I was one of the few people who was permitted to leave) feeling like I needed a shower. It was hard to hear of such pain.

But the class also gave me the opportunity to practice strong listening boundaries, something I had never had. Most importantly, it gave me the opportunity to practice being comfortable in others' pain, trauma and abuse, which is a huge part of the work I do today.

At the time, I left there not sure what I had gotten out of the program, as my love addiction was still there. Looking back, though, I know it was an important part of my training.

It was about a year later, when my friend who had crossed over came to me and we healed the decade's worth of pain we had caused each other.

I had been doing a lot of forgiveness work, getting more in touch with working with energy, and he started coming through from the other side. At that point, I was still healing from the grief and not very strong with trusting what I was sensing, which included reading energy and connecting with loved ones on the other side. He was persistent, though, and I instinctually knew that he was there and why. He wanted me to forgive him for the pain he had caused me. While I know when he was in physical form, he had had no idea of the impact his actions had on me, when he crossed over, my sense was that he realized this and wanted to make amends. The timing of me doing forgiveness work was perfect, and we ended up doing a forgiveness process together.

I remember the feeling of it like it was yesterday. I had my hands on my lap, face up towards the sky, and I felt him holding them. His energy was coming through, and I felt how truly sorry he was for the pain he had caused me.

I also remember being overwhelmed by his love. It felt open, comforting and warm.

It was beautiful and, while I didn't fully trust it, as I hadn't done a lot of this work with deceased loved ones, there was something about it that helped us both to heal and complete our roles for each other in this lifetime. I felt opened, and while it was hard to say goodbye to the person I knew in physical form, it was necessary.

All that was left from our relationship was love, appreciation and humor and goofiness, and he's now one of my Guides. This initially surprised me, as I had a belief he wouldn't care enough to help me, but looking back, I know that was the human side of him, and I now realize this is one of the unintentional benefits of losing a loved one. (I share more about working with your Guides and Angels in Chapters 12 and 38.)

LIFE LESSONS AND LEARNINGS

FINDING MY SENSE OF SELF

One of the biggest things that this man taught me was around having a strong sense of self. For years, in many relationships, I had merged with my partners. I would become who they wanted me to be, and in the process, I would go on a roller coaster ride with them. *This was not fun.*

This relationship was one of the key relationships I had that showed me how detrimental merging could be and I realized it was time for me to choose me and to start working on having a strong sense of self. As part of this, I began to develop stronger boundaries. I said no when I should, and I began to make myself matter more, vocalizing what I needed.

As part of this, my experience at The Meadows reinforced how defended and protected I was. I had been so conditioned to push outward and pretend I was okay, even when I wasn't. This blocked my connection to myself and to others. Again, too, I thought I was the only one who was struggling and who had experienced a hard life. This was simply not true, and what I was starting to really internalize was that everyone has their own version of struggle, and we're all just doing the best we can, until we can know, do and be better.

QUESTIONS:

- Do you have a strong sense of self? If not, why not? What are you scared will happen if you have a strong sense of self (i.e., if I have a strong sense of self, I may disagree with someone and they might leave me)?

- On the opposite end, if you have a strong sense of self, but it comes in the form of defense and protection, how does this impact your relationships? Do you block people from getting close to you? Alternatively, are there times when you hurt another because you're not willing to budge?

- As part of the above, where in your life do you merge? Why? What are you scared will happen if you maintain your boundaries? (For me, I felt scared to fully let go of my friend, as this would mean that I'd have to say goodbye, and at the time, I feared that I might not see him again.)

- Also, where do you have trouble with boundaries? Maybe you don't say no when you should or you don't vocalize what you need. Also, where do you take on other people's "stuff" as your own? Why do you do this?

TOOLS:

To start to develop a strong sense of self, especially if you've had a hard time with this in the past, it's important to continually keep refocusing on yourself, with questions like "How am I feeling right now?" and "What do I want in this moment?" or "Do I want to do what's being asked of me?" If your answer is no, it's important to notice this and determine if you want to actually say no or if you want to go along with it.

Either way, notice why you're doing what you're doing. Is it because you're scared to say no, worried about what someone will think of you if you do say no or even deeper, you're scared they'll leave you if you don't say yes? Alternatively, is it because you're wanting to do something for someone you care about? It's important to make the distinction.

This is especially key, too, when dating, as it can be common to get focused on them and what they want and what will make them happy to be liked, or even deeper, so they will stay. The truth is, though, this ends up creating the exact opposite of what you want and creates an environment of disrespect. Think about it. Have you ever met someone who is always agreeable or hanging on you? Does that make you want to move closer to them or push them away? Do you respect them? I don't know about you, but for me, many times, this pushes me in the opposite direction, and I lose respect for them. So, when you see yourself showing up this way, in addition to the above questions, asking what you like and dislike about this person and noticing how you feel being around them can be helpful.

DEFINING AND IDENTIFYING LOVE ADDICTION

With this, many people, especially women, though I have seen it in men too, have variations of love addiction, and usually it goes undiagnosed. It can include much of the dynamic I described above, as well as merging, obsessing and loss of self and boundaries. In essence, it's the willingness to do anything, even things that aren't healthy or rooted in self-love, to be loved.

Know, if you can identify with this, that it can be healed. I healed mine, and while it's not a perfect science, all of my relationships are rooted in self-love first. If I do slip, I don't beat myself up. Instead, I choose self-love again.

The questions and tools below are a great start to healing it. I also recommend Pia Mellody's *Facing Love Addiction*.

QUESTIONS:

- What are you willing to do for love and to be loved? Is what you're doing rooted in self-love?

- Do you set healthy boundaries in your relationships and are you willing to ask for what you want? If not, why not? What are you scared of?

Tools:

To start to shift this, I recommend the above tools under "Finding My Sense of Self." I also recommend starting to develop a relationship with the little girl or boy who lives inside of you. Throughout this book, I give you many ways to start to build a relationship with them. Here's another way:

1. See them in front of you or feel them inside of you.

2. Place your hand on your heart, and take some nice deep breaths. As you do this, feel and connect to their heart.

3. Ask them what they need and want from you when it comes to relationships. Then, from the "I" perspective, say this out loud multiple times, until it doesn't hold a charge for you (i.e., "I need you to protect me. I need you to protect me. I need you to protect me…"). It's likely, when you were in relationships, you broke their trust, so this is all about giving them the voice they've never had, honoring their feelings and rebuilding their trust. As part of this, they may need to know that you will respect and protect them and keep them safe. Also, this practice is meant to be a regular practice, not a one-off, to help you to rebuild your relationship with them and their trust, so doing this practice regularly, especially when you leave a partner or feel you have done something that wasn't honoring to you (and them) is crucial.

Listening to My Gut

This relationship also taught me to listen to my gut feelings. I've always had the mantra, "My gut is always right." Knowing this, though, and listening to it at all times, were two different things. In this relationship, because time and time again, it came in an indisputable form, there was nothing I could do but to start to truly tune in and listen.

QUESTIONS:

- Do you have gut feelings? If so, how do they come in? Do you listen to them? If not, what stops you?

TOOLS:

It's important that we start to pay attention to our knowings. When you get a feeling, you can do a quick check in to clarify if it's truth or fear. Like in the above story, while it may not always be easy to determine, it's important to tune in and begin to practice noticing and identifying why you're getting what you're getting and what's really true for you. The more you do it, the more you will be able to recognize the difference!

HEALING DIFFICULT RELATIONSHIPS FROM THE OTHER SIDE

Another beautiful thing that came from this experience was a taste of my ability to heal and connect with the other side. Up until this point, I didn't believe I could connect at this level, and while I still had a lot of practice to do to fully trust this (and it's a constant work in progress), experiencing this helped me to boost my confidence and it taught me that, on the other side, all that's left is love. In most cases, too, even people you may have perceived don't really care, actually do. Most importantly, even the hardest relationships and most difficult goodbyes can be healed, so they don't hold the pain, hurt or devastation they initially caused.

QUESTIONS:

- Do you have any relationships with loved ones who have crossed over that you are desiring to heal? Are you ready to let go and heal them now?

TOOLS:

Once you have taken time to grieve this loss, and you feel genuinely ready to forgive, heal and let go, let them know you are ready. (If you haven't already, I recommend doing the Forgiveness Process first, found in Chapter 11.) Once that is done, follow these steps:

1. Set aside a formal time to get quiet and present and to be with them.

2. Invite them in and let them know you're ready to truly let go and heal.

3. Ask them if they are also ready for this and sense their response. If they are, move to #4.

4. Open your body and your heart and hold out your hands. (Important to note: There is no one right way to do this. Do this how it naturally comes to you and however it feels right.)

5. Connect to your higher self. You can do this by bringing your energy up above your head. (We often do this naturally when we pray.)

6. Then, connect to their higher self, using the same process.

7. Once you've done this, say what you need to say and feel their love coming in, taking this in and allowing it to rewire the previous pain. (Also, important to note: Everyone, including beings on the other side, has free will. While it is likely that they will want to heal this, too, they have to choose it, just like you. If you don't feel them choosing it, make sure you are tuning into their higher self. If they're still not choosing it, it may be that you have more to work out with them first or vice versa.)

CHAPTER 20

When you let go of the pressure and simply believe, the Universe is like an amazing boyfriend who surprises you with the world, over and over and over again.

IT WAS RIGHT AROUND THIS TIME, TOO, WHEN I RECEIVED A CALL FROM MY DAD.

"Hey Deb, do you want to go to Australia with Patty (my stepmom)?"

The question took me aback a bit. While she was a flight attendant, I didn't realize her flight benefits were still open to me.

"You mean as a standby," I asked.

"Yes, as a standby," he said.

"Uhh, yeah," I said. Inside I was like, *Hell yes! You don't have to ask me twice.*

"Well, there's nothing guaranteed. There has to be space," he said cautiously.

It was then that it hit me that just a year earlier I had been planning a trip to Australia for this exact time frame, but because of the cost, I had put it aside for the time-being. As life does, though, I had moved on and completely forgotten about it, until I had gotten this call from my dad.

As I got off the phone with him, no matter what he'd said or how cautiously he'd said it, I knew I was going. *You don't know my relationship with the Universe,* I thought silently to myself with a big smile on my face.

And, on December 25, 2013, I went.

LIFE LESSONS AND LEARNINGS

BECOMING A POWERFUL MANIFESTER

As I began shifting the beliefs and things out of my system that were in the way of what I was desiring, and really, as I began rewiring the part of me that was operating from my childhood patterns, I was starting to become a powerful manifester. Now, I know I was actually returning to the powerful manifester I'd always been, that we all truly are, but have forgotten and shut down our true power around. Either way, though, this was one of the first and strongest examples of my return to this.

The biggest piece of this for me, too, was realizing that if I desired something and it was in my highest good, I didn't have to push for it to happen. I could let go and detach from the outcome, and it would happen on its own. All I had to do was be patient and believe.

QUESTIONS:

- What are you desiring right now? It could be something small or something big.

- Do you have any attachments to the outcome or it occurring? As part of this, what are you trying to control and where is this squashing what you're desiring from happening? Also, where does this stop you from living in the present, having fun and enjoying yourself? Also, where are you looking for a guarantee before you take action? (As we all know, there are no guarantees.)

TOOLS:

1. Put it out to the Universe.
When I talk about "putting something out to the Universe," it literally is that simple. Many times, I literally say out loud, "I'd like to create XYZ (fill in the blank here). Can you help me with this?" Then I take action to move toward it in my physical reality.

2. Let go of attachment to that specific outcome.
Once you've put something out to the Universe, if you feel attached to a specific outcome in an unhealthy way, it's important to let go of it actually needing to happen, or for that matter, how it happens— what Mike Dooley calls "the cursed hows." (The most common examples I see of this attachment are typically around love and it working out with a partner.) One of the best ways to do this is to become comfortable with your specific desired outcome not occurring. Then, instead, shift your focus to bigger possibilities and what you want to feel, instead of, for instance, who you want to feel it with or where you "have" to go. As part of this, keep expanding your perspective, so if you find yourself, for instance, focused on one guy, redirect your energy to the infinite amount of partners on the planet or alternatively, the desired feeling you will have with your partner.

Also, if you do find yourself attached to a specific outcome, it's important to practice letting go of this, as this attachment can squash the energy of possibility. To do this, while it may seem counterintuitive, I see my desired outcome not occurring. Usually when this comes up, I feel my chest tightening, and I feel myself wanting to push harder or "do" something to make it happen. Sometimes I do. At some point, though, I get to the place where I know the only thing that will serve me is sitting with the discomfort of not having it and really, surrendering. As I stay with this, which can take several minutes or more, I'll notice the discomfort and the feeling of control, attachment and holding on tightly start to loosen and open. This is an important key, as if you leave the feeling before it's opened, you'll still be in the attachment, and as Carl Jung says, "What we resist, persists." (This is definitely an advanced technique, so if you're struggling with this, it's important to reach out for support.)

The other piece of this is that you have to be genuinely okay with the thing you're desiring not happening. This is not faking that you're okay. This is not telling the world that you'll be fine if what you're desiring doesn't happen, even though this doesn't feel true for you. No, this is a genuineness in your heart that, whether it happens or it doesn't, you're truly okay with it. One way I like to do this is to refocus my energy on all of the good things that are happening in my life in that moment and to focus on the feeling and all of the possibilities of whatever it is that I'm desiring. So, in the above, I might focus on all of the wonderful places that I could visit or I might focus on how I will feel when I meet the right person for me.

3. See and feel your desired outcome occurring.
Once you've felt the discomfort and let go of any attachment, and with this, moved into an authentic space around being okay whether it shows up or it doesn't, then see your desired outcome occurring, and really feel this in your body, believing in every ounce of your being that it's going to happen. Again, I recommend being more general about this, and not attaching to a specific outcome, even setting the intention, "May this or something greater occur,"

keeping in mind that when you have a specific outcome in mind, you can block even greater possibilities. Also, if you notice yourself moving back into attachment, let go again, using the above process.

4. Do something to move toward it.
The next step, which is one of the most important steps, is to take multiple actions in that direction. It can be small or big actions, but our vibration is always matched, so if you're just sitting and waiting for it to happen, without taking any massive action, many times the Universe will match this vibration, which can delay your desired outcome.

5. Then, live in the moment!
This last step should be the easiest, right?! Either way, if you find yourself thinking about or obsessing about what you're wanting, take some deep breaths and focus on who and what is around you, what you're doing and how you're feeling to bring yourself back into the present moment. (If you find a fear is coming up around not getting the thing that you are desiring, use one of the many processes I describe in this book to work with your inner child to talk to them about their fears.)

It's important to note, too, that this process isn't necessarily linear, so you may need to do many of these steps multiple times not in any specific order.

Also, throughout this book, I've used both manifester and creator to describe the powerful force that's working with us to help us to create our reality. While it's subtle, I personally prefer creator, or even co-creator, as manifester has a slightly less powerful connotation. This is because with manifesting you're giving something over to the Universe to create it for you, while with creating or co-creating, you're creating it with the Universe as your co-pilot. Again, it's subtle, but to me, it's an important distinction since our words create our reality.

CHAPTER 21

When we try new things, we open new doors.

IT WAS RIGHT AFTER THIS THAT I FOUND ENERGY CLEARING, OR REALLY, IT FOUND ME. I was still in medical sales at the time, and there was a program that was talking about clearing my abundance blocks. I was curious, and, as the instructor was selling her program, I remember her saying something about how many times we let money get in the way of what we want. This really landed for me, and even though I had no idea what energy clearing was, I decided to invest in it.

As I began listening to the audios, though, I saw unexpected money starting to come in. This included everything from unexpected checks in the mail to business getting closed in my territory, typically with minimal effort on my part. At the time, I had no idea how it was working. I just knew it was working, and I was hooked! (The following year, I quadrupled my sales and increased my income by tens of thousands of dollars with this tool.)

As part of this, I also noticed that I was feeling better. I started to feel lighter and more positive. To put it simply, I was moving into a kind of flow that I had never consistently experienced before. *Hell yes.*

As this happened, I started diving deeper and deeper into the work. Unbeknownst to me, I was diving into a true soul journey. This journey would not be easy. It would be a journey to forgiveness, to feeling it all and to not leaving myself.

With the pattern of being left over and over, what I hadn't realized was that every time someone left me, I had also left me. Every time someone left me, I would blame myself and assume I had done something wrong. Every time someone left me, I would find myself struggling to get out of bed, in the fetal position again, shaking, with my heart feeling like a 100-pound weight had been dropped on it.

So, even though I had already healed so much, I thought I'd never fully heal this part of me. Really, I thought I would just have to cope with it for the rest of my life.

I went deeper, though, and I started to learn how to feel my feelings fully in a healthy way.

On a human level, I felt good, as I knew I was making myself matter. On a soul perspective level, I felt even better, as I started to know that I was living my soul's purpose in this lifetime. This purpose was the purpose of owning the full journey, not just the "good," and feeling it all, all the while growing, loving and forgiving. With this, I embraced it all, and perhaps for the first time in this lifetime, my soul was smiling.

LIFE LESSONS AND LEARNINGS

FEELING YOUR FEELINGS

I talk about this specifically in Chapters 5 and 15, but there are a few more things I want to touch on around this.

Just like so many of us, I used to not feel comfortable feeling my feelings. For so many years, taking on others' truths, I made doing this wrong. It didn't help, too, that it would feel like when something was coming up for me, and I started to feel it, that it could go on forever.

But, as I started to feel my emotions, instead of them taking me down into a never-ending bottomless pit, like I thought they would, I started crying less and less and feeling lighter and lighter. Intuitively, what it felt like was, each time I cried, there was a layer of untruth coming off me. It was like the black hole I had been in was opening and there was light coming in and I was beginning to climb out of it. For the first time ever, it felt like the crying that at one point I thought could go on forever started to actually feel complete. This wasn't because I had to stop. No, it was because I had felt what I needed to feel in that moment, and either the next layer of the pattern had been released or the pattern was gone completely.

As this happened, I felt freer than I ever felt. This makes sense, as our owning our truth frees us.

QUESTIONS:

- Are you scared to feel your feelings? What are you scared will happen if you do?

- Where do you find yourself upset about something, but instead of allowing yourself to feel it, you pretend it's not there and you go back to whatever it is you're doing in that moment? What stops you? What are you scared of?

TOOLS:

The key to this is practice. Initially, this is likely going to feel uncomfortable, scary or, at a minimum, out of your norm. The more you do this, though, the more "comfortable" you'll get with it, or at least, you'll see feeling your feelings won't kill you. For me, the more I do this, the better I feel, as my feelings open the door to the light.

With this, if you're struggling to feel, close your eyes, take some deep breaths, then:

1. Get connected to what you're scared will happen, if you express yourself or feel your emotions. Go there first. For instance, if you're scared you're going to get in trouble, maybe because your dad would yell at you when you were a child because he felt you were too emotional, start by connecting to this, seeing him in front of you, and saying out loud, for instance, "I'm scared I'm going to get in trouble." Alternatively, you can imagine a dial inside of you that's connected to that fear. Then, turn that dial up as high as you can, until the fear dissipates. (I know we are conditioned to think that, in doing this, it will never go away, or even worse, that we might die, but in my work, over and over, I see the opposite is true. When you turn the dial up, what happens in the energy field is the energy releases, so in this example, the fear actually begins to release.)

2. Once you've felt the fear, then go back to the feeling you were trying to feel initially. For instance, if you were feeling angry, go back to that and give yourself time and space to express that anger. For me, when I was initially letting go of the anger I had towards my dad, I used my voice and body, including screaming, punching, or kicking the air, to express my hurt. If this doesn't resonate with you, though, find what does. You can do anything from ripping up paper to screaming into or punching a pillow.

3. And, if you find you're feeling sad or upset, take time to talk with the little boy or little girl who lives inside of you and ask them what they're upset about. For me, when I was connecting with my little girl, she would say, "I'm upset that he left me. Why did he have to leave me?" Whatever she would share with me, I would say that out loud over and over, until I didn't feel the need to say it anymore. So, in the above example, I might say over and over, while staying connected to my body and what I was feeling, "I'm upset that he left me. I'm upset that he left me. Why did he have to leave me?" Sometimes, this would be the last time that this came up for me. At other times, though, she might have the next level of that feeling. So I repeated this process until it was no longer relevant for me.

4. It's important to note, too, if you feel hurt or sadness, but are struggling to access this, and it's not because you're scared, many times, it's because your anger or another emotion is blocking you from feeling this. If this is true for you, identify what this is and feel this first, and then you'll likely be able to access the pain underneath it.

ENERGY CLEARING

If you're curious about energy clearing and how it can help you to feel your feelings, in addition to the complimentary video I did to release the top patterns I see in my female clients, which you can get at bit.ly/childhoodpatternsvideo, and is a great resource whether you're male or female, you can also head to deborahacker.com for my energy-clearing audios as well as live and online energy-clearing workshops and programs.

One other thing I will say about energy clearing, and why it's so effective, is that it gets at the root of the issue. Many times when we go to change something, we try to change it in one of two ways: in the physical world or through mindset work. Here's why those ways aren't always the best method:

1. In the physical world:
Many times when we go to shift something in the physical world, like getting a new job or entering into a new relationship, while things can feel good for a while, we can end up in the same place. This is because when we change it in the physical world, which is only about 5% of the story (95% of the story is energy and our unconscious decisions, actions, emotions and beliefs), we're not taking the charge off of the underlying belief and why we're creating it in the first place.

2. With mindset work:
I always say changing the mind can change it, but changing the feeling will change it. This is because, many times, underneath our mindset can be a deep-seated belief or feeling that no matter how many times you try to rewrite this in your head or you say this out loud or in the mirror, if the underlying belief or feeling hasn't shifted, it doesn't work.

With energy clearing, though, you get to the underlying belief, and with this, the energy that has you creating it in the first place, so you can actually release it and create the reality you're wanting versus the one you're attracting.

CHAPTER 22

Just because you're born into it doesn't mean it's actually true for you.

AS I BEGAN TO STUDY ENERGY, I ALSO BEGAN TO GET CLARITY AROUND MY RELIGION. Growing up, I had grown up in a primarily Jewish family. While I wouldn't have considered any of my most-immediate family extremely religious, we did celebrate the high holidays, including Passover, Rosh Hashanah and Hanukkah, and at times, Yom Kippur. While I've always identified as culturally Jewish, which to me, included a strong sense of family, "bad" jokes that were oh-so-good and even a vernacular that has always made me feel right at home, I never truly identified with the religion piece of it.

As part of this, I remember when I was in sixth grade, when my mom asked us if we wanted to be Bat Mitzvahed. We hadn't really gone to temple up until this point, and she was asking, as we needed to start going, if we wanted to do this. We agreed, which, for me, was probably more out of a fear of missing out than actually a true desire for this experience. I do remember, though, as I was sitting in the temple, the distinct feeling of something not feeling right. Of course, at the time, I wasn't fully identified with what this was or why, as I was just following where I was being directed to go.

It would take a long time for me to understand why I was never fully aligned with my inherited religion, but as I dove deeper and deeper and started to get a better understanding of what energy was and how to work with it to move into deeper alignment on my path, I began to realize that I identified everything as energy.

With this, for me, many of the energies I associated with Judaism didn't feel good or true for me, so I chose not to identify with them. This isn't to make any religion, or in this case, Judaism, wrong. For me, this part of my journey was really about me understanding myself and understanding the incongruence I was experiencing throughout my childhood, as I studied Judaism and did activities at our temple.

Truth be told, I've had a similar experience when I've attended church with my stepmom and my dad, who ended up converting to Christianity. While the energies were different, the experience of feeling like I didn't fully belong there was the same.

But, as I began to understand this incongruence, and most importantly, to make peace with it, as I deeply wanted to connect and fit in with my family, and most importantly, to be like them, as I perceived this was how to be loved by them, I began to get the clarity and direction that I hadn't realized I needed or longed for on my path.

As part of this, the more I learned about Spirituality, which definitely had its overlap with many other teachings, including Judaism and Christianity, the more I felt aligned with it. To me, the beliefs felt light to me and were rooted in love, living our highest potential and not attaching to stories that felt like they held me back. To me, this was how I knew it was truth. In more recent years, many times, people have shared with me that I sound like a Buddhist, too. While I've never formally studied this, outside of a lesson in a high school history class, it's my sense that Spirituality and Buddhism have a lot in common.

LIFE LESSONS AND LEARNINGS

BEING TRUE TO YOU

Truthfully, I struggled with writing this chapter, as many of my loved ones and favorite people are identified with a religion. But, I wrote this chapter for the people who have felt out of place with the religion or beliefs they were born into, and yet, don't fully understand why or know what to do with it. For me, this chapter isn't about making any religion or person wrong. No, it's about helping people who are struggling with being true to themselves and yet, in the process of trying to fit in, have taken on others' beliefs and may not even know what's true for them. I wrote this to help you to open to why that might be and to help you to move toward clarity around what's true for you, not just in religion, but in all areas of your life.

So, first of all, what do I mean, when I say "energy"? I am defining energy here as what I feel when I'm experiencing something, in this case, a religion or belief. Examples of what I'm feeling when it comes to religion can include scarcity, control, guilt, shame or victim energy. As these don't feel good when I experience them, and I know we are meant to feel good, be happy and not struggle, for me, I know they are not rooted in truth or love, as truth and love always feel light in my body and heart. (For me, the only time when this hasn't been the case, and something has been rooted in truth and yet hasn't felt light, is when I'm scared of the repercussions of believing something that the people I love don't believe. This is when something that's rooted in truth may feel heavy in my body.)

So, as I got clarity around what I was feeling and why I was feeling that and then had the contrast of experiencing something that did feel true for me, and really, felt like a yes, this was how I was able to identify the right direction for me on my path.

QUESTIONS:

- Is there an area of your life where you've taken on something that you've learned that's not actually true for you? Why? Do you want to change this and identify and move toward what's true for you?

TOOLS:

How to Be True to Yourself
So, how do we be true to ourselves? While this is a never-ending journey, here's one process that you can use to start to dig deeper.

1. Ask questions to understand what you're experiencing and why.
Why am I feeling this way or resisting this? Is this because it doesn't feel right or is resisting and going against the grain a way that I feel seen (for example)? Is there another reason I'm feeling this way or resisting this?

2. Take action.
Depending on the answers you get above, take action accordingly. If it's not true for you, take action toward what is or to get clarity around what is. Also, important to note: Just because you're clear on what's not true for you doesn't mean that automatically this will give you clarity on what is true for you. It's important during these times to stay open and to keep investigating, learning and trying new things until you get the clarity you're looking for. Also, asking for guidance, whether from another person who's struggled with something similar or from the Universe, is always helpful in these situations.

How to Identify Your Yes, No and Maybe

Part of getting clarity on what's true for us, and as part of this, the direction to go in, is getting a better understanding of how we experience our yes, no and maybe.

1. Identifying your "yes."

First, think of times in your life when you've been a "Hell Yes!" toward something. Maybe it was around getting a new job, being with your partner or going on a vacation. As you experience these, notice how your "Yes" feels in your body. Does it feel light? Does it feel exciting? Is there a picture, color, texture or shape that comes up? Notice all of these and write them down.

2. Identifying your "no."

Then, repeat this process for your "No," bringing up times in your life when you were a "No" about something. Maybe it was a time when you went on a date with someone you didn't like or accepted a job or a role within a company that didn't feel right. Whatever the case, notice how you are experiencing this, again noticing how it feels in your body and any pictures, colors, textures or shapes that are showing up and write it down.

3. Identifying your "maybe."

Repeat this process again, identifying experiences where you were a "Maybe." Maybe it was spending time with a friend or family member or when you got talked into something that you weren't sure about. Whatever the case, notice this and write down how you experienced this in your body.

4. Return to your "yes."

Bring up your "Yes" feelings one more time. While this isn't mandatory, I always like to leave my body in a "Yes," as to me, this feels the best!

If you're looking to do more in-depth work on intuition, I recommend my Connecting to Your Intuition Workshop Online Recording, which you can get at deborahacker.com.

CHAPTER 23

There are no failures on the path—just many avenues to move you down it.

IT WAS RIGHT AROUND THIS TIME, TOO, WHEN THINGS WERE BE-
GINNING TO COME APART AT WORK. I had been in my medical sales
role for almost three years, and things weren't working as they once
had. For months, I had been getting the hit that my company was
going to be ending. (This ended up coming to fruition when they
were bought out and, in the process, they dissolved the company I
was working for.)

This was coupled with the internal feeling that there was
"something more" waiting for me. So, while I wasn't that sure of the
right next step, I knew I had to do something, and I started moving
forward.

Initially, it started with creating a fitness website. I remember
talking with a lot of people to get their advice and help. On the
inside, I didn't feel like I knew what I was doing, and I subconsciously thought, somehow, some way, someone else could give me
the answers. As I look back, I think some of this insecurity, and really
heaviness, was just because this wasn't the right fit. At the time, I
didn't know this feeling in my body, but, as I moved toward it, after

some time, I did realize something was missing. Later I would realize what it was: *flow.*

Things just weren't working. The company I had hired to do the website wasn't following through, and it stalled. The feeling that something wasn't fully aligned was growing. After months of this going on, while my inner nature is to keep pushing, I finally took a step back and started to listen.

With this, I still knew I needed to do something, though, but what was it?! I could feel the urgency and frustration building.

Then, the idea came through to try writing. I had always loved it, and I had decided to sign up for Writing from the Heart, a writing retreat with my now-favorite writing coach, Nancy Aronie. I really enjoyed the retreat, and when I got home, while I was writing a bit, it wasn't overtaking me. It was then that my therapist at the time made the very studious observation that "she knew writers, and the writers she knew had to write." *I did not.*

It was also around this time that I was starting to seriously work with my Guides and Angels. While since my mom had passed, I had a regular relationship with her, I was not really aware of this term and had not really reached out to any of my other Guides or Angels.

What are these? Many times, our Guides are our deceased loved ones and Angels are higher vibrational beings. Both are here to provide us with guidance and to help us create everything we're desiring and more, *if we ask.*

So, as I got home from my writing retreat, I decided to really commit to developing a relationship with my Guides and Angels, and I took my first step in trying it, and really, *trusting.*

It started off with my asking, "Show me that my current job is not the right job for me anymore."

I had just gotten back from the writing retreat, and while I was away was when my company had transitioned to the new company.

So, the first day I'm back, and I can't get on my computer—*for a day and a half.*
Message received!

I also remember, an alarm clock that I had wound before I left to take with me on my trip, but couldn't get to work, started ticking shortly after I got home. To me, the message here was clear, *"Time is running out."*
Message received!

My next step was to request, "Show me what I should be doing and what my next step is."

Within less than two weeks, I was sitting in a training with a high-profile coach in Los Angeles, and she was coaching someone from the stage. She opened it up for others to add input, and completely unconsciously, I started coaching this woman.

Following a break, the coach came up to me and asked me if I wanted to coach for the program I was taking.
Message received!

To be clear, prior to this, coaching was not even on my radar let alone moving toward it.

When she said this, though, I knew that was the guidance I had requested. I immediately began moving toward it.

LIFE LESSONS AND LEARNINGS

FAILURE AND FORCING THINGS

What happened with my fitness website and then the writing not "working out" was a powerful experience for me. I felt a bit of shame, especially when the website didn't work. I had told enough people where I couldn't avoid acknowledging my "failure." But what I was beginning to realize was that it was about the journey, not the outcome. I was beginning to realize that all of these things were leading me on my path, if I allowed them. I was beginning to realize that, really, there was no failure, unless I framed it that way.

What I was realizing instead was that these were just beautiful pieces on my path. Every time I chose something, I gave the Universe an opportunity to give me more information. If I had never chosen to do anything, the Universe couldn't guide me. That being said, it's important to note, even if you don't know the right next step, it's important to take some action, so you can get more information, guidance and feedback. I know it's easy to want to have the "right" answer or "right" next step, but truthfully, there is no one right answer or way. Everything is part of your path, and there are many avenues to move you down it.

Also, with this, the only way we can truly fail is by giving up. While some may have perceived that I "gave up" when I decided to stop writing or working on the website, had I continued with either of these, it would have been me forcing something that wasn't fully aligned. This is an important distinction to make, as sometimes, because we don't want to perceive that we've failed, we can force things that are just not in full alignment at that moment.

QUESTIONS:

- Where have you "failed"? How can you reframe this failure to see it as something that was just moving you along your path?

- Where have you forced something just because you didn't want to fail or be seen as a failure? Looking back, take note of these, so that, if this happens again, you can recognize what this feels like, taking a step back and making a new choice, if necessary.

- Also, if there's something you've been wanting to do, but have been caught up in trying to figure out the "right way," what's one step you can take to move forward? Take that step, even if you don't know if it's the "right" step, and then pay attention to how it goes and how it feels doing this. Course correct as necessary.

TOOLS:

1. Rewrite your failures.
Use the above reframes on failure to rewrite any stories where you've perceived that you failed. For example, my rewrite looks like "When my fitness business and writing didn't take off, this was the way I was being redirected to something better." Then, really feel this as truth in your body.

2. Choosing the right next step.
Again, while there is no one right way, when we take a step in our life or business, we can determine if it's in "flow" by noticing how easy or hard it is. Does it go smoothly or does it stall? Does it feel light or heavy in your body? We are meant to feel good, so while ease, smoothness, light and heaviness aren't always signs that you are going in the "right" or "wrong" direction, it can definitely be useful information. Then, you can use this information and, with this, the success of the task to determine future next steps (i.e., when you are thinking about your next step, notice if the feeling is similar to the way the step you took that was successful felt. If not, why not? Is it because you're scared or is it just because it's out of alignment for you?).

3. Determining when you are forcing things.
If you find something isn't working for you, it's important to take a step back and stop what you're doing. Walk away from the project—maybe for a day, a week or longer. Take some deep breaths and really get clear on why you're doing what you're doing. Is it because it's aligned, but you're just going through some growing pains? Or is it because you don't want to fail or be seen as a failure, so you're forcing something that isn't really aligned? Whatever it is, it's important to get clarity, so that you can make a clear decision for yourself.

WORKING WITH GUIDES AND ANGELS

The above story is a prime example of how you can work with your Guides and Angels. It's literally as simple as starting a conversation with them and asking for guidance. (For more on how to work with your Guides and Angels, head to Chapters 8 and 12.)

CHAPTER 24

If you choose to believe it, magic is right around the corner. You just have to show up for it.

AS I STARTED TO WORK MORE AND MORE WITH MY GUIDES AND ANGELS, MORE UNEXPECTED SYNCHRONICITIES WERE HAPPENING.

It was during one such time, when my grandparents were still living in Chicago, and my dad and his wife were visiting from Las Vegas, when I got to strongly experience this magic firsthand.

While I didn't have plans with them originally, I got an inkling to make plans with my family on a random Thursday night.

When I called them, they told me that we were going to try a new restaurant we had never gone to before, one that was farther away from my grandparents' house than was typical for them, as we usually went to one of a few of their favorites.

So, when I got done with work, I headed over to their house, and a little while later, we went to the Italian restaurant Grandma had picked out for us.

Little did I know the surprise that was in store for me!

As we sat down, I'm not sure when I noticed it, or really them, but at one point, I looked to my right and saw my grandpa Dan's niece, Jeanette, and her son and daughter-in-law, whom I hadn't seen probably since I was a little girl, sitting to my right.

Immediately when I saw them and went up to them, I knew this was the work of my Guides and Angels! I can't explain the feeling, but I felt giddy at the thought of the behind-the-scenes magic that had occurred.

I left the restaurant that day, having reconnected with an important part of my family, whom I'm still in contact with. This was magic, miracles and synchronicity at its best!

LIFE LESSONS AND LEARNINGS

RECOGNIZING MAGIC, MIRACLES AND SYNCHRONICITY

That day, I remember being in shock at reconnecting with my family. I almost instantaneously knew in that moment the amount of work my Guides had gone through on the other side to create this "chance" meeting.

To break it down, here are a few "behind-the-scenes" pieces that were created:

1. When I woke up that morning, I did not have plans to see my family that night. I'm not sure when or how it popped in, but at some point that day, the awareness, and really, the feeling to go see my family, came through, and, *most importantly*, I acted on it.

2. How my grandma was directed to that restaurant is crazy! It was not in the area where she lived. It was not a place she frequented, though my cousins did. I believe at the time she was looking for a restaurant that served chicken fricassee, and somehow had come across this place and decided we would go.

3. Then, of course, they also had to drop the thought in for my cousins to go, and not only for them to go, but for us to be there at the same time.

When you put all of these together, you begin to recognize just how much work on the other side goes into what we see as magic, miracles and synchronicity.

QUESTIONS:

- Would you like to create stories like these in your life? Is there anything that stops you from believing this is possible?

TOOLS:

Throughout this book, I share many tools to start to open, connect and create magic, miracles and synchronicity in your reality, but I want to add two things to these teachings:

To create more magic, miracles and synchronicities:
When something cool like the above story comes into your field, notice it and take it in, as whenever we put our focus on something, we create more of it.

If you don't believe this is possible for you, here's how to shift it:

1. Identify who you learned this from and around what age.

2. Notice if a specific memory pops up around when you stopped believing in magic, miracles and synchronicity.

3. See this memory and belief coming out of your body and replace it with light, love and a new belief—the belief in infinite possibilities.

This is just one of many ways you can shift this!

CHAPTER 25

When we choose to edit ourselves around another person, we choose them over us.

As I was working more and more on my self-love journey, side by side with creating my dream job, and most importantly, living a life of truth, I chose to start dating again. As I did this, I started to notice how agreeable I was and how most of what I said was around fitting in and being liked. On my truth journey, this was becoming more and more uncomfortable, and I had big dreams of a partnership that was deep and deeply rooted in truth.

It was on one of these dates that I made a commitment to this. My Guides were starting to put the bug in my ear about beginning to date again, and "coincidentally," this dating service that I had briefly used years ago had called me, wanting to fix me up with someone.

As I was thinking about this date, I knew it could feel like any other date I had been on in my dating career. But I was different, so instead I made a decision: I wouldn't shrink to fit. I wouldn't hide pieces of myself to make my date comfortable. I wouldn't pretend I was something I wasn't.

We ended up meeting at a rustic Italian restaurant that was a block from my high-rise. He was short, Jewish, successful and relatively attractive. As we sat down, this date started like most others. We were getting to know the basics about each other—jobs, interests and where we lived.

When he began to ask about me and my coaching work, though, I found myself sticking to my commitment and not holding back, maybe for the first time ever. Let's just say, I went big and let my freak flag fly! For me, this meant, sharing all pieces of my work, including the "woo" and "out-there" stuff. It meant no self-editing, no matter what. It meant being my big, fabulous self. I noticed, too, that without any worry of saying or doing the wrong thing, I was really enjoying myself and the conversation. It was exhilarating!

I remember at the end of the date, us walking out of the restaurant to say goodbye and exclaiming, "I had a great time!" He looked a bit bewildered, as the date itself had just been ok. What I had left out, though, was the "with me!" part. It was the one time on the date that I edited myself.

Either way, I had fallen in love with myself all over again.

LIFE LESSONS AND LEARNINGS

PRACTICING TRUTH IN DATING

If you're on a truth journey like I am, practicing speaking your truth and choosing yourself can be one of the hardest things to do, especially if you're used to muting yourself in any way. For me, it felt wrong to put myself out there, and be different and unique and to say the hard or uncomfortable things. For me, the more I did this, though, and put myself first, the more I learned that nothing really bad would happen if I shifted this for myself. Yes, people may not like it and some may even leave. But, with this, as I began to accept and truly love this part of me, so came people who reflected this.

These people had the same values as me and loved me for me, and not just because I looked or acted a certain way. It was beautiful and hard, but it was also exciting, as I was truly creating my world, including my relationships and friendships.

A side note to this story: Yes, while it's important not to self-edit, and this was a good start to being myself at all times, what I could have done better on this date was to be more relational, as I was likely talking more at him than to him, and I moved into a teacher role versus a peer-to-peer, partner-to-partner or friend-to-friend role. (For more on being relational, head to Chapters 32, 33 and 35.)

QUESTIONS:

- Where are you not true to yourself? Where do you hide pieces of yourself to be in relationship with another? Why? What are you scared of?

TOOLS:

If you're desiring to change this, the first thing I recommend is determining which relationships and friendships you want to look different. Once you've determined this, this practice is very similar to the practice I shared in my story with one more piece added: Set an intention around what you're going to practice before you see your loved one. This can be everything from speaking your truth and not modifying yourself to saying no when you mean it. Then, when you find yourself in the position of wanting to be liked or to fit in or when you're not sharing all of yourself, notice that you're doing this, and then take one step forward to change this. This will require a lot of mindfulness, and it may take some time to get this right.

Also, while I share more about this in Chapter 33, if you mess up, when you get home, see them in front of you and say what you wished you had said until one day, you find yourself sharing all of yourself in front of them in real-time. Important to note: it's important to be discerning of whom you're practicing this with. Not everyone is safe to share all of yourself with or ready for this, especially not initially, so if you find yourself wanting to do this with someone, feel into if this is something that feels right to practice with this person. If it doesn't feel right, one option is to have a relational conversation with them sharing that. You might start the conversation with something like, "I'm wanting to deepen our relationship, but I'm noticing I'm scared to share this with you." (Replace "this" with whatever you're scared to share with them.)

CHAPTER 26

Forgiving isn't letting them off the hook; it's letting you off of it.

IT WAS AT THIS POINT, TOO, WHEN I RETURNED TO THE FOR-
GIVENESS WORK WITH MY DAD. This was another piece I thought
I might never heal in this lifetime. It was hard to ever imagine I'd
ever get to a point where I'd fully forgive him. Forgiving him for
me meant letting him off the hook. *And I wasn't going to do that.*

It wasn't until I realized forgiving him really meant letting me
off the hook that I made a new choice. For decades, I had been carrying around the poison of anger, hate and hurt, and I was drinking
a strong dose of it regularly.

I had to let it go. *I had to let it go for me.*

My first retreat was the first stand I took for myself. This was
the next stand I would take, and I would do it because I was worth
it and deserved to be happy—fully, beautifully, unabashedly happy.

The process wouldn't be an easy one. It would mean saying
everything I needed to say to him. But I wouldn't do this in the
typical way of face to face or even writing a letter. I would do this
energetically to take the energy off of all the things that had kept me

attracting the same type of man.

With this process, I would need to realize I had chosen my dad. For the longest time, I didn't believe I had a choice with my parents. I thought I was just unlucky. This was a very painful way for me to think about my circumstances, though, as inherently, with this, I felt like the continual victim. As I started to grow, though, an interesting awareness popped in.

Before we come into physical form, we choose our parents.

This was an interesting idea, as this would mean I chose a lot of the struggle, craziness and hardship of my childhood. *Why would I do that?* Between my mom's codependence and her own version of love addiction, and my dad leaving and not taking full responsibility for his actions, it had been really hard. Years ago, I even had a therapist who told me, with the parents I had, I should have ended up with an addiction, suicidal or even dead. (My life had been living proof of this, as I had struggled with two of these three at some point in my life.)

This is where it was helpful to see it from my soul's perspective.

Of course, my human self would *never* choose the parents I had. She WAS NOT a glutton for punishment.

But, my soul, oh my soul, she had a different perspective.

She whispered to me, "This was the most powerful way for you to learn self-love. This was the most powerful way for you to clear your abandonment pattern, which you've had for many lifetimes. This was the most powerful way for you to learn you're a powerful creator."

What?! I'm a powerful creator?! How can this be true?!

"Yes," she hummed. (My soul has the voice of an angel.) "This experience you've created was all for you. It was meant to help you to grow. It was meant to help you expand. It was meant to help you to learn how to love yourself and others. You set it up perfectly."

I did? Oh, yeah, I DID.

This was key to my forgiving my dad and moving out of any victim mentality that I had just been unlucky.

After this concentrated work, for the next couple of years, as things would come up, sometimes with my dad and sometimes with someone who would show up with an energy or pattern similar to my dad, I would take time away from my day to feel whatever it brought up.

It was not always easy. It took dedication. It took tenacity. It took loving myself enough to not leave, even when it was hard or I'd rather relax or do something "fun". At some point, though, it became fun. After I would feel, and really "clear" something (to move to the next layer of the pattern or to clear the pattern for good), this lightness would wash over me. This was always lying underneath the pattern, and what I realized is this feeling was the feeling of returning to the truth of who I was, which was always light and love.

As I returned to this truth, life became easier. Things I would think about would just appear in my field. I found myself spending more time in joy, peace and ease, and when something hard did come up, I found myself more willing to go "there," feel whatever it was calling me to feel, seeing the lesson in it and opting to make a new choice.

And, all of this stemmed from one defining moment in my life: *my dad leaving.*

It wasn't too long ago, too, when I was told I could actually clear my abandonment pattern. (Any person with an abandonment pattern will tell you most of us spend our lives just trying to manage it.)

What?! I can clear it for good, so I don't have to take it into another lifetime?!

My Guides and Angels replied excitedly, "Yes, Deb. Yes, you can."

LIFE LESSONS AND LEARNINGS

CLEARING DEEP-SEATED PATTERNS

The key to clearing any long-term, painful pattern is staying with it. Most of us are conditioned to give up before we've cleared it because we believe it's not possible to fully clear it and it appears too hard. So we spend our life thinking our only option is to manage the pattern. But this is simply not true. Yes, for my abandonment pattern, it took years to clear it, but it was possible. I just needed to ensure I didn't leave myself in the process, and I stayed with it.

QUESTIONS:

- What patterns do you have that are defining many areas of your life? (While my abandonment pattern was definitely defining my relationships, it also defined the way I showed up for myself, the way I was treated—and expected to be treated—and many of my friendships. With this, too, I wasn't taking the stand for myself that I deserved, which many times also meant not fighting for myself and my worth.)

- As part of this, what pattern(s) in your life do you believe are impossible to clear and you just have to manage (i.e., what deep-seated patterns are defining your life in a negative way)? How does this belief serve you?

TOOLS:

How to clear a pattern or trigger:

1. Notice when you are experiencing something that isn't working for you or are being triggered and tune into what

this is. (This may take practice, as most of us for most of our lives have been practicing disconnecting from ourselves and pushing away what's bothering and not working for us. To shift this, it's important to start paying attention.)

2. Once you've tuned into this, ask why this is bothering or triggering you.

3. Then, feel what's bothering you until it's not present for you anymore. Are you mad, scared, upset? Why? Whatever that is, notice it and sit with it, and as much as possible, allow yourself to express it. (For more details on feeling your feelings, head to Chapters 5, 15 and 21.)

4. Once it feels clear, whether it's just for that moment or it's complete for good, see your body filling with light. (While clearing can feel different for everyone, many times you may notice it feels lighter, brighter and more open in your space and body.)

5. Repeat this, as any pattern comes up, until it's no longer relevant for you.

The only other thing I want to reinforce here is that in clearing any pattern, especially the ones that deeply define us, you have to stay with it until it clears, feeling all of the emotions that come up with it. It can take months or years, but truly, it's that simple. Of course, I love helping clients undo patterns, pain and abandonment, so if you're looking for support with this, reach out to me.

CHAPTER 27

Grandparents are the gifts that keep on giving.

It's interesting because as I look back at my relationships with my grandparents, while both sets of my grandparents were in my life from day one, I spent more time with my mom's parents in the first part of my life, and in the second part of it, my relationship with my dad's parents started to grow.

In truth, I was always looking for someone to comfort me and make me feel better. I was looking for someone (or something) to help me to feel whole inside. I was looking for the love I had lost when my mom had passed away.

I was searching, and one of the places I found it was with my dad's parents.

I remember going over to their house regularly, usually with laundry. Each time, my grandma Loretta would welcome me with a home-cooked meal, everything from brisket and latkes to salmon patties and kugel. My grandpa Izzy would be listening to his latest book on tape, and I would greet him with a kiss, usually on his forehead, before I'd wander into the kitchen to talk with my grandma. (He had suffered from macular degeneration years earlier and was losing his sight.)

Over these times with her, I would share the latest updates on whomever I was dating at the time and any other stories I would want to tell her exclusively. Sometimes, especially as I started working from home, I would meet her or stop by their house for a quick lunch. Many times, I would leave our time together filled to the brim with leftovers. (To know my grandma's love, all you have to do is look around my house, as I still have many of the things she would send me home with, everything from a needle and thread to sew my pants to an excess of Cool-Whip containers that I had brought much of her home-cooking home in.)

With this, too, if I shared that I needed something, she would often offer to go get it with me.

It was during one of these times, on a late Sunday in early December, that I shared something a psychic had told me about one of my grandma Loretta's loved ones.

Earlier that month, I had reached out to a psychic wanting answers about my own life. What would my future hold? When was I going to meet my significant other? What would he be like? Would I be happy? And, deep-seated underneath this: *Am I going to be okay?*

She had answered all of my questions, but then she said something I hadn't asked her about and wasn't sure I even wanted to know.

"Your mom is going to lose someone close to her in the next six months," she said. Of course, I was confused, as my mom had been gone for over 15 years at this point. "Okay, then," she questioned back, "Is there another mother figure in your life?" I thought for a moment and said hesitantly, "My grandma is a mother figure to me." "Well, she is going to lose an older gentleman close to her." Of course, I immediately thought she was talking about my grandpa Izzy. Besides her children, there were no other men in her life. Sadness, panic and preparation ensued. We can never be ready to lose our loved ones, and this was no different.

I finished the reading in a haze and got off the phone pondering what she had said, including what she had shared about my grandpa. Would her reading prove accurate? Was I really going to have only five more months with the man who had lovingly saturated my 33 years? And, should I tell my grandma? I had decided I would.

So, with darkness nestling in for the night, as my grandma and I were finishing up our boot shopping for my upcoming knee surgery at the local suburban mall, I worked up the courage to tell her.

"Thank you for the boots, Grandma," I said, as we dropped into my cool leather bucket seats. I started the car, but was not moving. "How do you feel about psychics?" I asked, somewhat abruptly. "Oh, I think they're fun to do every once in awhile," she said with a smile. I felt my heart drop a bit.

"Well, I had a reading the other night, and take this for what you will, but she told me someone close to you was going to pass." "Oh really?" she pitched back, perhaps in question, alarm or both. "She said it was going to be a male who was close to you, so I'm assuming Grandpa," I added. She didn't say too much after that. It had been a long time since my grandparents were close.

We headed back to her house, and the conversation was buried, but looking back, what I enjoyed most about conversations like these was finding out details about my grandma that otherwise I would never have had a chance to know. Yes, it was hard to share this news with her, and while of course at the time we had no way to know if it was going to come true, I think my draw to have this conversation was twofold—not only because I've always been curious about these topics, but also because these conversations helped me to learn new things about my loved ones. With this conversation, it was interesting to be able to own a piece of my reality, which had been such a rare experience in my earlier years, and with this, it was interesting to learn that she had an interest or belief in psychics as well, which I hadn't known until this conversation with her.

It did turn out that the news the psychic had shared with me came true, but it came in a different form. It was just a few months later when my grandma's sister Adele's health began to deteriorate rapidly. While my aunt Adele wasn't a male, her directive, strong-willed, stubborn style could read as masculine energy.

She did pass shortly after this, which was a big loss for my grandma. Her sister was her best friend, and I was grateful to be able to be there for her during that hard time and to have her for several more years after that.

Over the years, we became good friends, really the best of friends, and by the time of her passing in 2015, she was the one person in my life I knew I could turn to. She was the one person in my life I knew would drop everything to help me. Most importantly, she was the one person in my life I knew loved me unconditionally.

I remember the night my dad called to let me know she was getting ready to go. "We're moving Grandma into hospice, where she'll pass." My heart sank. I felt a mix of fear, sadness and confusion. The last I had heard, while she wasn't doing great, there was still hope.

I immediately flew out to Florida, where I met my family, to see her and say goodbye. I remember the flight there, in tears, trying to get used to the news I had just heard. It wasn't easy.

Over those next several days, I said the things I needed to say one more time, held her hand and combed her hair. I had already asked her what symbol would be a sign that she's still around. "*A piano,*" she said. "*I've always wanted to learn how to play one.*" (This was another time when I was grateful to be able to ask the questions that most don't ask, as, prior to this, I hadn't known that she had wanted to play the piano.)

When it came time to leave that week, I debated going.

But, I should get back. I need to work.

It felt like she could have a few more months. So I decided to leave.

She passed away a few days later, on a Sunday afternoon. The following week, when my family came in to celebrate her life, after her funeral, as we sat around the dining room table at my cousin's grandparents' house, sharing stories, I heard the keys of a piano playing for the first time in all of the years I had been at their house.

Hi Grandma.

LIFE LESSONS AND LEARNINGS

GETTING TO KNOW OUR LOVED ONES

As I lost more and more people in my life, I became better at really getting to know them as individuals and really ensuring the time with them was "quality time." So many times, especially when there's an age difference, we don't think of our elders as people with hopes and dreams, regrets and pain. My grandma Loretta was someone who I got to know past just the role of grandmother. I got to know her as a person and friend. From forgiveness to love, our times together would extend to all topics.

And, as we'd sit at her kitchen table or across the table at a restaurant, she really took an interest in all areas of my life. As I started to advance in my personal growth, she grew with me. It was during these times that we took these journeys into what really mattered, into the conversations most people don't think, or really, dare to have. I will always treasure these times together, and even as I sit here writing this, I am transported back in time to a time in my life when I was loved unconditionally by another, where my heart was held as closely as one holds their own.

QUESTIONS:

- What conversations would you have with your loved ones if you let go of social norms and taboos? How would you spend your time with them, and really, how would you make the time with them count?

TOOLS:

Make a list of questions to ask your loved ones (I've gotten you started below), and then, if it's important to you, make a plan to spend some quality time with them. If they live close, this could be thirty minutes or an hour a couple of times a month. If they live far away, make a plan to see them over a weekend or week. Then, actually be present with them. Ask them about themselves. Maybe even record your conversation. This can include lighter and deeper questions, including:

What were their hopes and dreams?

What was/were their biggest defining moment(s)?

What would they do differently?

What do they regret?

If they could do it all over again, would they change anything?

Looking back, what do they wish they had known?

What would they tell their younger self?

What advice do they have for you?

What do they believe happens to you when you die?

Do they believe in psychics? Ghosts? Signs from the other side?

What's the most interesting/exciting/scary thing they've ever done/ that's ever happened to them?

When did they first fall in love?

What's their favorite childhood memory?

Who was/were their favorite person/favorite people in their life?

Which of their parents are they most like and what were their relationships like with them?

What was their childhood like?

CHAPTER 28

Complaining about something doesn't change it.

To know my grandpa Izzy, you'd have to know about the challenges he faced in life. He grew up with very small means, which during his time, meant sleeping in the kitchen some nights. He lost his best friend in World War II, when he was only 19, a friend he had played high school basketball with, the center to his point-guard, so to speak, when he was part of the infamous Marshall High School Basketball winning streak. (He was later nominated into the Chicago Basketball Hall of Fame.) After college, he tried teaching, which didn't work out, and ended up landing a job delivering diapers. There, he worked his way up from nothing to become part-owner of the business. He and my grandma had four children, and while life wasn't always easy, and he made mistakes that hurt my grandma and impacted his family, he was always doing the best he could and he always chose to approach life, family and business with a positive attitude.

So, it's no surprise that when he got macular degeneration, he made the same choice.

It was several years ago now. He woke up one morning and the vision in his right eye was skewed. He went to the eye doctor and was diagnosed. Over the next three years, his sight began to shift until one day he was making a quick trip to the store and literally realized he couldn't see. Thankfully, he made it home that day safely.

But, that's when the real adjustment started.

He could no longer golf, which he loved to do. He could no longer follow some of his favorite shows or watch a movie and always understand what was going on. He could no longer drive or pay bills, which meant the loss of some freedom.

But with the loss of this freedom came a whole different freedom. Because with this loss came new choices. For him, the loss of his sight would not mean waking up every day complaining. It would not mean giving up his independence. And it would not mean the loss of his joy.

Instead, up until he recently passed away, he would:

- Take a twenty- to thirty-minute walk each morning.

- Make his own meals and meet his friends in the dining hall daily.

- Do what he needed to do to take care of himself.

All with a smile on his face—and many times, humming.

The last time I saw him, before he went into hospice, was at his nursing home for Father's Day. As we sat outside by the trees, listening to '70s music, he danced with me. While it was only for a few minutes, as he had been getting weaker, he got up twice, dipping me each time, which was his idea.

These are the times I will always remember with him—hearing stories about his life over a nice meal or while sitting on his couch, taking walks down the hall and listening to music and dancing with him. Of course, those, and our card games when I was a kid with him shouting, "We have a winner!"

Yes we do, Grandpa. Yes we do.

LIFE LESSONS AND LEARNINGS

It was humbling to me to see how my grandpa handled living without his sight. It's shown me that no matter what happens to us or in our lives, we always have a choice about how we're going to let it impact us, and really, we have a choice to choose joy or misery. I choose joy.

QUESTIONS:

- When something "bad" happens to you, do you allow it to take you down? Do you use it to make excuses for your behavior and how you're showing up? Do you allow it to define you, your attitude and what you can and can't do?

TOOLS:

Notice where in your life you're allowing something "bad" that happened to you, which may have happened decades earlier, to impact your life today in a negative way, and maybe even, to define you or take you down. Take a moment to take in if this is how you really want to show up, and if you want to continue to let what happened to you have a negative impact on your life. If not, it's time to make a new choice and redirect your energy. How do you want to approach today and how do you want to show up in your life? What is good about what happened and how can you express gratitude for this challenge? Get connected to this and feel the gratitude in your body,

194 • LIVING DEEPLY

allowing it to rewire you. Also, if you find yourself going back to your old ways, simply keep choosing to find the good again, and with this, the gratitude that comes with it, until this is your norm.

CHAPTER 29

Every experience carries with it new awarenesses, growth and the opportunity to expand. Could you ask for anything more?!

WHEN MY GRANDPA IZZY PASSED, IT HIT ME REALLY HARD HOW MUCH ALL OF MY GRANDPARENTS HAD BEEN THE SAFE HAVEN IN THE EYE OF THE STORM. In my adult years, with the passing of each grandparent, I would reach for the next one and they were always there to cushion me, and really, to cushion the blow of the loss.

But, when my final grandparent passed away, this loss, and with this, the loss of safety, security and unconditional love, was unsteadying in a time that was already full of uncertainty for me.

However, my grandpa Izzy's passing gave me two huge gifts.

The first one came at his funeral, where I made the choice that I was going to eulogize him. Before my grandma Loretta's funeral, I hadn't connected to the importance of this for me—in honoring my feelings, our relationship and even, the subconscious fears I had around speaking my truth in front of my family. With this, I hadn't realized that not only was this important for me, but that I knew my grandparents from a different perspective than their children did. This awareness hit me in the middle of my grandma Loretta's funeral, and I felt unprepared and deeply disappointed that I couldn't honor her the way I knew her.

So, just like I had done so many times before, when Grandpa Izzy passed, I made a new choice. Yes, I was scared to share my reality, and I was even concerned about how to bring my reality to a place where my family could understand it, and really, could understand me and our relationship. Truth be told, while I had been thinking about what I wanted to say for the entire week, I wrote, and really channeled, my grandpa's eulogy the morning of his funeral.

As I sat down to write it, I connected to my heart, and really to my pain and loss, and I let the words flow through me. It was a beautiful eulogy—one that did justice to the person my grandpa had been and one that honored how far I had come on my journey.

As I stood up to read it at my grandpa's funeral, I found myself, in some ways, scared to share my reality. With this, initially, I went into an old pattern and started to rush through it. Immediately, though, I stopped and paused, taking some deep breaths in my body (I could feel myself leaving myself). I even heard my grandpa's voice in my head, *"Slow down, Deb."* I did, and at the end of his eulogy, I found myself shaking. It was scary to say these words and own my reality in front of my family, much scarier to me than sharing my story with a million strangers. Yet, with this, I felt so seen and heard and so pleased to have been able to honor my grandpa's memory the way I saw him—as the loving, kind and joyful being he was.

The second gift was more subtle. At this point in my journey, I had had many experiences working with loved ones on the other side, enough so that when they would cross over, I had a sense of how they felt. I remember when I first heard the news of my grandpa Izzy's passing, I decided I was going to go for a walk, and on this walk, I could sense that he was still in the illusion of his physical body, jumping up and down, enjoying his newfound mobility and sight. (Fun side note: With his newfound sight, when I was getting changed to go on my walk, I didn't think to warn him of this, and I heard him go, "Whoa!") With that said, being on this side of the veil, he was still in the illusion of being in his physical body and was still experiencing other people from his human self. It's my sense that, just like we experience our deceased loved ones as we are, seeing them in a physical form, when we cross over, we experience our living loved ones as we are in that state, i.e., as energy.

It didn't dawn on me until the day after his funeral, though, that this was a sign he hadn't crossed over. I was talking with my sister and mentioned that he felt different from everyone else I had connected with who had crossed over. As I drove home from the shivah that night, crying and feeling the depth of losing him, I felt him sitting in the seat next to me. When I got home and in bed, lying down in my sadness for the night, it was then when it hit me that he didn't feel the same as everyone else because he hadn't crossed over. Not tuning in, I went to go help him cross over, the way I had done for a friend's father, ironically one of the times that I was staying at my grandpa Izzy's place. He didn't want to go, though, and feeling worn out and fatigued, I made a decision that I would fully tune in the following day to figure out what was going on.

The next day, I was texting with a friend I had trained with, sharing with her my experience, and she lovingly suggested I ask him why he didn't want to go. I did, and I got that he had some unfinished business here with one of his loved ones. I told him I could help him with it, if he wanted, and committed to doing this as soon as I could.

That's when it got even harder, though. I felt him around me throughout my days and evenings. He'd come with me to my classes at the gym. (Seeing him work out with me and how much he was enjoying it brought me so much joy!) He'd come hang out with me while I was working with a client or watching TV. And, he'd come lie down with me at night, when the deep grief would wash over me.

Every day I spent with him, it became harder and harder to say goodbye. It was almost like going through his death twice. And, while I was really enjoying his company, presence and this newfound relationship, I felt like I was holding him back from his next journey. To put it simply, I felt torn inside and guilty for wanting him to stay and not making the time to help him, like I had committed to.

So I decided I was going to sit down with him and help him do the work I said I'd help him do to bring his soul to peace. We did a beautiful forgiveness process, I said my goodbyes one more time and again, I sent him to the light. While initially it didn't feel easy for him to go, and looking back, I think, like most things in his life, he wanted to do it on his own terms, we talked it through, and when he was ready, he started his transition into the next world.

LIFE LESSONS AND LEARNINGS

TAKING UP SPACE

A big part of speaking at my grandpa Izzy's funeral for me was that it was okay to take up space in my family, and with this, that my voice and my truth mattered. For me, it was really important to embody this, as this is a huge part of my work and who I came here to be in this lifetime.

QUESTIONS:

- Do you hide or in some way diminish yourself?

- Do you believe it's okay to take up space in this world?

- If not, does this pattern come up during particular times? (Notice when.)

- Do you believe your voice matters? If not, why not?

Tools:

One of the biggest ways to overcome this is to choose through it. While initially if this is intimidating, like it was for me to speak my truth with my family, I recommend practicing this with people who feel safe, and if you desire, in arenas and venues that feel safe. As you continue to do this and rewire yourself and your old, deep-seated programming, trust, too, that this will get easier and easier.

Tuning Into Our Loved Ones

By the time my grandpa Izzy had passed away, I had had enough experience to know what a loved one feels like when they cross over, which is why I was able to recognize the nuance that he hadn't fully.

Question:

- Do you want to connect with and start to feel your loved ones from the other side? If yes, use the tool below to get started.

Tools:

Close your eyes, taking some deep breaths to bring you into the present moment. When you feel clear and calm, think of a deceased loved one and just notice how you experience them. How do they feel? What do you see? Is there a specific color you associate with them? Take note of all of these and anything else that you experience. Do this exercise several times with several deceased loved ones, and you will likely begin to notice a pattern of the way you experience your deceased loved ones as you do this.

BEING PRESENT

While I was pretty good at being present with my grandpa when he was still in his physical body and was able to be present with him some of the time before he fully crossed over, when I was working with him to cross over, looking back, I wasn't as present as I would have liked to be. While I thought I was present in the moment and did my best to be fully with him during this process, there was a part of me that wanted and, in part, needed to get back to my work. This was a different version of the same pattern that showed up when I initially had thought my grandpa Izzy had crossed over the week of his funeral and wasn't fully tuning in. In both situations, when I did get fully present and took time just to be, I was able to see clearly and recognize what was really happening.

QUESTION:

- Are you being present or is there something else that you can do, or alternatively, set aside, to be more present?

TOOLS:

I've mentioned many tools to help you get more present in your life, including stopping, pausing and taking some deep breaths. In addition to this, it's important to recognize what's really important to you in that moment, as this is where the truth lives. For me, had I taken just a few more minutes to take some deep breaths and get present with myself and him and then asked myself what was most important to me in that moment, this would have helped to pull any part of me that was focused on my book back to the present moment.

CHAPTER 30

When we high-five the Universe, it high-fives us back with its big Universe hands.

It was March 2016, and I had been working toward leaving my corporate medical sales job for close to two years.

The journey itself had had its fill of ups and downs. Along the way, there were many bumps in the road. For me, it meant many long nights and weekends working while I was still at my full-time job. It meant going against the grain despite what other people thought or said. It meant many times choosing discomfort, and really, fear, over comfort. I wish I had known that part of being an entrepreneur meant not knowing what you're doing, until you know what you're doing, and then you *still* don't know what you're doing. Either way, it was scary and exciting to be venturing off into this world.

But I remember the moment that it hit me, and this paradigm shifted.

It felt easier to go than to stay.

For the first time in a long time, I felt relief, and I knew it was going to be okay.

It was early in 2016 when I knew it was time to make an exit plan. My company was starting to micromanage us, and my manager at the time had stopped trusting me. This was a hard time for me, as I felt an internal conflict. I wanted to do right by my company, but I needed to do right by me first.

And, because of the nature of the corporate world, there was no space to share my truth. Looking back, I felt like someone who was impersonating a medical sales rep. Yes, I was doing well, and I was doing the things I needed to do to be successful and the things my manager was asking of me. But, many of these things were so far out of congruence with my truth, and even with what I knew would benefit my company and get the results my manager was desiring, I felt myself internally pushing against his requests.

It didn't help that he likely had his own version of this playing out. Instead, though, there was a lot of conflict and to put it mildly, we were not getting along. So while I was going to leave either way, his actions were providing a great motivator to leave sooner than later, and the Universe was giving me the nudge, *"It's time to go."*

All I needed to do was select a date. For months, I kept playing around with when I would put my notice in. On some level, I think this was a way of stalling. Having been in the Corporate World since my teens, leaving the safety and security of it was a big deal! I was scared. Looking back, *there was never going to be a right time to leave.*

On March 7, though, I finally decided to pull the trigger. I booked a ticket for a training in Los Angeles with one of my coaches along with a two-week vacation to Ecuador. I was a bit nervous, yet excited!

On March 8, my day started like any other. I was at a client's doing an in-service, and as I was leaving the hospital, I checked my emails. To my surprise, my manager, who had been with the company for close to 30 years (give or take), and, to my knowledge, had never worked anywhere else full-time, had put his notice in to go work for another company. I felt my heart sink. There was a mixture of relief, questioning and a bit of envy that he had done it before me. That little stinker!

Now I had a choice to make.

Did I want to stay a little longer, as it was likely going to be more manageable or did I still want to leave at the end of March?

The Universe has a fun sense of humor!

I spent that evening debating my decision and looking into the penalties if I did decide to cancel my trips. After all, work might be easier with him gone and was I really ready to leave? The penalties were minimal, so if I wanted to stay, the option was there.

Then, I looked at the energy of backing out of my decision. It was then that it hit me that my "reversing" was much bigger than just a couple of months of safety and security and an easy paycheck. I realized it was my saying no to my dreams. It felt like a ton of bricks had hit me. *I couldn't do it.*

It was the next day when I was on the phone with a friend of mine, and we were talking about my leaving my job. I casually, and somewhat jokingly, though there was truth behind it, said I wanted to get paid to leave. She's a coach, too, and suggested working on it to create it that way. (Genius!) So I asked, "What would it take to get paid to leave?"

At the end of that same week, I had a call with my manager. While we were never best buddies in our conversations, he felt unusually curt to me. Of course, I just thought it was because he was leaving, so he didn't think that he had to go through the typical pleasantries anymore. It didn't dawn on me it was because he was filing the paperwork to have me fired!

The following Wednesday I went to go meet with him to wrap things up before his final day. We were meeting at a deli out in the western suburbs of Illinois. We had met there before, so I hadn't thought twice about it.

As I walked in the door, though, and I walked up to him, he proceeded to introduce me to the HR manager, who was walking toward the table. He had flown in from North Carolina!

Oh, this is not going to be good. Or is it?

Immediately, I felt my stomach do flip-flops, the kind you get when you're at an amusement park, getting on your favorite ride. This was intermixed with a bit of a bruised ego and the disappointment of not being able to go out on my own terms, which meant feeling proud of completing my job and all I had accomplished while getting to say goodbye to the clients and colleagues I had worked with for over six years, and really, to honor my journey and where I was going.

With this, though, as they proceeded to go over everything, I had to mentally tell myself not to smile. And, when it came time to say goodbye to my manager, even with being let go, I was kind, as I had been practicing it for quite some time.

With this, while in that situation, it would have been tempting to get mad or be spiteful, I knew there was a huge part of growth there for me, if I chose it. I knew it was important to show up in a way that I could be proud of looking back. As part of this, deep inside my being, I know we're all connected. And, no matter what he had chosen, it wasn't going to change the final outcome, if I met him there.

So instead, I chose to see him from his heart, and the little kid that lived within him who didn't know any better. I chose kindness over being right. I chose love over hate. It was really hard. There was a huge part of me that wanted to stick it to him, and while this would have been tempting in that moment, I knew that, upon looking back, I wouldn't feel good about it if I chose to show up this way. I even gave him a hug before I left. Truth be told, I was really grateful.

So, with that, I closed the corporate chapter of my life, at least the one where I was working in it, and not surprisingly, the Universe answered my request to "get paid to leave" with a severance package, unemployment and an extra two and a half weeks paid time off!

A fun side note: As my relationship with my manager got more tenuous, and I was broadening my energy skill set, I started to read past lives. It turns out that we knew each other from a past life, and the energy from that lifetime reads of a lifetime where I stuck it to him. While I don't really believe in karma, as karma to me has a connotation of punishment and where for every good thing that happens, something negative is likely to happen in return and I personally don't believe The Universe wishes negative things on us or creates balance in this way, I do believe in past-life connections, vibration (i.e., being hurt and hurting another are the same vibration so it's highly likely that you'll magnetize both types of experiences) and healing anything that is not rooted in a high vibration or the true truth of who we are as light beings. That being said, one could say karma really is a bitch!

LIFE LESSONS AND LEARNINGS

CREATING MY REALITY

One of the biggest lessons in this for me was that it showed me that anything was possible and that I could create anything. When I asked, "What would it take to get paid to leave?" I had said it kind of sarcastically. I hadn't fully thought or realized it was truly possible, and even more importantly, that I could create it, let alone create it a week later. When it happened, it reinforced my belief in the Universe, infinite possibilities and just how powerful we all are as creators of our reality. I felt just how supported by the Universe I truly was in this decision.

I'm a firm believer, too, that once you decide something, truly *commit* to it and then move toward it, the Universe gets behind you tenfold. A huge part of this for me was putting a ton of energy into building my coaching business, and not giving up, no matter whether I felt scared, received negative feedback or how long it took. Then, of course, you need to move toward it *every damn day*. I call this *holding the pose* (i.e., no matter what feedback you receive, you keep moving toward it until your vision matches your reality).

QUESTIONS:

- What do you want and how committed are you to making it happen? What steps will you take? Will you give up if you don't receive immediate positive feedback?

- As part of this, if you could create something that you might perceive as impossible, what would that be? If you really want to bring it into creation, what steps will you take? (Letting go of attachment can also be a powerful step.)

- Also, if fear comes up during the process, what will you do with it? You get to choose if it will motivate you or take you down.

  It's also important to take note of times when you've felt supported as you have moved on your path and toward your dreams. (We'll use these in the Tools Section!)

TOOLS:

1. Set a goal around something you've been desiring or wanting to create in your life.
Pick one thing, big or small, that you've been wanting to create or do and write down the next three to five (small) steps to bring it to creation. Then, do step number one to move toward it.

If you find yourself feeling scared, use the inner child processes found throughout this book to connect to your little girl or boy to begin to clear your fear.

2. Using "What would it take to…?"
As part of creating my reality, one of my favorite tools to use, that

I got from one of my teachers is "What would it take to…?" What thinking this and saying this out loud does is open up and put out the possibility and desire to the Universe, without having to determine what it's going to look like or how it's going to happen. Examples of this might include "What would it take to make more money or create a new relationship?", "What would it take to find a new job?" or "What would it take to feel better?" I recommend saying this fifty to sixty times a day, when you're in the shower, when you're driving or any other time that works for you. While this may sound like a lot, it only takes five minutes, and this really puts your focus and energy on it.

Then, pay attention to what shows up while letting go of how it's going to happen.

Also, be careful what you ask for, as you just might get it!

3. Rewiring your body to always feel supported.
Take the above examples you came up with around feeling supported, and, one by one, take this in to your body and allow your body to rewire itself to always know you're supported. Then, see, and really feel this happening with what you currently desire, as this is a powerful tool in creating your reality!

WHAT ARE YOU PRIORITIZING?

Another thing I learned from this was the importance of being aware at all times of what we're choosing, not just physically, but energetically. Our choices are always telling the Universe what we want more or less of. For me, when I chose to leave, I was telling the Universe that I was ready for more in my life. Had I backed out, I would have been telling the Universe that I value security and comfort over my passion and doing what makes me happy. With this, the Universe may not have stepped up in the way that it did to support me. But, in choosing it, I told the Universe, "I'm ready. I want this." The Universe responded, "We want this for you too, and we want to make it as easy as possible for you."

Also, while I don't believe in tests, I do believe, with my old manager putting his notice in, I was being asked how committed I was to this new path. In saying "hell yes" to it and not reversing, I was telling the Universe what was important to me, and the Universe high-fived me tenfold with its big Universe hands!

QUESTIONS:

- What are you prioritizing, and is what you're prioritizing what you truly want? If not, you might want to consider shifting your actions and choices to match your priorities.

TOOLS:

1. Make a list.
The first piece of this is looking at your values and goals. Make a list of each and anything else that's important to you, in order of importance. This list may include things like family, friends, relationships, abundance/money, freedom, free time, security, fun and vacations.

2. Look at your current schedule.
The next step is to take a look at your current schedule and the choices you are making in your life. Are the priorities you listed in number one actually being prioritized, and if they are, are they being prioritized in order of what's truly important to you?

3. If the answer is no…
If you answered no to anything in number two, it's time to start

shifting your priorities and choices. Important to note here: Just like Rome wasn't built in a day, making changes to how you've been doing something and what you've been choosing may take time too. It's important to pick one priority you want to shift and just focus on that for the next several weeks or month(s). Once you feel good about it, you can pick another one and another one, until eventually your priorities and choices are aligned and you're truly choosing what you're desiring.

4. Choose your words wisely.

As part of the above, notice your language. If you're constantly talking about being broke or how hard life is, you will likely keep attracting this to you. Also, while it may be hard to jump from that to being a multi-millionaire, using transitional statements can be helpful. What does this look like?

"I'm starting to... (make changes, spend more time with family and friends, earn more money, get more clients, etc.) or, more generally, "Life is beginning to change or become easier for me," or to paraphrase Louise Hay, "Life is beginning to love me."

CHOOSING TO BE KIND OVER BEING RIGHT

The other piece of the above story I think is so crucial is choosing kindness over all else. There's a saying that smart people think it's better to be right than kind and wise people know it's better to be kind than right. For me, this is so true, and it's a great idea to center around.

With this, while of course, I wasn't always a perfect angel to my ex-manager, in closing our relationship in this lifetime, it did feel important to choose who I wanted to be moving forward, and, in that moment, I wanted to be kind, even though it may have "felt better" to be right.

I get it, though. I get that it can be easy to get caught in our own ego or righteousness, which is really our wrongness in disguise. I get that it can even feel good. I also get that our bodies can make us feel like we're separate beings.

For me, while we definitely came down here to have our own individual experiences and create our own world, the truth of the matter is really what we're saying or doing to another individual, we're really doing to ourselves. We truly are all connected, and this moment for me was about me owning this from within and acting from it.

Questions:

- Do you choose to be right over kind? If so, at what cost? While this can feel good in the short term (and sometimes it doesn't even do that), keep in mind, in treating another poorly, you're telling the Universe it's okay to treat you the same way. After all, what we're doing to another, we're really doing to ourselves.

Tools:

So, how do you choose kindness over being right, especially when it feels like that person has wronged you?

1. Feel whatever you are feeling toward them.
Before you can really feel that you want to be kind and are connected to this person, feel whatever you're feeling toward them. If you're angry or upset, feel that. With my manager, I had several times of feeling angry, which for me, many times meant kicking or punching the air, before I was able to really choose kindness from a space of truth.

2. See yourself in someone else.
Whether it's a stranger or your boss, when you're having a difficult situation with them, can you find one thing about them that you like, or at a minimum, can relate to? While this one can be hard, it can be so helpful in shifting a difficult relationship or moment.

3. Choose compassion.
Can we agree that, at most times, most people are doing the best they can? I know I am, and I bet you are too. So, in the moments when you're feeling frustrated or angry, can you find compassion for that person who is running late, is disorganized for that meeting or, in this situation, has you fired? While it may not always be easy, the opposite doesn't get you anywhere.

4. Be kind.
There's something beautiful that happens when we show kindness. If you're questioning this, think of a time when you received unexpected kindness and love from a stranger. How'd it feel? My point exactly. If you're still not convinced, take one moment to think about how your body feels when you feel dislike versus like towards someone or something. (If you want to test this, close your eyes and think of someone you don't like. Just notice what happens in your body. Now think of someone you like or love. Notice the difference. Feeling good things feels good, doesn't it?) With this said, if you can't do it for them, do it for you.

CHAPTER 31

The only way to fit in is to make yourself smaller than you were ever intended to be.

AFTER I COMPLETED MY CORPORATE JOB, AS A CELEBRATION TO AND FOR MYSELF, I DECIDED TO GO TO ECUADOR, AND I BOOKED MYSELF ON A GROUP TOUR.

I was super excited, as I love to travel and this was my "coming out" party. No more needing to hide a part of myself. No more pretending to be something I'm not. No more corporate world! I felt liberated!

So, as I started on the trip, at first, it started off like most, with polite banter and your usual "feeling-each-other-out" conversations within the group.

But, I could see it clear as day. People were starting to take sides, and visible divisions were beginning to form.

I had left the corporate world, so I wouldn't have to worry about fitting in, and then there it was—right in my face—*again*.

To be fair, I had struggled with not fitting in my entire life. From being in my high school gym class, where my sister and I would do different exercises from what the teacher was doing, and she would ask why we always needed to do things "differently," to moments when I would find myself with a group of old friends, making small talk to "try" to fit in, I've never belonged.

On the trip, I remember one such time ending up on a rafting excursion with some of them. Anyone who knows me knows I love water, adventure and rafting, but I was struggling. I definitely wanted to go, and I wanted them to like me, and yet I was also concerned about being on a body of water with no one who truly had my back. I did end up deciding to go, and it ended up going okay. The only eventful thing that happened was when we got thrown out of the raft and we were being pulled down the river and, for several minutes, there were three or four of us hanging onto the kayak who had been assigned to our group. [I remember making weird noises to calm myself and not panic (one of my signature fear sounds), and one of the other participants being kind enough to keep talking to me until we got pulled back into the raft. While I knew we would be fine, her concern was nice.]

I also remember getting sick on this two-week trip three times! While I didn't realize it at the time, I wasn't doing a good job of protecting myself from all of the toxic energy that was there, so I kept getting sick.

So, as the trip went on, while I found myself succumbing to my old pattern of wanting to fit in with the group, I finally gave in.

With this, I found myself mostly hanging out with the "outsiders" of the group, though I hesitate to call them that, as they were just people. On the opposite end, sometimes I would just do things on my own. Either way, I did find a few friends intermixed throughout the group and did my best to enjoy the rest of my trip.

LIFE LESSONS AND LEARNINGS

FITTING IN

I feel like the Universe kept giving me the opportunity to fit in for me to finally choose away from it. I can't even name how many times, earlier in my life, I desired to fit in, and really, how many times, I longed to be part of a group. This Ecuador trip was no different.

What I've come to realize since then is that I didn't come here to fit in. Fitting in is where we make ourselves smaller than we are supposed to be, and many times, to do anything that stands out, you have to be willing to go against the grain, and be big, really big. Not to mention, when we follow the masses, many times, it's like the blind leading the blind.

As part of this, for me, I like to think of this in terms of how old our souls are. Being a younger or older soul is neither "good" nor "bad." But, my sense of it is that if you are a younger soul, it will likely be easier to lean toward fitting in. This is because many younger souls are, understandably, seeking comfort, ease, fun and escape. This is not to say that older souls aren't also wanting these things, but the older you get and the more you've journeyed through various life-times, you can begin to gain a different perspective on why you are really here, what's really important and even what comfort, ease, fun and escape are to you. Yes, the older souls were once younger souls who craved the same things and thought and went about getting them in similar ways, but as they got older, they began to realize that this wasn't the complete story. In truth, they came here to have the full experience, finding a lot of juice in the difficult, challenging and hard, and that this was just as fun, if not more fun, than exclusively seeking the "good," as in this space, there was no trying to manage the environment or worrying about what could come their way. They knew, or at least, were leaning into, handling it all, and as they dove deeper, they realized they were reaching higher heights! I also believe this is why it takes some people longer than others to wake up (i.e., the older a soul you are, the more likely you are to awaken quickly, as you have a stronger memory of this).

I think it's important, too, to make a distinction between fitting in versus connection. For years, I thought of fitting in, which can include making yourself small and shrinking to fit, and connection, which I define as being close with another being, as one and the same. What I'm realizing, though, is I can create connection without fitting in, especially when I have similar values with another. One example: I have many friends and family members I spend time with who are ten-plus years older than me. Even though on the outside, we might appear to have nothing in common, when we spend time together, because we both have similar values, likes and/or history, we have a great time together. On the opposite end, last year I went to my high school reunion, and because my likes and values were different from most of my old classmates, for most of it, I didn't find the connection that I so strongly crave.

QUESTIONS:

- Do you desire to fit in? If so, why is this important to you and does fitting in match the goals you have for your life? (For example, if you dream of changing the world and yet you also want to fit in, those two things may not go together.)

- Also, if you tune into your journey, do you think of yourself as a younger or older soul? Again, neither is "good" nor "bad," but I found when I tuned into this, it helped me to better understand myself and my goals in this lifetime and why I struggled to fit in.

- With this, is fitting in what you really crave or is it really connection? If it's connection, what values, beliefs and interests, to name a few, help you to feel connected to another?

TOOLS:

Once you've gotten clear on the above, if you are wanting to break away from fitting in, here's what you can do:

1. First, ask yourself what you are craving in your friendships and relationships. What's truly important to you, when it comes down to it? For me, one of the biggest ones was not having to edit, minimize or mute myself to be in someone else's company. Another important one was deep conversation, as I really value getting to know someone on a deep level.

2. Once you've gotten clear on number one, then it's important to start choosing friendships and relationships that match what's important to you. With the example of minimizing yourself, if you keep choosing friendships and relationships where this is the case, you are telling the Universe to bring more people into your life who will also treat you this way, so be careful to choose what you want, not what you've had!

DIVISION VS. CONNECTION

Another thing that was so apparent, and really disappointing, at the end of my Ecuador trip, was the division, and really the separation, that occurred. Why do we choose to divide versus connect? More importantly, why do we need to make certain people wrong to make ourselves feel better? Instinctually, I know the answer to this—we have forgotten that we're all connected.

We've forgotten that what we do to another, we're really doing to ourselves. We've forgotten that what we put out there comes back to us tenfold. We've forgotten that we're all just humans doing the best we can. We've even forgotten that our differences are what make us beautiful and unique.

Also, important to note: If you feel what division, separation and really, what making someone else wrong feels like in your body, it will likely feel heavy and contracting (or some version of this). This is because this isn't the truth of who we are. Then, if you think of putting this onto another person, which is what was happening on my trip unconsciously, these are just a few of the energies that can lead to dis-ease and disease. This was one of the main reasons I got sick three times in the course of two weeks, which is HIGHLY unusual for me. In this happening, though, I saw and really, experienced, the impact of this type of energy over a prolonged period of time. And, while I know we're not trained to think of our actions in this way, I recommend thinking twice the next time you're treating another human being unkindly, as the net effect is it not feeling good to either party, even though it can feel temporarily satisfying.

QUESTIONS:

- As an adult, have you fallen into this? Have you treated someone else poorly to lift yourself up or have you subconsciously made someone else wrong to make yourself right? It's okay if you have. We all have, at one point or another. It's just important to notice this, and ask if this is the person you want to be moving forward.

- Also, what energy are you taking in and what energy are you putting out? If you're constantly getting mad at someone or someone is getting mad at you, it's important to notice how you feel when this occurs. If it doesn't feel good, and you want to make a change, start to monitor who you spend your time with and how you show up around them and vice versa.

Tools:

If you're ready to change this to connect with others, even with ones who may not always have the same beliefs as you, use these steps:

1. Find connection.
For me, amid the "popular group," there were people looking to have fun and find connection with similar beings. I navigated toward them and chose connection. As part of this, while it wasn't always easy and I wasn't always successful, I kept choosing to focus on the good in every moment, whether it was the people I was connecting with or the beautiful surroundings I was lucky enough to be enjoying.

2. Find likeness.
With the people I didn't feel connected to, as much as possible, I tried to see myself in them, recognizing that the opposite just expands the problem. As part of this, I could definitely identify with their desire to want to be liked and to fit in. For me, there were times I had chosen this, too, even at the cost of not being as nice as I could have been. In choosing this, though, it definitely helped me to choose love with them, when, at times, the opposite seemed easier.

3. Find compassion.
When I couldn't find something I could always connect with, I found it helpful to see the little kid that lives within all of us. This is such a helpful tool when we're having a hard time choosing love. Children definitely represent innocence, and while someone may appear to be "old" or "older," they may be a young soul in the scheme of things.

Also, understanding someone's need to put you in a box for his/her own protection can definitely help as well. What do I mean by this? As humans, it's natural when we meet someone to categorize them. Some simple boxes: single/married, black/white, tall/short.

This helps us feel safe and comfortable. In this situation, I totally got this, and the need to place people in the box of "cool/uncool" to feel secure. So, while it was not a perfect science, I chose to meet them with as much compassion as possible.

4. Find the opportunity.

As a coach, I believe everything in our field can help us see ourselves clearer and help us to shift the parts of us that aren't resonant with love. So, on this trip, I asked myself, "What is this meant to show me?" I then connected to the piece of me that still wanted to fit in and let her share her voice, using the inner child processes I discuss throughout this book.

5. Find kindness.

As part of this, it's important to be aware of the energy you're putting out, and if this involves treating another person unkindly, being aware of the energy you're putting on that person. If you wouldn't want to be treated this way, it's important to be mindful of this, treating the other with kindness.

CHAPTER 32

Embrace the not knowing, as it's the thing that you're going to miss most.

FOR YEARS, AS I WAS ON MY SELF-LOVE JOURNEY, MY GUIDES KEPT GIVING ME MORE AND MORE WAYS TO RETURN TO LOVE. Of course, we've all heard the saying that if you want love, you've got to love yourself. For me, I was doing the work and wondering when my love partner was coming.

It felt like he was coming closer.

He had to be coming closer.

Yes, yes. He would definitely be here soon.

It was around that point when my guidance decided they were going to work with me in a new way, a way they previously hadn't.

With this, they dropped in a question, and really a game, that I started to play.

For me, it started off one day quite innocently. I was on Facebook, and I saw a man I felt connected to, and decided to ask, "Is this him?" (I.e., was this the guy I was meant to end up with?) My inner story had always been that there was one specific person for me, so asking this question felt right. And, while it wasn't really conscious at the time, looking back, I liked the idea of checking in. In doing this, I felt safe and comforted and that I had some control over my reality. Not to mention that I was ready to finally find him. (Later, this story would change to him finding me, but in that moment, I still thought I had to find him.)

So, initially, as I started this process, the question felt quite harmless. I never thought I'd actually intuitively hear "yes" to my question, and even further than that, I didn't think about what happened if I actually did hear yes.

So, the game continued on for a few more months. In addition to doing check-ins when I would see someone I felt connected to, intuitively, I asked several questions about him.

Does he have brown or blonde hair? What color are his eyes? How old is he? What's his name? (They did give me a name, which I took with a grain of salt, as I had never been strong at intuiting names.)

It was one day in late summer, though, when it happened. I was on Facebook, and I saw someone I felt drawn to. So, while I almost didn't ask—he was really good-looking and seemed out of my league—as always, in my innocent voice, I asked inside, *"Is this him?"*

"Yes," my intuition, and really, my Guides and Angels, chimed back. That was odd. The only times when I had heard yes, I knew right away that my Guides were messing with me. This didn't feel like that, though. So, I asked again. *"Is this him?"*

"Yes," they replied again.

So, in this situation, I did what any good intuitive does. I asked the question about ten more times. Each time, I heard yes. I felt myself getting excited, even giddy. Was this really true? Could this really be possible? Was this really him?

Then, I did the next step that any good intuitive does, and I phoned a friend.

"Hey there. I got something really weird to ask you, and don't look up who this person is before you check in, okay? My Guides are telling me that this person is my person. What do you get?"

So, at first, she did what you'd want anyone who's reading something for you to do. She asked if it was in my highest good to know this information, and if so, if she would get an honest answer. When she got a yes to both, she then asked the question and also got a yes.

As she confirmed what I got, I felt my insides in disbelief. After all of these years of waiting, was he finally here?? Well, at least I knew who he was, so that should make it easier, right??

So, as the days followed, and I started to take in the information I had been given, I began to realize that I had all of these blocks to receiving the kind of love I was desiring.

I didn't believe I could have a super attractive man, and maybe I didn't even fully want one. After all, it would be safer to just have a "cute" guy. That way, it was my perception that he wasn't as desirable to other women. I also didn't believe this man would want me, which was interesting. When I asked why, I realized that, at some point, I had bought into a limit of the type of guy I could have. This was magnified with my twin sister dating extremely attractive men. Somehow I believed she could have them, but I couldn't. Perhaps the biggest block I realized I had, though, was that I didn't believe he would stick around. I had never truly, fully, completely had a man show up for me, so why would this time be any different?

It made me sad to think, even with all of the work I had done on myself, there was still more. It felt never-ending, and I felt like I would never get it right.

So, initially, as I started to see this man in my life, it was really hard to envision it. After all, I had never had a man who was really there for me not to mention, even growing up, I had never really lived with a man.

So, I started to shift these beliefs to open to the love I deserved and desired. (Whether it was him or someone else, I knew I desired and deserved to have a love without limits.)

As I started working with his energy, which, looking back, I believe was one of many possibilities, and that we even had a soul contract for this, if it did come up, I began to realize that there was something about him that was really familiar. I can't explain it, but I knew details about him that I had no way of knowing, and later, when I checked in, we had known each other in many lifetimes, even being married in one of them. I would imagine my Guides gave him to me, in part, because of this familiarity, as it made it easier to see him in my everyday life, and to believe, really believe, and *feel*, that this was not only possible, that it was already created.

With this, over the next several months, I began to notice several synchronicities. The initials of my first and middle name were his reversed. *Of course, I would have set it up for him to be my mirror reflection.* I believed his birthday was my half birthday. *This must mean that he's my other "half."* He even had a similar story about what love looked like and we have similar ways of being in the world. (He's a pretty open, public person on social media.)

So, I kept checking in and getting the go-ahead to keep using his energy. It was really helpful, too, as for the first time ever, I really *felt* what it was like to have a man show up for me. Prior to this, I had never been able to visualize a man fully being in my life.

Then, an opportunity came to meet him. You see, he's a coach, too, and he was hosting an event in Las Vegas with his business partner. As a huge part of my journey has been working toward truth, I had committed that I would only move toward something if it were aligned for me. I wouldn't do it just to meet someone, and in this case, him. *I had been there too many times before.*

So, while the energy read that it was too soon for us to "get together," my Guides gave me the go-ahead under the direction of doing the event for me and strictly practicing being in feminine energy.

You see, prior to this, for months, I had been working on moving out of the masculine energy that had helped me to climb the ladder and move into six figures in the corporate world, but had made me a disaster in dating.

What is masculine energy? It's doing versus being. It's "making things happen" versus allowing and receiving. It's busy versus calm. And, really, it's hard versus soft.

While it had helped me to be successful in business, it had been paramount to my former failure in relationships because when I was in masculine energy, a man couldn't feel me. For me, to be felt means to be truly vulnerable and open to really expressing myself, with my partner reciprocating. It means each of us is committed to going deep with ourselves and with each other. And, it means letting go of control and letting my walls down. Yes, letting go has been a big part for me.

Being felt is important, because when we can't feel each other, we're not connected. And, if we're not connected, the spark dies and the physical attraction, relationship newness and the excitement that comes with it, dwindles. We've all been there, and it ain't pretty.

This can be coupled with, when a woman is in her masculine, a man naturally goes into his feminine. And, to put it simply, *that's not hot.*

So, on this weekend, I would practice being true to myself and in feminine energy, which meant practicing keeping my energy in the lower half of my body and not initiating. Though initiating isn't always masculine, I wanted to practice receiving versus chasing.

I was excited. I was nervous. But, overall, everything went great. It was fun practicing "staying in my lane" and creating an invitation. I'd flash him a smile, flirting with my eyes that I had a secret to share and walk across the room bringing my energy in my hips.

I remember at one point in the weekend, too, seeing a bunch of scandalously clad women dancing in tight dresses. At that moment, it hit me. That's what masculine energy in a feminine body looks like; *that used to be me.*

So, everything was going smoothly until one of his staff members and I got into a fight. It was over something silly, but just like that, all of the energy that was feeling really good and open, closed, and that was that.

The next day I was processing the weekend, and I decided to go out for a walk in the hot Las Vegas heat. I hadn't gotten fifty feet from the door, when I felt this deep-seated emotion that had been boiling up all weekend come pouring out of me.

What I realized was that I had subconsciously been feeling like I had to be perfect, and really, *everything had to be perfect*. When I stepped into the summer heat that day, the sun was the activator that gave me permission to finally be able to let go of this and the excruciating belief that I had to hold it all together. This had translated to having to have exactly the right "feminine" outfits, which I had frantically gone shopping for just days before. It had translated to a fear that I could say or do the wrong thing and mess things up. It had also translated to a hyper-focus on feminine energy, so much so that I felt on-guard all weekend.

With this realization, I went back inside, and for a half hour, I cried. I cried for the part of me that believed I had to be perfect to get the kind of love I wanted, and really, to be lovable. I cried for all the times I believed I had to be something I wasn't to be loved. I cried for the part of me that believed I wasn't good enough just as I was.

And, with this, I released another part of me that was holding me back from fully loving myself, moving me one step closer to creating the deep love I was yearning for.

After I got back home, I checked in with my Guides and Angels for next steps. At this point, I wasn't clear that it was still a green light to keep working with him to create my partner, but they said it was. So I stayed with the practices—seeing him in my life, showing up for me fully and providing a space for me to be vulnerable, feminine and really, to let go.

It was a few months later when I felt it. I was lying in my bed doing a practice with his energy. Where, in the past, it was so easy to see his energy there, this time, it wasn't clear. I did a check-in and realized it was finally finished. *Our relationship was complete.*

I felt a bit of sadness, the kind you would feel going through an actual breakup. It was then that I realized the role he had played was the role he was meant to play all along. Whether it was a soul contract and/or just one of many infinite possibilities, I felt beyond grateful. What a generous offer. (My sense of him in this lifetime is that he does have a very generous heart.)

So, as we were completing, came the final exercise I would practice with him. This was the exercise of letting go of the long-held attachment that he was my person. *Truth be told, it was the perfect ending.*

Oh, and just before we completed, I found out one more interesting fact. In addition to being married in one lifetime, in another lifetime, the one he held the strongest memory of, I had been his mom.

And, I didn't want a man who was going to treat me like his mommy.

One more fun thing—it is my full intention to sit down with him in physical form and share this story. Oh, to be a fly on the wall for that one!

LIFE LESSONS AND LEARNINGS

WHAT DO YOU BELIEVE YOU DESERVE?

One of my biggest lessons in all of this was realizing the beliefs I had about what I deserved or could have. With this, as I was starting this journey with him, I almost didn't ask if he was a possibility, as he was really good-looking, and at the time, I had a belief that I couldn't have a "hot" guy. In some way, too, this was a subconscious protective mechanism I was using, so I wouldn't get hurt, as I perceived that hot guys would hurt you more. That despite all evidence to the contrary that it didn't matter whether I was dating someone who was classically hot or not, it typically ended in pain.

QUESTIONS:

- What types of partners are you drawn to? Now ask yourself, are you drawn to these types of partners because this is actually whom you're attracted to or because you have a belief around what you deserve or you just feel "safer" with this type of guy/girl? Take note of that.

TOOLS:

1. If you're ready to shift this belief to have more in your life, make a list of all of the qualities you'd like to have, but historically haven't chosen.

2. Then, connect with your inner child, either seeing them in front of you or feeling them in your heart, and ask them what they're scared will happen, if you actually are with a person with these qualities. Give voice to their fears. (I recommend doing this by saying these fears out loud.)

3. Once you feel like there's no more charge on these old choices, ask your inner child if it's okay if you make a new choice. If it's true for you, let them know that you have their back and you promise to stay with them, no matter what. Then, take this in, seeing your body filling with love and light.

ACCESSING YOUR FEMININE ENERGY

I remember when I first started this journey—I had no clue what feminine energy was, let alone how to be in it. Growing up, between always holding the masculine in my relationship with my sister and always being rewarded for overachieving, while I didn't realize this at the time, the masculine had been deeply embedded within me.

But, as I learned about the feminine and began to cultivate more and more, I felt calmer and more relaxed and life started to become easier. Why was this? Because instead of pushing so hard and needing to make things happen, things were coming to me. I was magnetizing opportunities, help and support, everything from small things like people helping me with my luggage and groceries to big things like new clients, speaking opportunities and more aligned love partners coming my way.

Also, where our masculine energy lives in our shoulders, chest and torso, our feminine energy lives in the lower part of our body. This inherently feels really good as we are more embodied when our energy is in our entire body, not just part of it. (I share more about this in the Tools Section.)

QUESTIONS:

- Are you more in your feminine or masculine, or are you balanced? (I've included a short list of each, if you're needing help defining this.)

- If you're not already, do you want to have more balance in your life around this and bring in more feminine? (If you're a man wanting to work on your masculine, email me and I'm happy to make some recommendations of teachers who can support you with this.) Important to note: This is not about exclusively being in your feminine if you're female or being in your masculine, if you're male. Most importantly, this is about balance and being able to use both of these as needed.

Masculine

Doing

Forcing

Making Things Happen

Pushing

Logic

Fixing

Thinking

Hard

Linear

Feminine

Being

Intuition

Feeling

Accepting

Receiving

Magnetizing

Nurturing

Soft

Vulnerability

Tools:

How to access more feminine energy:

1. Connect with your feminine energy.
Again, when I first started working on this, I had no clue how to access my feminine side. For so long, I thought it was positive to act like a man, which absolutely is understandable given how much I was rewarded for showing up this way. When I would receive feedback, for example, about how strong my handshake was, I actually thought this was a good thing, even attractive, and while it was working for me in my career, it was absolutely not working for me in the place that mattered most to me, my love life.

Accessing the feminine for me started with realizing masculine energy existed in the upper half of my body. This makes sense if you think of how men stand or even when you feel the safest (or the most scared) around a man—their shoulders are usually wide. For women, though, the simple act of bringing your energy and attention into your hips and relaxing and opening the upper half of your body can begin to shift this.

To do this, see your attention and breath going into your hips. You can even make figure eights in your hips as you do this. Also, relax your body, especially your upper half, feeling your heart opening.

As you do this, you'll likely notice right away that you feel more open, calm and relaxed. This is feminine energy at its best.

2. Be vulnerable. I mean really vulnerable.
So many times, we don't reveal parts of ourselves because we're scared and/or we don't know how. But, practicing sharing these pieces of ourselves is crucial to shifting into our feminine. How do

we do this? Begin to practice being relational with people who you feel safe with.

Being relational means sharing your insides and really allowing yourself to go deep, even if it scares you. A couple of cues that can help you get in touch with this part of yourself include "If I wasn't scared, I'd tell you…" and "What I don't want you to know about me right now is…" Then, go deep into why it scares you or why you don't want to share it. If you're just wanting to scratch the surface, notice this. There's a completely different feeling to "I'm uncomfortable" and "I'm scared to share this because I'm scared if I do, you'll leave me."

When we share from our truth and truly open up, we give a man the opportunity to hold space for us, and to really witness us, and trust me, there's something truly powerful and really delicious about this. For me, in moments when I've created this, I've never felt more seen.

3. Ask for help.
We can get so conditioned to being independent and doing things ourselves that we don't take help when it's given and, even worse, we don't ask for it. A crucial part in stepping into the feminine, though, is allowing ourselves to receive help. If you've ever said, "I've got this," or "I can do it myself," this one's for you.

4. Receive everything.
In addition to receiving help, we are constantly being given opportunities to receive. Think about the last time you received a compliment. How did you take it? Did it make you uncomfortable, or maybe you even felt the need to reciprocate? I've been there, too, and I know, many times in the past, I had a hard time just saying thank you, and taking it in. Instead, I might dismiss it or say something complimentary back.

Taken one step further, think about a time when someone wanted to give you something. Maybe it was something small like dinner, and maybe it was something bigger like a vacation. How did you respond to this gift? It's interesting to see how wrong we can feel receiving. One simple thing you can do to change this, whether it's a compliment or something bigger, is to take a deep breath before you respond and really drink in, internalize and receive, what they are offering.

CREATING AN ENERGETIC PRACTICE RELATIONSHIP

When I was initially checking in to "find" my person, I did not realize that this would end up creating a beautiful practice for me. Instead, this question was definitely rooted in my need to feel safe and my need to know. Of course, at the time, I had no conscious idea of what an energetic practice relationship was, let alone the actual intention to create one.

What this practice did, though, in addition to helping me to feel what it was like to have a partner in my life, was help me to identify so many of the patterns I had around relationship along with the energies I was taking into the partnership I was creating that weren't actually working to magnetize the type of partner I wanted. Most importantly, this practice helped me to clear many layers of my abandonment pattern and the places where I still didn't love myself enough and wasn't owning my worth (i.e., this was an important exercise in self-love).

As part of this, my question "Is this him?" was rooted in my need to feel safe. Inherently, this in itself makes it not a good question, as I wasn't trusting. I wasn't trusting that he'd show up. I wasn't trusting that the Universe had my back. Deeply rooted, I wasn't trusting myself or that I was desirable and lovable enough that he'd even want to show up.

This doesn't factor in the fact that my story is, you don't find your person, you magnetize, and really, create them by loving yourself and becoming the person you want to attract, not to mention that I believe in every ounce of my being that he will find me.

With this, when we're focused on something happening or worried it won't happen, many times, either of these focuses will create the exact thing we don't want to happen, if we're coming from a lack mentality (i.e., if I'm focused on getting something, I'm automatically putting separation between the thing I'm desiring and me. There's a saying, "You can't have what you want." This is because in wanting something you're not in the "have" vibration, which includes not matching the vibration of the thing you want, and, remember, like attracts like. So, instead, what this does is puts you in the constant vibration of wanting it, instead of having it, which makes it hard to manifest and is completely frustrating!). (By the way, to have it, you have to go into the feeling that it's already happened, and really believe this in every cell in your body.)

Along with this, wanting to make it happen is a strong masculine energy, and for someone who was moving into my feminine and from that, wanted to magnetize a partner who could lead me, again, this was not an ideal energy to be creating from.

I love this part of my journey, too, as it was such a fun way to play with energy to create my love partnership. I love that I believed it so strongly. I even love that, in telling people about what I knew, when I realized it wasn't true, I had to reconcile the part of me that didn't want to be wrong.

When I look back, there was such perfection in it all. It was a beautiful exercise to clear the blocks I couldn't see without having someone in my actual physical world. It was deliciously helpful in my truly believing that someone could and would show up for me. And, it was exciting! It was a win-win-win all the way around!

QUESTIONS:

- What blocks do you have to creating and magnetizing the right partner for you? Where are you settling for less than you desire and deserve? (If you're not sure, one good way to identify some of your blocks would be to close your eyes, seeing your ideal partner in front of you. Now, notice what you believe about yourself and their desire for you, including why you can't have them and/or why they don't want you, if this is true for you. Include what they're saying to and about you (which is just really a reflection of your own internal beliefs).

- As part of this, where don't you trust that you will meet the right person for you? Why? What do you need to shift and get clear on to believe this is possible? (To shift these blocks, I first recommend using any one of the many exercises found in this book. After working with these on your own, if you choose to, creating an energetic practice partnership can also help to heal these and will show you more patterns.)

- Do you want to create an energetic practice relationship?

TOOLS:

Below is how to create an energetic practice relationship. If you're looking for further support around clearing relationship patterns and any of the practices, tools and methods I share in this book, especially around relationship, this is a specialty of mine, so don't hesitate to reach out.

Step One

If you are desiring to create something similar to what I described above, especially if you, too, don't know what it's like to really have a man show up for you (i.e., identifying someone in physical form whose energy you can work with to practice being in relationship with and feeling what it feels like to have someone show up for you in a real and true way), the first step is to ask your Guides and Angels if this is aligned for you. (If you're not used to communicating with your Guides and Angels, use Chapters 8, 12 and 23 to get you started.)

If it is, then ask them to guide you toward someone you can practice with. While I was guided toward mine through social media, there are infinite ways that this person can come to you, including at work, in a social circle or through other online platforms. An important key to this is ensuring this person is not already partnered up. You do not want to be activating this energy with someone who's unavailable. I happened to get lucky with the person I was energetically practicing with. In addition to being very attractive, he also had a very kind, loving and open nature to him. This helped me to feel safe, to really open myself and trust. This is possible for you, too, and just trust that, if this is the right thing for you and you're truly sincere about your intentions, when you ask, your Guides will bring you the perfect person for you. Of course, once you've asked, it's important to pay attention to whom they put in your field. If you need to, ask for clarity, if you're unsure if the person they give you is the right person's energy to practice with.

Alternatively, depending on where you are in your journey, you don't need a person in physical form to do this with. Initially, they gave me a real-life person, as they knew it would be hard for me to visualize without this. The more I did this, though, and the more I opened up to having a man in my life, the easier it got to visualize this happening and feel someone's presence, without needing to have a specific person in mind. To me, feeling this person is one of the most important pieces of the exercise, and in general, to creating a love partnership.

Also, if they say no to this exercise, I'd definitely ask why. Maybe you're not ready for this exercise or this exercise is simply not the right exercise for you. If so, I'd recommend asking for help as well as other exercises from your Guides and Angels to create your love partner and to work with this process, if it calls to you. Then pay attention.

Step Two

If you do end up doing this exercise, once you've identified a person to work with, notice what comes up for you when you are "introduced" to them. Are you surprised? If so, why? Do you believe they are too good for you? Do you have blocks around being worthy enough? Do you think they won't like you? It's important to notice all of this and feel the emotions that come up when you actually try to picture this person in your life. (Again, if you're struggling with feeling your feelings, use one of the many tools found in this book to dive deeper into this.)

Step Three

Once you've felt and cleared anything noticeable that stops you from believing something like this is possible, start to see them in your everyday world. See all parts of your life with them—having breakfast, brushing your teeth, eating dinner, watching television, going to bed and everything in between. See yourself traveling and spending vacations with them, enjoying all of your adventures together. See yourself on holidays with them. See yourself finding new places together—restaurants, destinations, views—see it all. Again, the important piece to this, too, isn't just seeing them, it's feeling them. Are they rubbing your feet after a long day, giving you a hug and kiss before you leave for work or cooking you dinner? Feel their comforting, playful, open, deep, loving, kind self and how you feel and show up in their presence. Experience it all! (Again, you don't have to have a specific person in mind, if you're able to feel the energy of having this person around, and with this, all of the feelings that you want to feel in this partnership.)

Important to note: This is an add-on exercise to anything you're doing in your physical world. This is not meant to replace dating, and it's important to recognize the fine line between practicing and get wrapped up in someone's energy that you're exclusively meant to practice energetically with. It's important that the exercise feels real, but if you find that you are shutting yourself off from reality or getting too caught up in this fantasy as truth, I recommend stopping the exercise. When my Guides and Angels gave me this exercise, they knew I had a strong enough sense of self that it would serve me, and if I did find myself in an unhealthy behavior, that I would know when to stop. It's important for you to determine your version of this. Only you can know what's truly right for you and where your boundaries lie. Again, if you are looking for support with this, this is a huge piece of the work I do with my clients, so don't hesitate to reach out. (Also, if you notice you think you can or need to do it all yourself, asking for help might be part of your process to let your walls down and move more into the feminine, as being able to ask for support is part of being in the feminine!)

LETTING GO OF PERFECTIONISM

The other thing this process helped me to let go of was my need to be perfect. While I thought I had already cleared this pattern, I didn't realize that a piece of me still believed that I needed to be perfect to be loved. Seeing, and really feeling how I showed up in this person's presence, helped me to see that this pattern still existed in me, and most importantly, it helped me to see how exhausting holding this pattern was.

QUESTIONS:

- Do you need things to be perfect in your life? If so, where? How does this pattern impact your relationships and life and how do you show up as a result of this pattern?

TOOLS:

Are you ready to let go of your perfectionism pattern? If so, begin by feeling what comes up for you as you think of letting go of this pattern. How has this pattern served you? It could be keeping you safe and protecting you from having a real relationship. It could be keeping you from fully putting yourself out there. Notice what's true for you and feel the fear that comes up, as you imagine letting go of this and people seeing the real, perfectly imperfect you. This may be a multi-layer process. You may shift one layer today and then find another layer shows up tomorrow. Just keep choosing it, by choosing through this pattern, whether that means allowing someone to come over to your house when it doesn't look perfect, leaving the house without makeup on or being willing to share or post something online, even though it could be "better." If you find yourself still struggling, continue to feel whatever comes up for you and *breathe*.

For how to let go of attachment, head to Chapter 20.

CHAPTER 33

It's one thing to know your truth. It's another to communicate it.

I LOVE ALL OF THE TOOLS THAT MY GUIDES AND ANGELS HAVE GIVEN IN HELPING ME ON MY SELF-LOVE JOURNEY TO HEAL MY ABANDONMENT PATTERN AND CREATE MY DREAM RELATIONSHIP.

It wasn't too long ago when they gave me another unique tool to do this.

It was mid-May 2016, and I was brand-spanking new into doing my coaching business full-time. I had had a rough week, and the guidance that came through was simple:

Get out of your house and do something fun.

Fun to me many times includes learning, and I found an intro workshop in the area on Conscious Love. At the time, I'm not sure if I knew the workshop was Tantra-related or not, but either way, the title spoke to me.

So, on Thursday of that week, I headed to the evening workshop. As I began hearing the teachers speak, I felt pulled in, really called, to their teaching style. There was something about how real they were; they were vulnerable and in the yumminess of life, and yet, they were

242 • LIVING DEEPLY

unabashed about their challenges and experiences. They had such joy, and you could see that they really got that it was all about the journey, and, with this, that it didn't matter what people thought. They were going to let their "freak flag" fly and be who they were with no apologies. I felt giddy seeing how free they were. It was such a breath of fresh air, and I just knew that I had to be at their longer, weekend workshop, even though when I had gotten there, I had no intention of signing up for their full-immersion weekend.

So, I said to my Guides, and really the Universe, if it's less than $400, I will do it. No questions asked.

A few minutes later, I looked down at the card they had handed out about the weekend, and the investment was more. I felt disappointed, but I was prepared to stick to my original internal commitment.

It was when they were wrapping up the class that they announced that they had too many men for the weekend. (This, by the way, NEVER happens at these type of events.) With this, they were offering the women a discount, if we wanted to do the weekend. I felt my stomach flip with the internal excitement one feels when it is beautifully reaffirmed how truly supported they are. *I knew I was meant to be there, and I was in!*

As we started the weekend, I had no idea what to expect. They were teaching us Tantra, and while for many, Tantra has a sexual connotation, for me, while I was definitely aware of the sexual connotations, I knew there was more to Tantra than that. As the weekend went by, I learned that Tantra was really about breath and connection. I was definitely a hell-yes to having a deep partnership that included deep breath, connection and hot sex too!

It was Saturday afternoon when I was getting the sense that we were going to have the option to do something that was *way* out of my comfort zone. Anyone who knows me will tell you I'm usually very comfortable out of my comfort zone. This time was different, though. I didn't fully understand what was going to happen, but I knew we were going to have the opportunity to pick a partner, and the night was meant to be all about us.

The in-between part was unclear, though I did know, whatever it was, the women were calling the shots, the men were being coached explicitly on what was and wasn't okay and it would be up to us as to how far it would or wouldn't go.

As the night approached, I got a bit clearer on what *could* happen, and *I was terrified*.

I began talking to myself to calm my little girl. "We don't have to do anything that we don't want to do or are uncomfortable with and we can leave anytime we want, okay?" It helped a bit, but who was I kidding? There was nothing I or anyone else could say to ease my nerves.

With this, though, my intuition knew that this would be a healing experience for me, if I could let go of having to know exactly what was going to happen, and really if I could let go of *control*, and trust that this process was for my highest good.

So, that night, as we stood in a circle picking our partners (it was women's choice), while there had been men who had alluded to their interest in "partnering," I picked the man who felt safe and familiar. (This was definitely one of my relationship patterns.)

As we went off, we were both chuckling nervously. We hadn't known about this "exercise," and we were both petrified. *Neither one of us had done something like this before.*

Our evening started with sushi and the grocery store, where he picked up some things to "set the tone" for the evening. (They had been guided to create a loving, safe, romantic space.) As I sat in the car, it took every ounce of my being not to go running out of it and back to safety multiple times. I stayed, though.

We ended up at his house in the northwestern suburbs of Chicago. I had a sense that our assignment might make quite the mess [another relationship pattern of mine—avoiding the physical (as well as other) messiness in my relationships], and I didn't want that, or a stranger, in my house. For some reason, too, it felt more comfortable to be on his turf than on mine. I felt like I could leave anytime I wanted, and I would be less OCD in his space.

The night itself ended up being more healing than sexual. I was guided during our time together to have him say out loud to me, "I'm not leaving you," which he said generously, over and over. Something in hearing it from the opposite sex out loud helped me to rewire the piece of me that had believed that I would always be left. I definitely felt like a different person that next day. I felt a new calm and openness, no longer on edge waiting for someone to leave.

The workshop finished the following day, and at the end of the day, he pulled me aside to see if we could be Tantra partners.

I was open to that but was also very clear that we would not be a good long-term match for each other. More importantly, for the first time ever, not only was I very clear about this, but I was able to successfully communicate it to a partner. I felt proud of myself and excited for what we were creating.

He called me a couple of days later, excited to connect. As we were on the phone, talking about making plans, he casually mentioned that he was also talking to another woman he had liked at the event, and since we didn't have an exclusive relationship, they had made plans to go out that weekend.

I immediately tensed up and noticed the conversation I was having in my head when he said this. With this, I noticed myself going into an old pattern of desiring someone's time and attention and only getting scraps from them. *It didn't feel good.*

That's when I explained to him, that while I knew our relationship wasn't a "forever" relationship, that if he was going to go out with her, which was totally fine, I couldn't also go out with him. For the first time ever in a relationship, I knew where my no was, and really, I knew my self-worth, and, most importantly, I honored and communicated it. *Plus one for self-love!*

As part of this, I knew that, given my abandonment pattern, it would not be healthy for me to be dating someone who was dating someone else, no matter what the parameters of our relationship. I told him that he was free to date her or anyone else. I just couldn't date him if that was the case.

That's when another first happened—*because I chose me, he chose me.*

So, we started dating and what started out under the guise of a Tantra relationship ended up turning into a beautiful practice partnership. I had shared with him that one of the things I was working on was being in more feminine energy and receiving more. He helped with this by doing everything from cooking for me to picking me up at the airport, all of this while I practiced showing up in truth and really being myself, instead of doing what I thought would make him want to stay. Yes, at times it was really hard. For me, we were at different parts on our growth journey, and so what triggered him, I saw as serving him, which meant at times feeling like we were in two different realities. Also, we had different priorities in our lives then, so there was a constant push-pull, where I felt pressured to spend more time with him and he felt like I wasn't spending enough time with him.

Overall, though, it was a beautiful practice, and one of my favorite things about the dynamic was that we could be real with each other. This meant putting down the normal fronts that we put up when we're getting to know someone and wanting to put our best fronts forward, whether it's to get laid, for long-term partnership or both.

While our relationship ended six weeks later (we really did need an independent third-party to help guide us through our triggers and the missteps that would come up, as we were navigating this process), it was a valuable practice that I would recommend to anyone looking for an original way to create and be in partnership.

LIFE LESSONS AND LEARNINGS

CREATING A PRACTICE RELATIONSHIP

This relationship helped me to realize that everything is a practice relationship, until it's not. I think we're so conditioned as a society to think that if a relationship doesn't work, we've failed, instead of looking at each relationship as helping us to learn and grow and to likely, be more of ourselves. For me, this was the relationship where this really got cemented and where I changed my definition of a successful relationship.

What I realized, too, is that in any other scenario, I could have easily defined this relationship, without the word "practice" in front of it. In truth, it looked like a lot of the relationships I had been in, with one big distinction—I was truly conscious of and sharing my truths with my partner. Unlike the past, I wasn't scared of the consequences of sharing these, as I already knew it was going to end at some point. While, looking back, this may have been a way to keep myself safe, this allowed me to relax in a way I never had before. (Imagine always worrying and being focused on someone else leaving you. This definitely makes for a hard time relaxing. Whether we're conscious of this or not, as well, the person we're dating can feel this.)

I learned, too, that, while, as a coach, I could see most of what was happening in our relationship clearly (and the pitfalls that were coming up), it was too hard to take care of myself and overcome these challenges.

Also, while in this situation I did communicate to my partner that this was "practice," you can take this idea into any dating scenario, as again, that's what dating is until you meet your person, and really, it's still practice, even after that. (I.e., while it's ideal, if possible, to communicate your desire to practice with them, especially if you know that it's short-term and you know that they are capable of staying with it and respecting you through the process even if they know it won't lead to something more, you don't have to necessarily communicate that you're practicing to get the benefits of this exercise. Also beware if you're putting up the parameter of it just being "practice" more to protect yourself, so you don't get hurt, or if it is just your sincere intention. I've heard of long-term couples who have gotten together under this guise, so it's important to stay open.)

With that said, I've listed some good guidelines and tools below to getting you started, if this is something you're feeling called to do, and of course, if you're looking for third-party support, I love facilitating my clients in this practice.

QUESTIONS:

- How do you typically define a successful relationship? Can you change the idea of a successful relationship being one of growth, truth and one where you honor yourself, the other and set boundaries versus a successful relationship being one that doesn't end? As part of this, can you choose love, kindness and respect over all else? At times, this will be very hard, but when you create from this foundation, it's a beautiful thing.

- How would it change your view of relationships and the pressure you put on yourself if you viewed all relationships as practice?

TOOLS:

Here are my recommendations, if this is something you're desiring to create your own version of. (By the way, these questions and recommendations aren't only for practice relationships, as they are also good for any relationship that you're creating or are in.) Also, important to note: Just because this is practice and you don't see yourself spending your life with this person, this doesn't mean that you should pick someone who isn't nice or kind to you or who doesn't respect you. This is still crucial in creating a safe, loving space.

1. Set rules and boundaries.

I recommend setting rules and boundaries. You can do this by discussing the following questions:

What are your intentions for this relationship and what are you hoping to get out of it?

What are your values and how will you bring those into this relationship? (I.e., respect, honesty, kindness, love, etc.) (This may seem simple, but when you're at the heart of a heated argument, it'll be important to have these as your foundation.)

What are your expectations, needs and desires?

What areas are you needing support in? Where are you looking to grow? What are your typical relationship patterns that don't work for you? (For me, I needed support in knowing he wasn't going to abruptly leave, as abandonment had been at the heart of all of my relationships. Also, for me, I was looking to grow by moving into more feminine energy.) Whatever the case, it's important to establish these at the beginning, as rewiring yourself and working through old relationship patterns is one of the things this can help you with.

Of course, too, it's important to communicate these, as you don't want your partner unintentionally re-wounding you.

How often are you going to see each other (i.e., one to two days a week) and for how long (i.e., a month, six weeks, more?)? (I find it helpful in this context to set a certain time parameter. Of course, too, the parameters of this relationship can always change, and you may even find that it moves into something more, though it's important not to go into the relationship with any hopes or attachment to this idea.)

Also, are you going to see other people? What are the rules around this?

What are your typical triggers?

How will you communicate when challenges and conflict come up, which inevitably will?

2. Do regular check-ins.
As part of this practice, it's important to set up conversations for regular check-ins, outside of the time you will be spending together. When you are initially setting these up, talk to your partner about what you will need during these regular check-ins. Either way, this framework creates an opportunity to address anything you need to change as well as anything that's come up that's bothered you that wasn't brought up immediately. Initially, I recommend once a week.

3. Get help.
If possible, get a practitioner who can act as a moderator. I recommend a therapist, coach or another practitioner, who can help you see yourself and the other clearly and can help you address

any issues that come up. (Again, I love facilitating these, if you're serious about this and looking for support.)

SAYING NO AND CHOOSING YOU

Another important piece to talk about in this story was my no. For years, I had said yes to things that didn't always feel good because I was worried that if I said no, I would be left. But, when I said no this time, I learned the truth—that my fear of someone leaving me when I didn't say no was actually creating that exact thing and that when I finally chose me, like I did at the beginning of this practice relationship, that's when it would get reflected to me by a partner and they would choose me too.

QUESTIONS:

- Where do you say yes when you mean no? What are you scared will happen?

- Where don't you choose yourself and where do you let something that doesn't feel good or acceptable occur? How would you show up at all times if you truly loved yourself and you weren't scared of any repercussions in your relationship? (Please note: This doesn't mean being cruel or unkind. This is about setting boundaries and respecting yourself.)

TOOLS:

Throughout the day, especially when you are around your partner or practice partner, though this can be a good practice in all relationships and friendships, keep checking in with yourself. What do I want right now? How am I feeling? How can I honor myself? If I was being true to myself, is this how I'd show up? As you do more of this yourself and practice this more and more, you'll find that you'll also see this mirrored in all of your relationships too.

With this, it's important to note that saying no and choosing you is ever evolving. You are not going to always do this right, nor do you have to. The important piece here as you practice this tool is, if you don't get it right one time, pick yourself up and try again. Just like with being relational, I also recommend seeing that person in front of you, back in the scenario you were in when you agreed to something that didn't feel good, and saying out loud, as if it's in real time, what you wished you had said in that moment, if you were being true to yourself.

One other important thing to mention: While my getting a read on if someone could be a long-term fit is usually accurate, and it's important to trust our gut, there is a way that this can keep us protected and blocks real love from coming in. If you do this, too, while it's important to trust that feeling, I would invite you to practice the art of surrendering and going with the flow for a bit. This will allow you to see if that feeling is right while practicing being relational in the process.

LEARNING HOW TO RELATE

When I communicated that I didn't see us in a long-term relationship, maybe for the first time ever, I was being relational. I defined this in Chapter 32, but this was a practice I initially learned from one of my therapists. She defined being relational as sharing your experience and bringing yourself, your feelings and, really, "your insides" (i.e., what's going on inside of you), into the conversation.

As I worked on this with her, she helped me to continually practice sharing my personal experience with someone, so I could speak my truth, and most importantly, so I could be in relationship with them. It took me a long time to fully understand this and, most important-ly, to put it into consistent practice in real time, but I kept working on it until it became easier and easier. Don't get me wrong, while it's not always easy and I don't always nail it, I know that every time I practice this, and it is all practice, I am one step closer to my love partnership, as I am actually *being in relationship* and communicating my truth with another human being.

So, many times, with this, I am choosing discomfort over comfort. I am choosing truth over being liked, and I am choosing owning and honoring my feelings even if it might be hard for someone to hear. This is a beautiful practice in putting me first, and choosing deep intimacy, even if it's hard, and the more I do this, the more this gets reflected in all of my relationships.

QUESTIONS:

- Where aren't you relational? Why? What are you scared of and what do you do instead? (This can include avoidance, defensiveness, shutting down or escaping, to name a few.)

- Moving forward, what do you want to choose? Be really honest with yourself here. It's okay, if you're not ready for this yet, but if you are, check out the below tool to start practicing!

TOOLS:

If this is something you're wanting to implement, the only way to do this is to practice, and then practice some more and then some more. I can't tell you how many times I had the intent to be relational and share what was going on for me, but when the opportunity would come up in real time, I'd be scared to say what I was feeling. When I "missed" these opportunities, later in the day, when I was home, I would imagine them in front of me, having the conversation we were previously having that I had wished I had been relational in. Then, I would say what I wanted to say. I kept doing this until one day, I started to say it when the person was actually in front of me. (As I briefly mentioned in Chapters 25 and 32, this tool can also be applied to speaking truth, as speaking truth can be very similar to being relational.) Important to note: You may not always get it right, but it does get easier and easier over time. With this, too, always be as kind as possible and remember that there's a person with their own heart and soul, who also has feelings, sitting in front of you.

CHAPTER 34

Good or bad, right or wrong, every time we say yes to something, so does the Universe.

As I started to move more and more into feminine energies, one of the biggest pieces of guidance that I was given with this was moving toward joy and away from obligation. For me, my entire life I had moved toward obligation. As part of this, I functioned heavily from logic and doing the right thing or what made the most sense. This is just what our family did.

With this, up until this point, this did have its place in my life. After all, it was necessary in taking care of my grandma Roz and her affairs. Of course, too, I had to do what my work asked of me. Also, in general, I had to say yes to helping my father's parents, my grandparents, whenever they asked. Of course, a part of me wanted to do all of these things. My guidance was just beckoning now that there was more for me, and really, that there was another way.

I remember when I initially received this guidance being scared of it. My whole life had functioned from doing what others wanted and saying yes when I meant no. *Could I really do it? Could I really say no at the cost of letting someone else down? Most importantly, could I really be that true to myself?*

It was during one of those times that I was given the ultimate opportunity. My coach had sent me an extremely juicy proposal to spend time walking, playing and sleeping amongst wolves at a wolf sanctuary with a group of my peers, and most importantly, people who I felt connected to and who I could connect with, which at this point in my life, wasn't a common occurrence.

As I saw the invitation, I imagined myself under the stars, connecting with the wolves and building new friendships. I felt my heart light up, and I just *knew* I had to do it.

Then I saw the date—it was the same date as my girlfriend's wedding. I had known my girlfriend for close to 15 years, AND I had already committed to her wedding. Anyone who knows me knows that, prior to this, anytime I've committed to something, I commit 100%. Historically, I've never backed out—*ever*. (This was part of the reason why my Guides and Angels were inviting me to make a new choice. No more choosing my commitments, and really, others, over myself.)

So, with this, I had a difficult decision to make.

Do I keep my word and choose my friend's wedding or do I follow my heart's desires, my knowing and really the energy of my future? I knew that in choosing the energy of my future, I was telling the Universe to bring me more of this. I knew that it was the chance to choose me over obligation. Most importantly, I knew this was the chance to choose my future over my past.

So, while it wasn't easy by any means (I was truly excited for my friend's future, and I would have loved to have been there, if the timing had worked out.), I leaned into *my* future and truth and told the Universe exactly what I wanted. Awoooooo!

LIFE LESSONS AND LEARNINGS

Moving Out of Obligation and Choosing You

For years, I had unconsciously created my future. I said yes to things that felt heavy or weren't aligned for me because I wanted to be a good person, and at times, as part of this, because I was a people pleaser. Don't get me wrong, inherently in being a good person and doing the right thing, I felt good about myself and there were many times I did want to be with or help a family member or friend, even though it felt hard. But, what I didn't realize was, inherently in saying yes to these things, I was telling the Universe to bring me more of it. Yes—more obligation, more putting others first and more putting my wishes, desires and dreams to the side. With this came the realization that it was just as important to recognize my no as it was to recognize my yes.

I also didn't realize that I had the ability to create my reality however I wanted it. Yes, I could live in a reality of obligation, and there would be nothing wrong with that, as long as I was *consciously* choosing that, or I could live from my desires and truth. While in many lifetimes, I know I chose obligation, in this lifetime, I came here for the latter.

Questions:

- Where are you choosing from obligation? How does this feel? Is that what you really want?

- Also, what do you want to experience more of? What are you saying yes to? Is what you're saying yes to aligned with the future and relationships you're *really* wanting to create in your life? If not, why not? Do you really want to live your life this way? If not, what do you want to start prioritizing and whom do you want to start choosing and putting first?

TOOLS:

For anything listed above that you're saying yes to but isn't true for you, start saying no when you can, and even, back out of any obligations that aren't true for you. As you do this, take note of how the Universe begins to align you with your true desires. This second piece is important, as what we focus on, grows.

Also, use the questions found in Chapters 5, 19, 33 and 39 to help you determine what's true for you in every moment.

MOVING OUT OF MY HEAD AND INTO MY HEART

Also, for me, this was one of the first times I didn't do what was "logical" or what most would have considered to be the right thing, just because it was "the right thing" to do. Instead, I followed my heart. This was huge, as much of my journey had been around using only the logical, and really, my mind, to make my decisions. This was because it was more "concrete," and at the time, I believed this was the only way. In doing this, though, I dismissed valuable information that could have made my journey smoother, easier and getting "there" (wherever there is) quicker. It didn't help, too, that many of my family members were attorneys! This process, though, was beginning to help me to know that logic was only part of the puzzle.

QUESTIONS:

- Are you desiring to let go of the logical, in favor of your heart? If not, why not? What are you scared of? What's one way in your life that you've been guided by something that wasn't tangible that worked out for you? (If you can't remember one, ask for some help from your Guides and Angels.)

Tools:

If you are desiring to make the journey from your head to your heart, especially if you've typically chosen the mind and logic first, it's important to keep checking in with yourself and asking:

- What does my heart want right now?

- Am I choosing this because it's safe and logical or because it's what I'm truly desiring?

Other ways to make the journey from your head to your heart include building a relationship with your inner child and shifting and undoing your childhood patterns, as many times, it's what we've learned that blocks us from following our heart. Tools for both of these can be found throughout this book.

CHAPTER 35

Sometimes gifts come in the form of triggers.

IT WAS JUST A FEW MONTHS LATER THAT I WAS GIVEN A GIFT. This wasn't your typical gift of chocolate, a new book or money. No, this was a gift delivered in the form of an eight-hour non-date date.

To be clear, this could have been a date. In another time and place, it would have been.

In this time and place, though, it was an opportunity to clear one of the last pieces of my abandonment pattern, and it was an opportunity to relish being single one more time.

I had the feeling I wasn't going to be single much longer. While I was excited for this new chapter of my life, after all, I had been single for a *really* long time, I was also feeling reminiscent, and maybe even a bit sad, as this chapter was coming to a close.

I had connected with this man through Facebook a year or so earlier, and through my radio show, we had had a chance to speak live. Since we didn't live that far from each other, we decided that we would arrange a time to meet.

It was a Friday, and on this eight-hour non-date date, we spent the entire day walking around one of the most beautiful places on earth. Well, at least, it's definitely one of the most beautiful places in the Chicago area: the Botanical Gardens.

Picture vividly colored tulips, roses and lilies that go on for miles with a sweet smell that overwhelms you in the best possible way.

We had never met in person before, and we lived just far enough away from each other that it wouldn't be easy for us to just fall into the pattern of dating, just because it was easy. No, if we wanted it, we would have to truly choose it.

He was good-looking, in a similar profession with similar interests and, even more perfect, though I wouldn't realize this until later, his energy was similar to my father's.

It was the perfect set-up for disaster or magic. It would be both, depending on what angle I chose to look at it from.

The day went perfectly, or so I thought. We had spent eight hours together, and he was the one who kept extending our time. No one spends eight hours with someone they don't want to see again, I told myself.

Though this wasn't a date, there would be another date. *There had to be.*

When I got home, I felt the excitement you have after you spend that kind of time with someone you don't know very well, feeling the anticipation that comes when you know you could like someone a lot, if given the opportunity.

Also, even though I knew he wasn't the one, I was filled with the anxiety you have when a date goes really well, and you really like someone, and you think they could really like you, but then it doesn't finish with a clear "I'll see you again."

It triggered me, and I felt conflicted. I definitely wanted to see him again, but I also knew that we weren't meant to be, so I questioned if there would be any point to this, though I was beginning to fully take in the value of connecting with someone, even if it was just "practice." (Again, I hesitate to call it practice, as everything's practice until it isn't.)

Either way, though, my abandonment pattern needed to know that he would call.

"Of course, he'll call," I said, comforting myself. *"There's no way you spend a full day with someone and not want to see them again."*

After he dropped me off, we texted a bit into the following day, and something he said or didn't say put up my red flags and full on activated the abandonment trigger he had touched when we had left each other.

This was good, right?! (Insert sarcasm here.)

I spent that next day feeling what had come up. He hadn't given me a definitive no on going out again, but I had ridden this ride far too many times to not recognize the warning signs.

But, this time, instead of pretending everything was okay, I sat with it. Correction: I curled up in the fetal position. It was uncomfortable. It was heavy. Really, it was agonizing. All I felt was fear. At many points, it felt like there were a ton of bricks on my chest. But I didn't leave it. *Really, I didn't leave me.* I didn't try to escape. I didn't try to pretend it wasn't there or that I was okay. I wasn't okay, and I finally wasn't pretending that I was.

As I sat there in a ball, that's when it hit me. This was a perfect opportunity to use this experience for all it was worth. Yes, it would be great to see him again, but either way, him showing up this way for me was the perfect way for me to clear the last piece of my abandonment pattern.

So I did what any awake person would do. I used it with every ounce of my being. I sat. I cried. I shook. I felt—deeply.

I don't remember how long it took, but within a short period of time, I moved back into me. As always, this me was carrying a little less weight, and a little less of her story around, so she was more available to the love that was meant for her.

He eventually did call, and we eventually did talk. Truth be told, I had let it go, so his calling confused me. Our conversation ended in an old relationship pattern for me, with me questioning, or really, cornering him. After that call, I made a decision that this was the last time I was going to show up this way, and I haven't showed up this way since.

Also, after processing everything, the clarification I got on his actions was this: On our date, he had done something that is very common of people who read energy, but is also very unhealthy and really, unsafe, in relationship dynamics. He was reading me without being in relationship with me. In his own way, he was trying to protect himself and read if it was going to work out before he had even given it a chance. While I can definitely understand this response, as I've shared that I've been guilty of this many times too, as I briefly mentioned in Chapter 33, I don't recommend this, as when we do this, we take ourselves out of relationship with each other, and with this, all of the juicy, fun, exciting and potentially scary growth that's waiting for us, if we're willing to dive in! Also, while it wasn't appropriate to ask him about it, energetically, it did read that something else that was major was going on with him that caused him to choose to protect himself in this moment and to show up the way he did.

LIFE LESSONS AND LEARNINGS

READING SOMEONE AND NOT BEING IN RELATIONSHIP WITH THEM

When we were at the Botanical Gardens together, while I wasn't fully aware of this at the time, something did feel off. For me, he kept extending our time together, which I took as a good sign. What he was doing as he did this, though, which I didn't connect to until later, was trying to read the energy, instead of just simply asking me his questions. (Looking back, I knew the exact moment he made his decision, and not only did I wish that he had been relational around it, I wish, in that moment, I had been relational with him about what I was sensing, not because it would have changed the outcome, but because it would have been good practice for me, and it would have been me bringing myself into the conversation, standing in my truth and connecting to and owning my insides, including what I was feeling and sensing in that moment.)

As part of this, it's very common if you're intuitive to read if something is going to work out before you take action on it. As I've shared, I've done this many times myself. Doing this, though, can lead to making assumptions about people and situations, assuming we know the full story, not even bothering to ask them what's going on for them or share with them what's going on for us.

Inherently, though, this can take out the opportunity for the magic and real connection, and with this, we can end up shutting off the energy of possibility and creating it the way we read it happening, missing out on all of the fun.

Being on the receiving end of this felt very unsafe, which makes sense. If we are constantly reading someone versus being in relationship with them, it doesn't give them the space to feel safe and relaxed with you and for them to process, too. (This isn't to say to stop checking in with yourself or reading the situation, as it is important you are using your intuition and inner guidance system to guide you in every circumstance and relationship. It's just important to have balance and boundaries with this.)

Trust me, too, I definitely get it, as I've also done my fair share of "reading" in relationship, in an effort to feel safe and to not waste time. But, I've come to realize that part of the journey is not knowing, and really, that nothing is 100% guaranteed to work out, as even if it's reading as such, it's only reading as such in the present-day moment. With this, the only constant is things are always changing and being able to lean in and follow the flow is part of the journey!

QUESTIONS:

- Where do you read someone instead of having a conversation, taking yourself out of relationship with them? Why do you do this? Is it to feel safe and to protect yourself? Is it so you don't waste time? Is it because you're scared of getting close to someone, and really, of getting hurt?

- If something has felt off with the person you're with, have you shared your reality with them? If not, why not?

TOOLS:

1. Let go and surrender.

If you find yourself trying to read someone to protect yourself, practice the art of not knowing or needing to know. With this, you can embrace the mantra, "I don't know, and I don't need to know." (If this doesn't feel true for you, I'd ask why it's not true. What are you scared of?) As part of this, practice surrender and letting go. I know this can be a scary process, but it is definitely one of the reasons why we're here—to learn how to let go of control and our need to be safe to trust ourselves, others and the Universe.

Also, in this story, one example of this could have looked like simply being more present in the moment versus trying to analyze if it was right or not. (Also, to be fair, while I wasn't reading him, as I was trying to figure out if we were going to see each other again, I did have my own version of this playing out myself.)

2. Have a conversation.

So, instead of reading someone, what do we do instead? I recommend simply having a conversation. In the above example, either one of us could have said something like:

"I'm sensing (fill in the blank) (i.e., "you don't want to be in a relationship," "we're not the right fit" or "something's off"). Is what I'm making up true? What's going on for you?" This would have given us the opportunity to share what was going on and then we could have talked about it.

Putting Things in the "Boxes" of Good and Bad

The other awareness that came over me with this experience, which is similar to the way we can view success and failure, was the fact that we spend our whole lives defining things in the categories of "good" and "bad." If a guy we like wants to go out with us again, that's "good." If he doesn't, that's "bad."

What I realized, though, was that the truth is, the only good or bad that exists, is when we define it as such. With the above, I was learning what I wish I had known all along. *Everything is supporting me, even the things I don't think of as "good."*

Whether the outcome is one that I want or don't want, it is all for me, and I might as well use it as such and allow myself to feel whatever it brings up. After all, if I can't feel it, I can't heal it.

To be clear, in the above story, I could have pretended that he liked me in "that" way. I could have stayed focused on my disappointment. I could have gone into an obsessed place to try to "make him" want to date me. While, yes, initially after and when we did eventually talk, I did find myself in moments where I was in old patterns around this, I moved out of them quickly, and instead, I chose to move forward versus staying stuck in the past.

QUESTIONS:

- Where do you put things in the boxes of "good" and "bad"?
  How does this limit your perspective? How can you use
  something that you might define as "bad" to feel and heal a
  piece within you?

TOOLS:

When something comes up that you wish hadn't happened, ask
what good is in it. Maybe it's helping you to clear a pattern. Maybe
it's because the Universe is redirecting you toward something better. Maybe it's because it was never meant to be in the first place.
Whatever the case, it's important to start seeing that everything is
working in your favor, as the more you see it this way, the more you
will create it.

MOURNING MY SINGLE LIFE

One other piece that came from this experience was realizing I was
actually feeling sad to let go of my single life. For 20 years, *not* being
single was all I wanted. But, for the first time ever, I wanted to stay
a little longer. I was no longer trying to get "there" (i.e., married),
and I was enjoying the "here." This was powerful, as it took me back
into the present and into being grateful for where I was. And, one of
the biggest tools that can help to create what you desire is gratitude
for where you are.

QUESTIONS:

- Where in your life do you live in the future, trying to get
  somewhere, not enjoying what's right in front of you?

- What can you do to be more present and grateful of where you are now?

Tools:

One of my favorite tools that helps keep me in the present that I use right before I go to bed is gratitude. I've nicknamed this tool "Putting gratitude on the day!" and each night before I go to bed, I think of the things in the day I'm grateful for. Then, I say them out loud and even get excited for what's occurred. It's important to note here: It doesn't need to be only "good" things. You can be grateful for the way someone showed up for you, even if you didn't like it, because it helped you to heal something within you. You can be grateful for a pain you have in your body, as your pain has a message for you. You can be grateful for something you were looking forward to getting cancelled, as maybe you needed to rest that night. Also, important to note: if you miss a day (which I often do!), don't beat yourself up. Just pick up where you left off the following day.

CHAPTER 36

Anything that feels like an attack is an opportunity to love—you, them and it—more.

THE LAST PIECE OF MY ABANDONMENT PATTERN CAME A COUPLE OF MONTHS LATER WHEN I WAS AT A WEEKEND WORKSHOP WITH TWO OF MY TEACHERS. They had generously given the students in the class the opportunity to teach their students. As I'm always desiring to teach and reach more people, which in this situation included a desire to show my skills to my peers, and really, *to be seen*, I decided to take them up on it.

They had asked me to write out an agenda for what I was planning to teach. At the time, being eager to please, I agreed to it, even though the nature of energy clearing is about what's present, i.e., you can't plan it. So, while I didn't realize it until after the fact, in trying to plan what I was going to do, I was stifling the energy that wanted to come through.

I found out Sunday morning that I was going to do my exercise that morning. As I sat in front of the class, with my nerves heightened, as I had just been told a few minutes before that I would be teaching right then, I began doing the energy clearing, just like I had committed to do.

As I did the brief exercise, while I couldn't feel exactly what had happened at the time, I could feel that my exercise wasn't landing. Later, I realized that, in trying to plan and give my teachers what they wanted, I disconnected from the actual energies that were in the room, which is typically where the magic lies.

It was later that evening when I had the opportunity to receive feedback. I'm one of those people who loves feedback, even when it's not good, or at least that's what I've always told myself. In truth, I do love improving, and I do feel really seen when I receive feedback. Of course, I prefer it to be good.

That night, as we sat in the circle, I waited with anticipation for the feedback, which I already knew wouldn't be great. To put it mildly, though, let's just say that the feedback did not go well. While I know it wasn't intended that way, I might as well have been getting verbally stoned. I don't know how long it lasted, but the entire time, my Guides were whispering in my ear, "Don't take this on. This isn't yours to take on." I kept breathing, and I felt clear about this.

Even with all of this consciousness, though, I still left myself.

As hard as I had tried, I had merged again, and in the process, I took my peers' and teachers' side and believed their truths over mine. There was only one problem with this—in the process of doing this, *I wasn't on my side.*

Later that evening, I got back home to my cousin's house, where I was staying. That night, as I lay on my blow-up bed, I felt just as deflated as it was. I was shaking and scared. My heart felt really heavy. Initially, I didn't have any explanation for why I was feeling this way. I recognized that this was my abandonment pattern, but I was so used to this occurring in the context of a man or a date, that I didn't see the connection. It was then that it dawned on me that I had left myself during the feedback I had received. *Ouch.*

So, as I sat in the dark feeling terrified and alone, yet grateful that my cousin was not in the room with me, I cried, as I allowed myself to feel and clear the last pieces of the pattern.

In truth, I felt ashamed and disappointed. Part of this was the fact that I wanted my peers to have a good experience of my work, as I knew how powerful it could be. It was also hurtful, as I felt, in part, that the teachers were scared of my work and what I was going to do. The last part of this shame and disappointment was that I had taken on their words as truth, even though I was conscious that most of what was being said wasn't true. With this, I hadn't had my back or stood up for myself. It was hard to know what this would have looked like had I, but I still wished I had the presence of mind to have my own back, or at a minimum, to communicate what I was feeling around the experience.

As the tears washed over my face, my little girl knew everything was going to be okay, even though my heart was broken.

When I woke the next morning, though, after the prior evening's intense session of feeling everything, I felt complete. There was a calm that had washed over me. With this awareness, I realized that all that was left of my abandonment pattern were a few tendrils that would resonate themselves out over time. The pieces that would have me re-experiencing this pattern over and over, curled up in a ball, crying, scared, with the heaviness that comes with depression, and with no one to help me through it, were gone. I couldn't believe it!

LIFE LESSONS AND LEARNINGS

Staying Open and Allowing for Healing

With everything that happened that night, it would have been easy to go into defense mode, blaming everyone else and taking the position that I hadn't done anything wrong. While I hadn't, and in truth, neither had they, I realized that, if I was open to it, instead of focusing on them, how they hurt me and how what they'd said wasn't true, which is a super common way to deal with things when we are hurt, I could use what happened to heal the final layer of my abandonment pattern.

I know it can be easy, especially when we feel attacked or unsupported, to put what's occurring on everyone else. But, inherently, this isn't what I call radical responsibility. And, for me, my journey is taking radical responsibility for *every single thing* that's in my field, including the good, the bad and the ugly.

It's in this space, and in this space *only*, where we have true control of our lives. And it's here where our power lies.

QUESTIONS:

- Where have you blamed someone else for something that happened to you, and really, for something that you created? Are you willing to look at this and take responsibility for your role in this? Most importantly, can you see how it was serving you, even if it might have been painful, hurtful or uncomfortable at the time?

- Where have you been criticized or attacked and with this, where have you taken their side over yours and left yourself? This might look like not standing up for yourself when you're getting picked on (and even also criticizing yourself in your head for the same thing) to going along with something that doesn't feel right to you. Did you believe what they were saying?

- Also, what does leaving yourself feel like in your body? It's important to recognize this, so when this happens, even in a non-traditional way, you can identify it quickly and sit with what's up for you.

Tools:

If you find yourself being criticized or where you feel like you're getting attacked, here's what I recommend:

1. While it's occurring, tune in to see if you believe what they're saying. If you don't believe it, even if you don't say anything to them, make sure, as it's occurring, to reinforce within yourself that it's not true. If you do believe it's true, when you are alone, if it wasn't constructive criticism or if it still hurt you, it's important to tune into your inner child, and ask them why they believe this about themselves. Maybe this was something one of your parents said to you, as you were growing up or maybe this is how you learned to survive, or even to be liked or get attention. Whatever it is, it's important to become conscious of your reason and to give voice to this, and if appropriate, to start feeling your feelings around this, using one of the many tools found in this book. (Of course, if they were just giving you constructive criticism, and it genuinely was kind and true, and you just felt like you were getting attacked because you're not comfortable with this yet, I recommend looking at why you're not comfortable with this, then working with it. This may include taking in the parts of their feedback that you felt were true, incorporating their changes or in your mind, seeing them giving you this feedback again, while you practice keeping your body and heart open.)

2. Once you've felt your hurt around this and it's dissipated, tune in to see if you feel like you left yourself in this conversation in some way. If so, it's important to reintegrate yourself back into your body by:

a. Seeing any parts of you that you left in that conversation coming back to you. You can do this simply by seeing that part of you where you left it, which is likely where you received the criticism and then pulling it back to you, which is as simple as it sounds. You can picture it physically or just see it energetically coming back to you. Typically, I like to gather the energy from where I left it, which to me, looks like a cloud or bubble, and then I see it filling my body.

b. Then, fill your body up with you by simply running your breath through your body. I call this "breathing yourself in." You'll notice as you do this that you'll likely feel more open.

Also, if something happens in your life, whether it's around feeling unsupported, hurt or attacked, when you are out of the situation, especially if you notice you're defensive or you're focused on or getting mad at the other party and what happened and with this, projecting your feelings outward, it's important to stop and instead ask yourself how you created this and how what happened is serving you and in your highest good? Is it there to help you to heal something within you or to grow? Whatever it is, after you've really honored your feelings and hurt around it, take note of this and allow yourself to take in this support, even if you didn't feel supported at the time. (In Chapter 41, I talk more about how to start to recognize that we are creating everything and that everything is supporting us.)

One more important thing to note: Just because someone's in an authority position or giving you feedback, like I received, doesn't mean that what they are saying is absolute truth. Each one of us is on our own journey and at a different point in our growth. The most important thing when working with someone or receiving feedback is that they can offer you a higher vantage point and are maybe even farther along in their growth than you are or at a minimum, farther along on the topic you're learning. (Before I was fully connected to this awareness, at times I worked with coaches or received feedback and coaching where this wasn't the case and ended up making disconnected decisions because of it. I learned from this, though, and it reinforced within me that no one has more answers about my life than I do, to always take some someone else's guidance with a grain of salt, and most importantly, to always check in with myself.)

CHAPTER 37

Seeing it can change it, but feeling it will change it.

IT WAS LATE 2016, AND I HAD JUST FINISHED MY WEEKEND TRAIN-
ING WITH MY TWO COACHES.

I was playing major catch-up, including a call with my Virtual
Assistant. I also needed to head out to catch my flight home from L.A.

Anyone who knows traffic in L.A. knows that when you're
flying, you don't want close calls out of LAX. *That includes me.*

It was running tight, but I would make it, I believed, as I ran
around my cousin's apartment frantically tidying up loose ends and
putting the last pieces of my stuff into my suitcase. I think I was
sweating as this point, and inside, I think I may have been freaking
out a bit, but my history of close calls was telling me, *No problem,
Deb. You've got this.*

So, I left his place and got on the highway. I was relieved to
see that it was moving, and while it looked like there was a bit of
congestion, I thought to myself, *You should be fine.*

Then, all of a sudden, out of nowhere, we're stopped. While I
shouldn't have been surprised, I was. We might as well have been
parked. With this, conveniently, or not so conveniently, my GPS is

updating minute by minute. *Well, this is a first,* I thought to myself.

So, I decide to do what I always do when I'm running late and starting to panic—I check that the Universe has my back with a quick intuitive check-in. This time, this meant me asking, *"Am I going to make my flight?"*

"Yes," I hear.

As often occurs in these types of situations, I don't believe it. In reality, I might as well be having a screaming match with myself.

"What do you mean, yes? We're at a standstill here," I yell inside.

"Okay, okay. Don't panic," I start to tell myself. (Of course, I start to panic.)

Okay, calm down. It's going to be fine.

Then, yelling inside my head again, I ask my intuition one more time, *"What do you mean I'm going to make the flight? Are you fucking with me?"*

"No," it responds innocently.

Okay, okay, remember the tools. This is an opportunity to trust. I've had some close calls before (we're talking like getting to the airport 19 minutes before a flight close calls), but I've always made it. At least, I've always made it since I started doing this work and playing in the world of magic and miracles.

We're still not moving.

Okay, back to the tools. What would I do, and really, how would I feel if I had plenty of time? I feel my body starting to relax. I get in the vibration of calm and ease. I take in fully and completely that I have plenty of time.

AND, the next minute, I kid you not, I get an update from Southwest that my flight had been moved to 2:22!

Bingo—just enough time to return the car, go through security and get some food.

Damn, I love the Universe!

Fun fact: 222 is an Angel Number. Its meaning, according to Doreen Virtue's *Angel Numbers 101: The Meaning of 111, 123, 444 and Other Number Sequences*, is "Trust that everything is working out exactly as it's supposed to, with Divine blessings for everyone involved. Let go and have faith."

Have faith I did.

LIFE LESSONS AND LEARNINGS

CREATING MY REALITY TO WORK FOR ME

My biggest learning in this was really in creating my reality to work for me. I remember distinctly stopping dead in my tracks, as I was panicking, and the feeling of a "download" coming through. The download was beckoning, "Deb, you can create your reality however you want. What do you want right now? Whatever you want, get in the feeling that it is happening right now. Believe it with every ounce of your being and then you will create it."

While I had played with many ways to own being a powerful creator, this was the first time that it had hit me, and really, it had landed, in real time, to simply choose the feeling or vibration I wanted to be in to create it instantaneously. From that perspective, too, in that moment, it felt truly easy. I didn't have to worry how it was going to work out; I just had to know it would and choose from that energy, and really, the feeling I associated with my desired result.

QUESTIONS:

- Do you believe you can create your reality like I did in this example? If not, why not?

- As part of that, where don't you trust? If there were something that could make your life a lot easier, yet you didn't know if or how it could happen, would you let go of those details and move into trust that, if it's in your highest good, it will happen?

- What do you want to really be creating in your reality? *Choose that.*

TOOLS:

Anytime you're wanting to create something, it's important to not only see it happening that way, but to feel it happening that way. Our feelings are one of the most powerful generators to creating our reality.

As part of this, a huge key to creating our reality is clearing out our childhood patterns, pain and trauma/abuse, and really the density our bodies hold, that often keeps us tied to this reality. This is important because, in this reality, there are certain constraints to how we can create something. As you clear the above, though, you return to the truth of who you are and as part of this, to the powerful creator that we all came here to be, and not only are you able to create everything you're desiring, you're able to create what you're desiring quickly.

To understand this further, when we are not in our physical form and just in an energy state (i.e., when we are "dead"), literally when we think of something, it's right in front of us. This is one of the reasons why, when we come down here, we have the same expectation that something that we are desiring should happen immediately. But, most of the time, this doesn't occur, that is, until you start to clear out the density you hold in your body, which many times, stems from the fear, guilt, shame, control, anger, you name it, that we took on during our childhood. As you address and shift and clear these, though, which is the work I do with my clients, you move up into higher energetic states, like light, love, peace, joy and gratitude. Then, this is when, "all of a sudden," things you think about literally appear in front of you. This is when you realize there are no coincidences, only synchronicities. This is when the magic and miracles occur—*regularly.*

Important to note: If you are using this tool, and don't feel like it's "working," there may be a subconscious belief or beliefs that are blocking it. For instance, in the above example, if I believed that life didn't work this way and, instead, that I was life's bitch, so to speak (i.e., that I was at the beck and call of life and, really, life was happening to me), it may not have resulted in the same outcome. When this is the case, one way to shift this is to use one of the many inner child processes that I share in this book to address it and clear it from your body and belief system.

CHAPTER 38

Our Guides and Angels are like our own personal concierge who are "dying" to support us.

As I started to do more and more of the work, and really clearing out the pieces of me that I had learned growing up, I was loving myself more, and I felt myself becoming more and more connected.

It was one of these times that I chose to take an intuitive coaching training. I was excited to take my intuition to the next level while learning many tools, including how to connect further with my Guides, Angels and loved ones on the other side.

I remember the first time my teacher walked us through meeting our Guides. As I closed my eyes, and she walked us through the process, one of the Guides that stepped forward was my mom. I would recognize her energy anywhere! As she came forward, I felt excited, but there was one thing that confused me. At that point, I thought my mom had reincarnated. (I have a cousin whose energy reads similar to hers.) I remember asking my teacher if it was possible to be reincarnated and to also be a Guide. She thought yes, so I didn't think too much about it.

It was on a practice call during this class, though, when this was clarified for me. We were connecting to our loved ones, and one of my practice partners was reading me. She began describing what, or really, whom, she was seeing. She said, "I see a woman with curly blonde hair." I immediately went to my grandma Roz, who fit that description. She told me she was younger, though. Well, I know that when we cross over, we can choose to look and be whatever age we want, so that could be her. My practice partner was getting a different sense. As we continued on, my next guess was my mom. While my mom had stick-straight blonde hair when she was in physical form, she was always jealous of my sister's and my curly blonde hair. *So you have curly hair in heaven, Mom?! Cool!*

After we clarified this, she told me that my mom had been trying to get a message through. She had, in fact, not crossed over and was committed to being with my sister and me until we crossed over, but as my practice partner told it, "not in a creepy way or anything." *That was definitely my mom's voice.*

I felt immense excitement at connecting with her like this, as to put it mildly, it was really hard to lose my mom, and it felt like forever until I would be able to see her or connect with her again.

This dialogue comforted me for many reasons. First, I was grateful to know that she hadn't reincarnated, as in some way, my human mind couldn't comprehend feeling as connected to her on the other side if she was in the body of a human I barely knew. Also, it was comforting to know that she wanted to be with me every step of the way, and with this, that she was acting as a Personal Guide to me. Of course, too, as I was beginning to open my abilities to connect with her on the other side, while I still missed her in physical form, being able to connect with her in this way was starting to ease the pain of losing her, and it was very healing for me.

It was a little while later when I realized just how invested she was. I was on a call with that same practice partner, who had now become a friend, and she was reading about my love life. She always gave really fun love readings.

"I see your mom, and she's stirring a pot of possibilities," she said, in relation to possible love matches.

Really? My mom is my matchmaker?! I hadn't thought of this so much as a possibility, but how fun! Hopefully, too, she'll have better taste in men than she did when she was in physical form. (I love and adore my mom, but she did not have a high success rate in love.)

As she continued on, she told me she was putting together a bunch of possibilities in Chicago, so if I could stay there for a little while longer (I had been wanting to move to California), that would be helpful. "It's okay to leave," she stated. "Just know if you leave, it might take her a little bit of time to get her bearings in the new place."

"Oh, okay. I guess I could stay a little longer," I replied. Yes, I was eager to move to California, and I was also eager to meet my partner. Most importantly, though, for me, the decision to move was more about it feeling in full alignment, which it hadn't yet, than waiting to meet my partner, though for a long time, it had felt like Chicago would be a good place for me to meet this person.

My friend then began describing one of the next men my mom had had in mind for me. My mom had been working on many possibilities for quite some time, and at times, I would feel someone's energy come in, but then it would disappear before I had met that person.

"He's tall, athletic, has a thick head of brown hair, light eyes. His build is similar to Tim Daly's." *Way to go, Mom.*

Hearing this, it was another opportunity to trust. *It's all happening.*

288 • LIVING DEEPLY

LIFE LESSONS AND LEARNINGS

WORKING WITH YOUR GUIDES AND ANGELS

Before I started this journey, while I knew my mom was around me, I didn't know anything about working with and connecting with my Guides.

As I started learning about these, though, I realized that there was another whole Universe out there, and really tons of support that I was missing out on, if I didn't choose to connect to it. To me, I like to think of my Guides and Angels like my own personal concierge, and they are dying (pun intended) to help us and support us on our journeys. For me, when I opened to these relationships, I opened myself to more support than I could have imagined, which included an easier life (*hell, yes!*), and being able to release any fear of death and much of the grief that comes with death.

With this, came the ability to heal parts of my grief that I previously couldn't touch. For the longest time, I missed my mom so much, and it felt like there was nothing that could take this pain and longing away from me. For me, sometimes I just needed my mom, and no matter who else was there for me, while they were wonderful to me, they couldn't replace this loss.

So, as I found this way of being in the world and was actually able to develop a strong relationship with many of my loved ones from the other side, all of a sudden I found my grief had lessened, and really, had virtually disappeared. It was wild!

This doesn't take away from the fact that with any loss, especially significant ones, the grieving process is extremely important. Grieving allows us to honor our pain and to connect deeply to ourselves and our feelings. While initially it can feel like the depth and breadth of the pain will never dissipate, and while I've never found that it's gone away fully, it does lessen. Plus, in being willing to go there, this is the key to feeling the most alive.

It's also important to note the importance of not spiritually bypassing this by jumping straight to the idea that they haven't really gone anywhere and that they are still around. With this, give yourself time and space to be with and feel your feelings and grief. At this point in my journey, I had spent over fifteen years with my grief, really feeling it, so I was ready for the next level. That being said, there is no guaranteed amount of time it takes to heal your grief. Depending on where you are in your journey, it may take years, a lifetime or you may never get over it. In truth, I believe we never fully "get over it," but it's the being with it (along with time) that helps us to heal and move forward. Then, if we choose to, this allows us to create a new relationship with them on the other side.

For me, now, I can always tell when my mom is around me, and while I can't physically touch her, and really, hug her, which sometimes, I truly need, I can always talk to her and I feel like I'm truly being guided by her. So, while of course it would be wonderful to have her in physical form, there are some benefits to having her on the other side, especially since she is so invested in my journey. (As I type this, Bob Seger is playing, which is one of the ways she always likes to come through to me.) (The only other important thing to note here is that, just like us, our Guides have free will, so, once you've asked for help, it's up to them to choose this too.)

QUESTIONS:

- Do you believe in Guides and Angels? If not, why not? If it was weird, but it could help you and make your life easier and better than ever, would you open yourself to this possibility? (Many times we can get caught up in something being weird or worrying about what someone might think, and to put it bluntly, this is where we get in our own way. I used to feel the same way, until I realized that most humans are just winging it and no one has more answers about my life than me.)

- With this, do you want to start to connect to your Guides and Angels?

TOOLS:

I talk about variations of this in earlier chapters, but if you are wanting to have a relationship with your Guides and Angels, and yet you don't have any clue where to start, start by saying that out loud. Our Guides and Angels are always around, but they won't interfere unless we ask for their help. So, with the above, this might look like "Hey Guides and Angels, I want to start communicating with you," "Hey Guides and Angels, can you give me a sign that you're here?" or "Hey Guides and Angels, can you help me with X?" Then, pay attention. You may hear a song that you haven't heard in ages (our Guides love to communicate with us through electronics and music) or you may keep seeing a number over and over (Doreen Virtue's book, mentioned in Chapter 37, is great for understanding the meaning of these) or you may see something that reminds you of something or someone. The important thing here is to pay attention to what appears and to take note of what you see or what pops in (which may not be immediate) and to not dismiss it.

You'll find that the more you do the above, and the more you communicate with them, asking for guidance or help, the easier this becomes, and the more tuned in you become to the signs that they are giving you but we're not always tuned into.

Important to note: Long before I knew of Guides and Angels, or was working with my intuition or inner voice, I would connect with my mom in the above way, just using the word "Mom" in place of "Guides and Angels." Of course, time after time, she never let me down.

CHAPTER 39

When we choose to exit, we open the doors to something much greater.

It was over a year later when I finally met one of the people that my mom was working to connect me to. As it read, she had been working on this particular possibility for about six months, and this was the first person, of all of the recent possibilities she had been working on, that I was going to meet in physical form.

Even before we met, I was tuned into the fact that my mom had brought us together. Knowing this, I felt excited and nervous to meet him. On some level, it felt like a lot of pressure, and I remember stalling leaving my house that first evening we were going to meet. *Would this really be my person?* I was going to find out.

Our first date went really well. It seemed like we were on the same page. *At least, he was saying all of the right things.* In the physical, too, we appeared like a great match for each other. He was a coach, too, and we had similar life goals, including wanting to move to San Diego with both of us having studied some relationship and intimacy practices. His presence (he held a nice masculine space, which felt very safe and comforting, and had been a good part of why I had been studying the feminine—to attract a masculine man) made me feel very seen and heard, and he was genuinely curious about me. I didn't feel criticized or judged, either, even when I shared my inner reality, which included sharing that my deceased mother had played a role in setting us up, and that my grandma, who was also deceased, popped in at the end of our date to express her joy.

Truth be told, while our date did go well, there were some things that I should have noticed that I chose to disregard, things about his past relationship history and choices that were major red flags.

In wanting love so badly, though, I ignored all of it. And while I didn't realize it at the time, I subconsciously shut down my intuition almost immediately to be with him. I shut down the voice of my little girl. I shut down my knowing and my ability to see clearly.

To be fair, I was still learning how to be in relationship with someone with these newfound gifts without shutting them down. With this, I was figuring out how to stay connected to myself and my truth while also being fair to the other person, staying in relationship with them and not always just reading what was going on. Most importantly, I was figuring out how to trust myself and be all of me in the space of another human being.

So, on this first date, and for the next month while we started to get to know each other, I subconsciously broke my trust by trusting him and not listening to my intuition that, prior to our first date, I was so determined to stay connected to. I thought because my mom had sent him to me that he was "good peeps." With this, I had assumed I didn't have to date him to get to know him, that she had vetted him for me, and it was already done.

So, I let my guard down. I wanted love so badly, and I didn't realize what I was willing to accept to get it. As the month went on (I was out of town for most of it, so we were going on "video" dates), I kept generously opening up my heart to him, and it felt like he kept doing what felt right for him, which sometimes factored me in and sometimes didn't.

Yes, initially he was all in, at least I perceived as much as he knew how to be, where he was, but it was within a couple of weeks when things started to change.

He came to me one evening on one of our calls, sharing with me that he was feeling smothered. While initially I took this on as my own, it felt like he wasn't taking ownership of his feelings. With this, as I started to reflect, I felt deeply that I was just following his lead. He had said that he had wanted to work towards making a life with me—that we would move to San Diego in a little over a year, if things were working out. He was determining the frequency of when we spoke and when we didn't speak. He was taking all of the initiative and calling all of the shots. And while I did bring this up with him, he couldn't see it.

So, as this started to become more and more of a "physical-world, reality-based" relationship, I was starting to feel like I wasn't "enough" for him. While it took me longer than I would have liked to realize this, I was starting to recognize that this was not what I truly desired, which was really a soul-based relationship. (My old self was so conditioned to going along with things, and while I was checking in regularly, I missed a lot of things because I really did want the fantasy of us to work out.)

It took him going on a trip with his ex and cheating on me with her to wake me up. Even with knowing this, I didn't cut it off immediately. I justified it by saying we didn't really know each other, and he didn't owe me anything, but even writing this now, I feel a bit of shame around this. I had done all of this personal growth work on myself, and yet I was still struggling to get it right, and really, to own my worth.

It was the night before Valentine's Day, and we were both finally in the same city again, and we had committed to getting together. Having just found out about what had happened with his ex, I was mad at him, but I was also curious. We had spent the last month getting to know each other while we were both on the road, and it felt like a waste not to get together at least one more time to see if there was something there, and really, if the spark I had initially felt was still there. In truth, there was a part of me that had such high hopes and felt disappointed in myself for not setting better boundaries and really not just telling him to work everything out with his past and come back to me, if and when he was *really* ready. It hadn't yet dawned on me that this was a place where I was still hanging onto "crumbs," even knowing that I deserved better, so, with this, I agreed to see him.

When I got to his house, I was experiencing a mixture of actual anger and pretending to be angry. (After all, this is what you do when someone breaks your trust, right—you get angry with them?) Later, I would realize my anger was rooted more in breaking my own trust.

When I got there, though, everything seemed to go okay. He had bought me flowers for Valentine's Day. While I don't remember what we talked about, we talked, and I felt the safeness and comfort I had felt when we first met. Everything *appeared* to be fine. He was saying all of the right things and doing all of the right things, and while my radar was up a bit, I was still doing my best not to read him.

I ended up staying over, and while we did sleep in the same bed, we didn't sleep together, though I still cringe at the thought of any intimacy with him, knowing what I now know and can see very clearly.

That morning when we woke up, my radar was still not going off. Overall, I had felt very comfortable being around him. It was then, though, that he told me, quite casually, that he wasn't into it and he still had feelings for the ex he had traveled with. (Later I realized that even though a day earlier he was still saying he wanted things to work out with us, he likely already knew where he stood with us.)

So, as he said these words, for a brief minute, I went into a pattern of bargaining to try to salvage what was left, but the biggest thing that struck me was, as he was ending things, I felt nothing. No trigger. No internal feeling of needing to hold on. No fear of letting go. While my old self went to my old way of showing up for a few minutes, my true self knew I was going to be okay.

When he mentioned staying friends (he had a strong pattern of wanting to make every woman he came into contact with a life-long friend), it was my old self who agreed to this and to hanging out with him that day, so we could talk about what a business partnership would look like.

It was shortly after this, while still at his house, that I called a dear friend, and she helped my old self walk off the ledge, so that my true self could make a clear decision.

I said to her, "I have to leave, right?"

"Yes! You have to get out of there—*now*," she replied.

"Okay—I'll have breakfast, and then I'll go."

As we sat at breakfast, this mixture of disappointment and sadness, mixed with the wondering if I would ever get it right, started coming up. As it did, I let myself feel it, and I began crying, with him as my witness. I didn't care, though. I didn't care that he was seeing this. I didn't care that I knew he wanted to get back to work, and I was taking up his time. Really, I didn't care that I was taking up space. This was a big shift for me, as typically I would have chosen to do what I had perceived he wanted, even if it wasn't what I wanted.

While this was happening, I believe he was holding my hand, looking at me in amazement. It was my perception that he hadn't seen anyone go this deep. With this, there was a part of me that felt *deeply seen*, even if it was being seen by the wrong person.

It was after I finished this vulnerable process, and I was sitting over the oatmeal he had made for me, procrastinating from leaving, that I saw a vision—one of my (hot) Guides was standing outside of his house, ushering me out. He was waving his hands in the air,

298 • LIVING DEEPLY

joyously jumping up and down. To me, at the time, I couldn't tell if this was my Guide or a potential future partner, but what I did feel very strongly was that he was beckoning me out of my past and into the excitement and possibilities of my future.

With that, this girl who always had trouble exiting, left.

LIFE LESSONS AND LEARNINGS

INTUITION, TRUST AND SELF-LOVE

It had been a long time since I had dated someone, and even longer, since I had dated someone who could potentially be my future partner. Truth be told, I had no idea what it looked like to be my intuitive, true self AND be in relationship. As I shared earlier, I've been in other dynamics where people have read me without my permission, and it's never felt good. So, I've struggled with, what does it look like to be in relationship and not shut down my intuition, and really, to have my own back, mixed with being fair to the other person.

This time, what I realized after the fact was that it was like I had his back more than I had mine. I shut down what I knew and all of the warning signs I saw to be with him. I betrayed my little girl and what she felt was right. I broke my own trust, giving him trust before I really knew him. Over and over, I let him violate my boundaries and did things that subconsciously didn't feel right in the hopes that he would stay.

In doing this, and breaking my own trust, he ended up breaking my trust. The lesson I learned through this was that's it's okay to use my intuition in relationship, and while it's important to have healthy boundaries around "reading" another, that we are all wired with a guidance system, and it's important to stay connected to this as I'm dating.

As part of this, I got clarity on how my mom was picking partners for me. She had picked this particular person because he was in a high vibration, and likely, too, because we had previously known each other before in other lifetimes. Living in another dimension, though, she had not "vetted" him, so to speak. That was my job.

There were many times, too, even when he would say something small, complimenting me, that I knew he was lying, and really just saying what he thought he should say and what he had been conditioned to say to get his way and make him appear to be a nice guy. (As part of this, later, I realized he was displaying the signs of a classic narcissist.) It was during these times that I felt instinctually that he was lying to me (I remember even hearing inside, *He's lying!*), and this relationship reinforced my need to listen to this inner voice in relationship. With this, it was another practice in maintaining my sense of self, no matter who's around, what they are saying or how bad I want something in my life.

It also reinforced staying connected to my little girl throughout this process. She had some strong words for me around what was happening and what I was allowing to happen, but I wasn't listening. This was a great lesson for me for future relationships to keep checking in with her and asking her if she was okay with my decisions.

QUESTIONS:

- Where have you broken your own trust and allowed something to happen or someone to treat you in a way that didn't feel good? Why? What were you hoping would happen? Was there some benefit to allowing this?

- Where have you tuned out your inner voice and not followed your gut or intuition? Why? Again, was there some benefit to shutting down your inner voice?

- Do you check in with your little girl/boy, especially when you're dating or in relationship with another? (This is important in all relationships, not just love partnerships.)

TOOLS:

In any relationship, I recommend doing regular check-ins and asking yourself the below questions to ensure you stay focused on you and what you're feeling and needing, no matter who is around you. While it's good to do these when you're around the other person, it's also good to do these when you are alone, so you can ensure your answers aren't being subconsciously influenced by them. Here are some good questions to get you started:

Intuition
To connect to your intuition, you can ask:

- What am I feeling right now? What do I want right now? Is what they're saying true?/Can I trust this person? (Especially if something is feeling off or there is a history of dishonesty in the relationship/friendship, in which case, you may need to reconsider if this is a relationship you want to be in.)

Little One
When checking in with your little one, you can ask:

- Is this okay with you?/Are you okay with this? Is what's happening right now okay? What do you want right now?

(This can be around everything from whom you're spending time with to what you're doing with that person.)

SCARCITY

Another huge lesson in this for me was the place where I was still accepting less than I desired and deserved, and really, the place where I was still accepting crumbs. Even in knowing my worth, I got to see the places where I still went along with something that wasn't honoring of my worth.

QUESTIONS:

- Where haven't you owned your worth? Why? If you've let someone disrespect you or treat you poorly, this is a place where you haven't fully owned your worth.

- As part of this, even when you've known you are worthy of more, where have you gone along with something that was less than you desired and deserved? Why? What were you scared of?

TOOLS:

1. The first key to this is awareness around where you are not owning your worth and where you are settling for less than you desire and deserve.

2. The second step is making a new choice. So, if you find yourself in a relationship with someone who is treating you this way or at a job that isn't valuing you, if you are ready for it to change, start taking a stand for yourself. Start asking for more in your relationship or at your job. This can be

small at first and then get bigger over time. One good way to tune into this is by asking, "If I was owning my worth, how would I show up right now and what would I ask for?" This can include everything from asking for more time to talking with a partner to asking for a raise or promotion at your current job.

3. Of course, if you are taking this stand for yourself and aren't being met with the same response or gratitude, you may need to exit that job or relationship, if this feels right to you.

EXITING

For me, exiting a relationship has always been challenging. What I realized, years earlier, was my inability to exit a relationship was in direct correlation to my perception that when my dad left, he had exited our relationship so easily. This had caused me so much pain that I had subconsciously vowed that I'd never do that to anyone else. In the process, though, I stayed longer than I should have in relationships, causing myself more pain than necessary, and when I eventually did exit, or more accurately, they left, the little girl in me would want answers around why they were leaving. This was really rooted in wanting answers around why my dad had left, and the subconscious blame I had put on myself that it was my fault that my dad had chosen to leave. Of course, then, when someone I was dating was leaving, whether we had dated for a month or longer, I would go back into this pattern of wanting to know why, and I would borderline corner them to find out. Understandably, they didn't have answers for me, at least not the answers I was looking for.

This time, though, when he told me he didn't want to be together, while I asked a few questions around why, I felt myself let go easier than I ever had. I actually was able to leave, and while maybe this was made easier by the talk of getting together over the weekend to figure out about possibly working together, really, this was a huge step for me!

(By the way, most ruminating, obsessing and overanalyzing patterns are rooted in blaming ourselves for something that wasn't our fault in our childhood. Then, to take control of something we didn't have control over, we start this pattern. This is one of the core patterns I help people walk out of, so if you're looking to shift this, and I've personally seen over and over the impact that releasing this has on the quality of one's life, don't hesitate to reach out to me.)

QUESTIONS:

- Do you have trouble exiting relationships? Why? If you let go, what are you scared is going to happen? What's one thing you can do to begin to shift this?

- Where have you been loving to another at the expense of loving yourself? How will you choose you moving forward?

TOOLS:

When you're feeling a trigger around exiting (and really, anything), using your breath and taking your time in responding is important. So many times, we respond out of our old conditioning or discomfort, but when you can take a moment (or more) to pause, and even walk away, to make sure you're responding from your truth, and an open, loving place, this can be a helpful tool in creating authentic responses and not falling into your old responses and triggers. (Of course, using many of the tools in this book to clear this pattern is key to truly clearing the trigger.)

As part of the above, staying in constant communication with the little one inside you is also a very important step.

CHAPTER 40

Sometimes the only loving thing you can do for yourself is to walk away.

AFTER I LEFT HIS HOUSE THAT DAY, HE MESSAGED ME THAT EVE-NING. I was already starting to get the clarity, though, that I didn't trust him, and if I didn't trust him, it was starting to hit me that I was definitely not going to be able to be connected to him in any capacity. So, instead, I settled into the idea that we weren't going to be in any kind of relationship, love, work or otherwise, and, as I settled into this idea and got full clarity, I told him I needed space.

Even after this, though, he kept texting me. Truth be told, while he had "officially" left, which he later said meant that I must still have more of my abandonment pattern to clear, it felt like I couldn't really get him to leave; he kept pushing for contact. I eventually agreed to talk with him, which looking back was another violation of my boundaries (and maybe I even knew this at the time, though, again, I was curious). During this conversation, we ended up having a huge blowout. I was really angry, and while I was angry with him, I knew I was even angrier with myself for what I had allowed to happen.

When we ended that conversation, though, I got off the phone and almost instantaneously, I felt joy. I didn't love how I had shown up, but compared to the way I would have shown up a decade earlier, I did love that I had my own back, and even more than that, I felt so clear and free!

It was only as I had more time to think about what had happened that an old version of myself started to creep in, and I felt more uncomfortable with the fact that we hadn't left things nice and neat, and in my mind, that the door was definitely closed. This, and the fact that I had not shown up on that call as my best self, and while this may have been warranted, two wrongs don't make a right.

While, after this blowout, I wanted to reach out to him, and even a part of me wanted to apologize, I knew it wasn't in my highest good (and maybe not even loving to myself) to do so and that it would definitely take me backward, not forward. So instead, I sat in the discomfort.

Later that week, when he did email me unexpectedly, while I wished it hadn't had any impact on me, as I read his email, I felt my body relax. Even though I didn't want him in my life or even like him as a person, it made my old self uncomfortable to be in the dissonance and to fully let go, as I always liked to keep the door open.

Instead of writing him back, though, and disrespecting my boundaries again, when I knew staying in contact with him wasn't healthy or even loving to myself, I just left it alone and that was that.

LIFE LESSONS AND LEARNINGS

NOT HAVING TO EXIT NEATLY

For me, this entire exercise carried so many good lessons in exiting. One of my biggest fears with exiting in the past was that the door would be shut. As part of this, even when someone had really hurt me, I avoided conflict or sharing how I felt about what they had done and how they had impacted me because I thought that people leave when you're not nice to them. What this situation showed me, though, was that this isn't always true.

Also, while my whole life, I had tried to always be kind, nice and really, agreeable, as I had perceived this was love, what I realized in this conversation, is sometimes you can't love yourself and another at the same time. Could I have been nicer, and a bit softer in this closing conversation? Absolutely. But, the most important thing, and my biggest intention in this final conversation, was me loving me.

QUESTIONS:

- Do you have to exit every relationship and friendship neatly? If so, why? What are you scared is going to happen? What does not having a conversation that's wrapped up neatly mean about you and why does this make you uncomfortable?

- With this, how do you feel about conflict? If it scares you, what are you scared will happen if you have conflict with another? (For me, conflict has always meant that the door is closed on a relationship, and this finality has always scared me.)

TOOLS:

Use any one of the many tools found in this book to clear any of the fears and patterns that come up around conflict.

Then, in having a challenging conversation:

1. Lean into the difficult conversation and lean into the conflict, noting that it doesn't actually have to be hard, difficult or messy, unless you choose it to be.

2. With this, before you get on the call, see, and really, feel, the conversation going well. Set the intention for an easy conversation, including being loving to yourself and if possible, the other as well.

3. If it works for you, before the call, write down the things you need to say, in a clear, concise and kind manner, so you are ready to go.

4. Before you get on the phone or see them, open your heart space by relaxing your body and breathing into your heart. See them as their best self or even see the little child that lives within them, having compassion for them.

5. When you do get on the phone, speak as clearly as you can, and if you find yourself feeling triggered, take some deep breaths, and if necessary, exit the conversation, asking, if you desire and it feels right to you, to pick it up at another time.

WE ARE A CONSTANT WORK IN PROGRESS

As you can also see from this story, we are always evolving. That being said, there isn't always one right way of showing up and choosing what's best for us isn't always black and white or super easy. For me, as I moved from my old self to my true self, my process in letting go in relationships was fluid and a constant work in progress.

With this, in my relationships, I didn't always show up perfectly and sometimes my old self took over or I made decisions that weren't in my highest good. Then, while not being hard on myself, I would have to choose out of it and remind my little girl, that it's okay to be human and that we had shown up the best we could, until we could do better. Also, each opportunity was an opportunity to practice and just get better and better at something. After all, for me, this was always the real reason for the journey anyway (i.e., we didn't have to do it perfectly all of the time).

This is really important, as many people think of change as black and white, and if it doesn't work immediately or they get it wrong the first time (or even the tenth time), that it didn't work. But much of our deeply embedded patterns take us making a constant choice, over and over, to choose out of it, until it's fully integrated in us.

QUESTIONS:

- Where have you struggled with how to show up? Was this because of an old pattern that hadn't changed or was it for another reason? Take note of whatever this is and if you're ready to clear it, use one of the processes in this book.

- Also, when you haven't shown up as you would have liked to, do you beat yourself up and assume things aren't working for you and that you haven't made any progress? Alternatively, do you stick with it and do you choose to focus on the progress you've made, even if you're not 100% "there"?

TOOLS:

As we are changing, it's important that we take note of what's changed and that we're not hard on ourselves, if we find ourselves back in an old place. This doesn't mean that we're back to square one. It just means we are somewhere in between where we were and where we want to be, which is why taking note of what's working and what's changed is so important, so that you don't get discouraged.

Also, constantly choosing from your new self until it becomes part of you is key. In the above example, my new self knew that he wasn't right and I could let him go, but my old self was used to showing up by holding on and not trusting. So, I had to keep choosing from my new self that knew there was more for me, if I chose it, until it was integrated in me. With patterns that we've had since birth (or soon after), this may not be an overnight process, and it's important you're gentle with yourself, as you are evolving.

CHAPTER 41

Nothing has ever been as it appears.

THROUGHOUT THIS BOOK, I DESCRIBE MY JOURNEY OF TRANSFOR-
MATION, CONNECTING TO MYSELF, AND WITH THIS, THE MAGIC
AND MIRACLES THAT ARE IN STORE FOR US WHEN WE ARE WILLING
TO DO THE WORK AND ALIGN WITH OUR SOUL.

It's important to note, though, that even just a short time ago,
this wasn't my inner experience. Just like most of us, I was very ana-
lytical and spent a lot of time in my head, just trying to get through
the day-to-day, and while I had done personal growth work in the
form of therapy, I did not feel connected to myself, my truth and my
soul, though I was not aware of this at the time.

As part of this, for most of my life, while I was intuitive, I did
not consider myself really intuitive, which is pretty comical if you
know me now. Really, I believe that we're all intuitive, and the more
we undo our childhood patterns, and we heal our childhood stories
that conditioned us to believe that what we knew wasn't true, the
easier it gets to tune into that little voice that lives within us that is
one of our most important tools.

For me, one of my first memories of using my intuition was, on the Fourth of July, when I was eleven or twelve years old. I remember the date because, often times on the Fourth, to get out of the heat, my mom, sister and I would go to the movies. This was always a treat and a fun way to spend time with my family. This time, we were going to see *Pretty Woman*.

We sat down, and I remember there not being anyone in front of me in the movie theater. This was good, as it was in the days before stadium seating, so sometimes, always being petite, I found my view obstructed, depending on who was there.

About halfway through the movie, though, a couple came into the theater and sat in front of us, blocking my view. Being on the verge of my teenage years and to quote my mom's loving phrase, the "little stinker" that I was, I put my feet up. Slapping my knee, my mom sternly whispered, "Put your feet down." That's when I said, loudly enough for them to hear me, "They didn't pay to be here." (This was back in the time when movie hopping was very common, as the movies had gotten really expensive. In case you're not familiar with this, this is where you'd buy a ticket to one show and then hop from movie to movie.)

In that moment, though, as I said this, they got up and left. I remember my mom asking, "How did you know that?" In my body, I just knew.

What I would realize decades later, though, was that this was my intuition talking. As I got older and learned how to hone this invaluable tool, too, moments like these did get more memorable and more common.

It was one such time, several years ago, I was in an online community, and someone I had never met posted about moving to New York and that she was looking for a job. She included a bit of her experience, and I got a hit to tell her about a newer fitness company in New York that I had heard was hiring. She applied, and she ended up getting the job! She moved to New York not long after, feeling super grateful for the guidance.

Since then, I use my intuition for everything from deciding where and what to eat (one of my friends always comments that I pick the perfect place) to making all kinds of business decisions and facilitating my workshops and trainings.

LIFE LESSONS AND LEARNINGS

CONNECTING TO OUR INTUITION

For the longest time, I, too, just like most of us, believed that only certain people had psychic or intuitive abilities, and I wasn't one of them.

I remember when I was eighteen years old befriending one such woman. We were good friends for two decades, and throughout that time, time and time again, I gave my power away to her and would ask her to tell me what she saw. Most of the time it was regarding love or connecting with a deceased loved one, but anytime I had a burning question, she was there. It wasn't until after I had my awakening and started listening to energy clearings that I realized that I was intuitive and even psychic, which I define as being able to see clearly and being willing to know the truth in all moments, and with this, being able to tune into all levels of consciousness, and I realized I could also connect to the other side. It's important to note, too: I am not the only one; we all have the power to access this. Most of us start off with some intuition, and then it can get blocked during our childhoods. If this does happen, it can be unblocked, and the more work we do on ourselves, and the more we undo our childhood patterns and pain, the more it paves the way for us to be connected and in truth and clarity at all times.

Another interesting piece of this was how my Guides progressed the way my intuition came to me. When I was first starting this, it mainly came to me in the form of Yes/No answers. As this progressed, though, they started to move me away from everything being so black and white. Instead, they started writing messages to me in my head and at times, even used shapes, though I found this confusing, so I asked them to make it clearer. Again, your intuition and guidance will come to you in the form that you understand, so it's important, as this comes through, that you trust yourself. Also, just like me, if you don't understand what you're getting, ask for it to be clearer.

The other important piece of this is that, according to Bruce Lipton, approximately 95% of our programming is subconscious. This means that most of our reality is based on things that we're unaware of. When we can tap into our intuition, though, this gives us more information and another piece of this puzzle.

QUESTIONS:

- How do you feel about intuition? If you think it's "out there," why? From whom did you learn this? If you knew this could help you beyond your wildest dreams, would you begin to let go of any negative beliefs about intuition that aren't truly serving you?

- Also, do you think of yourself as intuitive? If not, why not?

- Where have you given your power away to another being? (This can be with a parent, teacher, partner, friend or even a psychic or healer.) If so, why?

- Where haven't you trusted yourself or a sense you had about something? Why didn't you? As part of this, where did you dismiss something you knew? Why?

- On the opposite end, where did you trust yourself or a sense you had where it worked out for you really well? Whatever the case, whether you followed it or not, take note of the times you got an intuitive "hit," as these are important keys to beginning to recognize your intuition.

Tools:

There are many important pieces to accessing your intuition. In addition to what I've shared throughout this book, below are some additional ways to begin being able to see the truth and really, through the illusion, at all times.

The Importance of Asking Good Questions

One key that's super important as you start tuning into your intuition is, when you're seeking answers, asking clear questions. I remember one of my teachers saying that you can ask about anything in your life, everything from everyday questions like what movie to see to if you should take a job or not. As I started doing this, and tuning in to how my intuition would respond, I got stronger and stronger around asking better and better questions to get clearer and clearer answers. This isn't something that happens overnight, so keep practicing. As you do, you'll find you're able to tune into the truth and start to distinguish how your intuition communicates with you.

As part of this, it's important when you're checking in to differentiate what voice you're hearing. Is this your intuition, your Guides, your inner child, your fear or even your ego? Initially, they may all feel pretty similar, so it's important to differentiate this.

Clearing Our Energy Blocks

The other key to working with intuition is clearing your energy blocks, as doing so paves the way for a deeper connection to your intuition and with this, connecting to the truth at all times. This is because, as we clear these blocks, we move up to higher levels of vibration, and this is where it's easiest to tune into the intuition that's always coming through, but can be harder to connect to if we're carrying around a lot of anger, guilt, fear, shame and control, to name a few.

With this, as part of clearing your energy blocks, it's important to look at the negative beliefs you've identified above around intuition and where you decided to stop trusting yourself and shut down what you knew. Why did you do this? Who was there when you decided this? Common examples of these might be that you subconsciously chose not to know something because you were scared of punishment, being laughed at, left or not being loved. After all, if you told your parent about something you experienced and they denied your reality, it would be scary to keep owning what you were experiencing, as subconsciously, you might be scared that they wouldn't love you if you didn't share their reality. While, of course, this might seem crazy to you now, as you know your parents love you and would never do anything intentional to harm you, at the time, this would have been a completely understandable (and subconscious) conclusion to take on.

One example of this for me was when I was a young girl, when I knew something 100%, I would be wrong. Inherently, I made the decision to never be 100% about knowing something again.

Once you've identified a belief that's not working for you, see this belief or pattern leaving your body and being replaced with light, trust and truth as well as using many of the processes I discuss in this book to shift these patterns and beliefs.

Tuning Into the Unseen

Another important piece of this is, if the unseen, including the unconscious and subconscious is 95% of the story, how do we begin to tune into this part? My simple answer is to ask yourself the below questions throughout your daily life. These questions are some of the same questions that can help to move you into being a powerful creator and can be applied to everything from why you're showing up a certain way to why someone is showing up a certain way for you. These questions include:

- Why is this in my field? What is this here to show me within myself? How is this here to help me to learn, grow, expand and love more? And, even, how did I create this?

So, for instance, say you're getting disrespected at work by a colleague, where they are putting you down. If you start to tune in and ask yourself why this is in your field, you may realize that this is just a reflection of where you are putting yourself down or you don't believe in or respect yourself. With this, this is just an opportunity to love yourself, and this piece, more.

Also, for me, asking myself these questions has become automatic and it's been a great way for me to see the subconscious and unconscious pieces of me. (Important to note: I shared similar questions around identifying and clearing patterns as well as understanding the roles others play for us, as these are all part of seeing ourselves clearer.)

Again, there are so many details to intuition, and by no means, does this encompass everything, so if you're looking for further support, you can get my Connecting to Your Intuition Workshop Recording as well as other recordings on my website at deborahacker.com.

CHAPTER 42

There are many dimensions to our healing—when we're ready for them.

So, AS I'VE BEEN TAKING THIS JOURNEY AND MY SKILLS KEEP GROW-
ING, MORE RECENTLY, I'VE HAD THE STRONG AWARENESS OF WHEN
I'VE KNOWN PEOPLE IN OTHER LIFETIMES.

Now for you, this may not even be in your realm or on your
radar, but I can tell you, that for me, starting to identify these has
added an extra level of depth, dimension and richness to my life.
Through this understanding, I've made closer connections with
people, and it has helped me to understand why I feel the way I feel
about certain people. In times, too, when I've felt uncomfortable or
felt resistance, unkindness or bad energy coming toward me, when
it hasn't appeared warranted in this lifetime, it's helped me to get
the clarity that I've needed to understand and shift this. Also, when
I've felt in danger, I've been able to know why and more importantly,
when it's felt like it could carry over to this lifetime, I've gotten the
hell out of there!

As part of this, what's been interesting is some of the main
people my Guides keep bringing to me are past-life killers. Some
of these people have killed me intentionally and some accidentally.

Also, there are some I've killed as well. My sense of why my Guides are doing this is to heal past-life energy and bring me to what I call the "zero point." This is the point where we literally have worked through everything, in this lifetime and beyond. Since this is in my awareness, I'm assuming this is possible at some point on my journey through time and space, but either way, these experiences have been very interesting.

With this, the first one started a couple of years ago. I had decided, a bit begrudgingly, just because I'm scared of heights, that I would take an early morning hot-air balloon ride in Albuquerque.

When I got to the site, after I checked in, we were asked to wait in a room as they were getting everything ready for us. I found myself immediately drawn to this man, who was with his father. (They were traveling together to celebrate the father's 79th birthday.) In part, I was looking for someone non-intimidating to sit next to, and in part, I was also looking for someone who was either there by themselves, or at a minimum, not there as a couple, as it was a bit overwhelming to be there by myself, doing something that scared me.

So, as I sat next to him, we easily fell into conversation, and he immediately took an interest in me, which felt comforting. Our conversation continued as we boarded the van to go to the site, where they would fill the hot-air balloons. We ended up in the same balloon, and while we didn't talk, after the ride, he found me again to talk some more. He ended up getting my number, which surprised me, as he lived in Denver, and I in Chicago. As we said goodbye, I didn't think too much of it.

I did hear from him shortly after that, though. He was in California, and he wanted to see if I was out there, as I had been talking about moving there. I wasn't, and that was that.

Truthfully at the time, I didn't think I'd see him again, of course because of our distance, but also because I felt nervous at the thought of seeing him again. He had invited me out to Colorado, and the thought of spending time with him like that made me a bit anxious, as while I wasn't aware of this at the time, I didn't fully trust myself to say no if it didn't feel right. Also, understandably, I wasn't sure how I felt about him, as we hadn't spent a lot of time together. (In New Mexico, while it had been nice to have someone show interest in me like that, having a conversation with someone and spending time with them one on one for an extended period of time are two different things.)

It was almost a year later when I had decided to take him up on his offer. Even heading out there, the thought to see him hadn't been on my radar. But, as I approached Denver (I had been on a road trip from Phoenix through New Mexico to Denver), he popped into my consciousness.

I still felt nervous at the thought of reaching out to him, but when I got to where I had planned to stay, and realized she hadn't cleaned the sheets prior to the previous guest (Yuck!), I decided I would take a risk. My Guides were definitely encouraging me to go have some fun too.

So, we made plans to get together the following night. As I started to check in to see if we had known each other in any other lifetimes, a pattern I had recently started to fall into, which I was finding quite fun, especially with men I would go on dates with, my Guides told me gently that I didn't want to know. So, I let it go.

We did have fun, and when I was at my next destination, I decided I was going to ask about our past-life connection. That's when I got he had been my father and had abused and killed me in that lifetime! I could definitely see why my Guides had told me not to ask! I could also see why I felt some nervousness around the idea of seeing him and a bit of fear around him, especially when I felt particularly vulnerable. On the other end, I also felt very comfortable around him and very taken care of, and what I loved most was how laid-back and easy-going he was. Hanging out with him was definitely easy.

We ended up seeing each other a couple more times, and our comfort with each other grew each time.

It was in between our second and third visit when my Guides guided me for the first time to Red Rock in Las Vegas.

One thing about this that fascinates me is, while my family lives in Las Vegas, and has lived there for close to two decades, and I typically hike in most places I travel to, in all of the years I had been there, it had never even dawned on me to go for a hike there, until late 2017 when my Guides knew I could handle the information they were about to share with me.

It was a beautiful late-November day, and my dad had given me his car to take. As I started to enter Red Rock, and was driving through the mountain's winding roads, I started getting visions. Now, to be clear, visions come to me all of the time in my sessions and if I'm intentionally focused on it, but these kinds of visions weren't the norm for me out of this context up until this point. But, all of a sudden, this Denver man's face popped in, then I saw an American Indian's face, whom I instinctually knew was the Denver man in another lifetime. In the vision I was seeing, he felt like the father figure. Then, I saw a young American Indian girl, whom I instinctually knew was me in that lifetime. Then, I saw a penis. It felt like I was on the ground, and I felt this father figure over me. I'm not sure how much more detail they gave me, but I definitely knew at that point this is where he had killed me.

Of course, this experience at Red Rock was definitely a weird one. While I know most people would be horrified by these visions, and it was definitely a fair amount to process, with our relationship in this lifetime, I feel at peace with everything. In this lifetime, he has been kind and generous, and I was able to clear the energy this past life experience held. Oh, and on our most recent visit, I did ask him if he believed in past lives. While he didn't have a strong opinion either way, he did say something during this conversation that was quite profound:

I don't know how you can believe in love and not believe in God.

While, up until this point, we hadn't had very deep conversations, this really stuck with me, and it helped me to see, too, some of the healing he had done in this lifetime.

It was about six months after this experience in Las Vegas when these past-life occurrences started to happen regularly. While I don't have a recollection of asking my Guides and Angels for help clearing these, my sense is that I had a soul contract or agreement to help in clearing this energy, so that I could move even higher vibrationally and to free myself even further, if and when I was ready. Either that, or in a roundabout way, I had asked for this, and they, always wanting to help, obliged.

It was in April, and I had booked a new place to stay in Santa Fe, as my usual place wasn't available. While I typically check in intuitively anytime I'm booking a new place, I remember looking for a quick solution and forcing it a bit, just so I could check it off my list. I do also think I was meant to stay there, so I wasn't meant to see it clearly ahead of time.

I have to say, that in my head, before I arrived, I was thinking she was one of my "peeps." When I say one of my peeps, many times, as I'm traveling, I run into older women who are into spirituality. Her picture matched this idea that I had in my head, but when I arrived at the door, while I was hoping for the best, I didn't feel connected to her, at least not in a good way.

As she began to show me around her place, she had a very particular, strict way about her, even at one point pulling me aggressively into the bathroom to make sure I saw the conserving water sign. This made me uncomfortable, but I didn't think too much about it, as I was staying with her for three nights and my old pattern is to override my inner feeling and pretend everything is ok, even when I am beginning to sense differently.

So, I started going about my business, and everything initially started out okay. I had plans to meet a friend that night, so I got ready and headed out.

When I got back, I walked into the bathroom and noticed all of my stuff had been moved. I don't like when people touch my stuff without my permission, and she had made it a particular point to mention the "private bath." So this, coupled with the fact that it was clear someone had used the bathroom, while my non-confrontational self almost didn't, I decided to ask her via text if we were sharing the bathroom. She came running out of her bedroom, insisting that this wasn't the case, that she had a half bath in her room. To someone who reads energy, her response felt protective, and really that she had been "found out."

To be clear, I didn't care that we were sharing a bathroom. What I did care about, though, was if she was lying to me. While it's abusive to lie to anyone, it's especially abusive to lie to an Intuitive, as they can shut down their truth and reality. When this happens, an Intuitive gives their power away and can think that what they know or are getting isn't true. Then, they make themselves smaller to be around this person, contracting their body and moving out of their own truth. Understandably, this is a very unhealthy and unsafe place for an Intuitive to be, as they can shut down their gifts with this.

Personally, I had had enough experiences with this, and I wanted to make sure this didn't happen again. For me, too, even outside of this, I have a particular charge around being lied to. Yes, I know no one likes getting lied to, but, for me, being lied to takes me back to the pain of my childhood and living in an environment that was full of subconscious lies, the biggest of which were me lying to myself about how much I had been hurt and that things were okay, even when they weren't.

Her response to my question was coupled with the fact that it was clear she didn't trust people, which included everything from the fact that she didn't give you a key to her house to none of her silverware being in her kitchen. There's an old saying that what people say about and do toward others is really about them, and this lack of trust to me implied she wasn't trustworthy.

In any case, I brushed it off. After all, I didn't want to get in a fight with her, as I still had a lot of time that I was staying at her place.

When I got back the next night from being gone all day, I noticed the toilet paper roll had been changed, which was odd, as when I had left, I remembered there being almost a full roll. (I have a photographic memory.)

I was pretty convinced at that point she had lied to me, but I decided to Google her property to reinforce my knowing. Of course, it did pull up as a two bedroom, one bath.

At that point, I remember feeling really angry. *Why was she lying to me?* As my anger built, her lying threw me into an old obsessing pattern, which continued late into the night.

When I woke up the next morning, I remember listening for the toilet. I thought about "busting" her, but it didn't feel like a good use of my energy, and truth be told, I was feeling less and less safe around her. If she was willing to lie about this, which I assumed was for the money, what else would she be willing to do?

So, I went about my day and made a decision I would leave it alone and just get through the night. I was leaving early the next morning, and I had planned to be out most of the day and evening, so I could make it through just one more night.

Best-laid plans.

That night when I got back, she started offering me random information I had never asked about and didn't care to know about, things like the fact that her toothbrush and toothpaste were in the refrigerator because of the centipedes in the bathroom. This wasn't the first time she had done this, and to me, again, this was just another telltale sign that she was lying.

So, I went against my better judgment and ended up asking her again about sharing the bathroom.

"My, you're suspicious," she responded. (I instinctually knew she was projecting her stuff onto me.)

She walked into her bedroom, and as I started to prepare my dinner, while it didn't happen right away, a strong fear started to build inside of me. I went to the bedroom and realized I couldn't lock the bedroom door. I started thinking about her lack of knives in her kitchen. I started thinking about how I was in the middle of nowhere. I also started thinking people had killed for less.

It was in that moment that I had a strong fear of death staying in her house. The awareness was coming through me that she had killed me in another lifetime, and I didn't want history to repeat itself. I knew I had to leave—*immediately.*

I began quietly packing my things. I was honestly terrified she was going to come out and hurt me.

One by one, I took my stuff out to the car, being extremely careful not to drag my luggage across the floor or make any noise.

I checked to make sure I took everything that I really wanted—*I was not coming back*—and I left and drove off into the pitch-black night, a mixed sense of heightened adrenaline and relief rushing over me.

It was later that night, as I was safely lying in my hotel bed in Albuquerque, that the awareness came through me as to why I was drawn to this woman.

It's important for you to clear this and, really, the energy of killing, in your field.

I was exhausted and heading back to Chicago early the next morning, but I made a commitment to myself that I would clear this and heal this within myself. (Looking back, while I know my reaction to her and sharing the bathroom wasn't rational, I believe I was meant to remember this past-life energy, so that I could heal it.)

The third time I had another past-life meeting was when I was in Michigan finishing up my book, just a few weeks later. I was staying at this beautiful house on a lake in Michigan, two hours from Chicago. From the pictures, it looked like the perfect place to have some quiet writing time and relaxation.

Everything started off just fine. I got there, and the house was pretty much how I expected it. The view was breathtaking, and while I had been having a week that had thrown me off, I was prepared to relax and get to work.

The next morning, as planned, I started writing. I wrote for several hours, and around lunchtime, I decided it was time to sit outside, to really enjoy the beautiful day and view. But, as I walked through the sunroom, an infestation of stink bugs overwhelmed me, so much so that I emailed the owner, in fear that I had left something open and they had snuck in. He told me this wasn't the case, though, and no matter what they did, they couldn't keep these bugs out of the house. Yuck! He mentioned asking the next-door neighbor, whom I'll call "John" and who was also the groundskeeper, for bug spray.

So, I went about my day, and headed outside, trying to pretend the bug situation inside where I was planning on staying for a week wasn't a big deal.

It was then that I ran into John. He was on his lawn mower. He seemed friendly and wanted to make sure he wasn't disturbing me, though almost immediately, I detected this strong, dominant energy coming from him that didn't feel quite right. I instinctually knew, though, that he was "safe" and that I wasn't in danger, and on the outside, he appeared to be very kind. I just was keenly aware that a big piece of what I was experiencing was an energy from a past life.

Throughout the course of the week, I'd occasionally see him outside and we'd be friendly. He even invited me to borrow his kayak, which I wasn't sure I'd take him up on, only because I felt the need to be "all-business" and hyper-focused on my book.

It was late Friday, my last day there, when I decided I was going to take him up on his offer and take the kayak out that evening. I went down to where it was and realized it was too heavy for me to

328 • LIVING DEEPLY

carry on my own, so I went looking for him. He popped out of his house (literally!) and came down to the water area to help me get the kayak in the water.

It wasn't too much later, sitting out in the water, that I finally had a chance to be present with what was, and asked about my past-life connection with John. At this point, I had been on a roll running into past-life killers, so one of the first questions that came up to ask was this. We had been a couple, and yes, he had, but it was an accidental killing from regular physical abuse. In that moment, I knew I was brought to him to make amends with this. So, as I sat on the lake, watching the sunset, listening to Joe Cocker (one of my faves!), I decided I would look at this further when I got back to Chicago.

Three hours later, I pulled the kayak back in, and his beautiful dog, with white fluffy hair mixed in with some brown and black lines, came running up to me to say hello. He came out, and we started chatting.

It came up that he was previously in the advertising specialties business with his wife, and that his wife and I had worked at the same company. *Small world.*

What I found most interesting about our conversation, though, was that he kept mentioning how I should meet his wife, implying she was inside, though I instinctually knew she wasn't. *There was no one else inside the house.* I wondered why he was saying this, though I didn't press it, as I was leaving the next morning. It did feel like he was covering something up, though, and I couldn't tell if it was his pride, perhaps because she had left, or because he was trying to cover up something darker. My gut said she had left, but what's the old saying about history repeating itself?

That following morning, after I loaded and was sitting in my car, with my head down, getting directions for my next stop, he was standing outside of my car and surprised me. He was trying not to scare me, but since I wasn't looking, I jumped, which to me, was an interesting reflection of the energy that I had perceived.

He had come up to say goodbye, and as he did, he shared again that his wife wanted to meet me, which to me was weird, as if she wanted to meet me, and was *really* there, wouldn't she have just come outside? I didn't push any further, and before I drove off, he invited me to stop by his place anytime I was driving through to meet his wife. While it was a generous offer made from the right place, I knew I wouldn't take him up on it for many reasons, including our past-life history and the fact that he was acting strangely about his wife, and in the event she wasn't there, I didn't want to find out if history would repeat itself for me.

It was after this occurrence that I started asking my Guides to bring me "softer," less intense ways to clear this past-life energy; I was sick of living with and next to my past-life killers. They obliged and started switching it up, bringing me people I had killed in other lifetimes.

The first time this occurred was on a flight to Boise. It's so interesting how, in this life, you don't know you know someone, but you're immediately drawn to their energy. Such was the case with this older woman, who was sitting at the end of a row at a gate at O'Hare Airport. I was looking for a place to sit and was pulled to her. We looked at each other and smiled, and she offered that I could use the plug to charge my phone, though I didn't have my charger handy and didn't think much of it.

As we boarded the plane, I realized we were seated next to each other. At first, I felt relieved. Oddly enough, or not so oddly, while there were a ton of empty seats on the plane, when I went to go assign a seat, the only seats that were available they were charging extra for. I live in an inherent state of trust that things are always working out for me, so I went through the check-in process, and a window seat was auto-assigned. No big deal, I thought, figuring I'd try to get an aisle seat again at the airport. They were only showing window seats there as well, though, and since I was looking for an aisle, I left it alone.

So, initially, as I sat down, we started talking like old friends, which when I had run into her inside of the airport, I thought we actually might have been in another lifetime.

Either way, she seemed nice, though the conversation quickly turned when I started talking about my work. Typically, I'm very careful about what I say about my work, but intuitively, I heard what to say, so I shared it. She immediately shut down, and that was the end of us talking.

In truth, in that moment, I felt set up by my Guides, but I knew it had a purpose, so I relaxed into it. After all, I was starting to get used to "weird" interactions, and I was starting to get hyperaware of whom I was being drawn to, and most importantly, *why*.

It was about halfway through the flight when I started to get visions. I saw myself as a tall, big, African-American man with a chain around my neck, being dragged by this woman, who felt like the woman who was sitting next to me. Then, I saw myself killing her.

Oh, that's why we're sitting together.

I found myself amused, obviously not because I had killed her, but because this was becoming a regular occurrence, and her response to me was priceless. I only wondered what her reaction would have been had I shared *this* with her.

The last time I had a past-life occurrence was on my most recent trip to Boise. I found myself at a Saturday night dance and, while you could tell that most of the people were used to their regular cliques, one of the ladies there was immediately friendly, so much so that at the end of the evening, we got each other's numbers and decided to go on a walk the following day.

On the walk, we felt like old friends. We each were sharing vulnerable pieces of ourselves, and we were talking openly, which was quite nice. I was really enjoying my time with her.

It was at some point during that walk or shortly after, when, again, I started getting visions. Of course, I was already being hypervigilant about checking in around past-life killers and killings, as I knew, at this particular juncture in my life, I was being called to clear these.

So, as I checked in, I would see her coming at me, but then when I would ask if she killed me, I would get a no, which was confusing to me. Then, when I asked if I killed her, I got a yes, but what I felt was that she had initiated the fight, which ended up in her death. In any case, I marked it on the docket to be healed.

LIFE LESSONS AND LEARNINGS

How to Identify If You've Known Someone in Another Lifetime

Six years ago, when I initially started this journey, if you had told me that I would be able to read past lives, this would have seemed very far out there for me. But, what I think most of us don't realize is that everything is energy, and being energy beings, we have the ability to read energy, including past lives, when we are tuned into it.

Would I consider this more of an advanced technique? Yes, I would. But, is it possible, and even likely, especially the more work you do on yourself? Absolutely.

Before this, while I wasn't tuned into past lives per se, I was tuned into my connection with another person, and I did have a sense, especially when I felt strongly about someone, that I had likely known them before. I just never took this any further to look at it and investigate it, as I didn't have the skill set at that time to really dig deeper.

That being said, I always believed in past lives, as while I couldn't always tell you what these were, I just knew in my heart that these had been part of my journey.

QUESTIONS:

- Do you believe in past lives? Why or why not? If you don't, is this because it's something you've learned? If so, does believing this feel true for you or do you believe this for fear of being made wrong for your beliefs or being outcast or not loved? (One way to tell this, is truth often feels light in our body. That being said, if we're scared of subconsciously being persecuted for a belief, our wiring may get mixed up and this is where truth can feel heavy. For example, say your parents believe it's wrong to have tattoos. If you have a desire to get a tattoo, but it feels heavy or like a no in your body, it may be that subconsciously you took on your parents' beliefs around the idea of getting a tattoo. From this perspective, it would be hard to tell what's really true for you, especially if you've taken on their beliefs as your own or you're worried about not being loved, or maybe even abandoned, for doing something that they don't believe in.) Important to note here: All there is, is love, and we are meant to be happy, so anything that is the rooted in the opposite of this is generally not love or truth. Of course, this is a much more in-depth conversation, but again, if something feels light in your body AND it's rooted in love, it's generally based on universal truth. Either way, whether you believe in past lives or not, both are completely okay. Right now, where I am on my journey, this is my truth. Wherever you are on your journey is great. Own that. I'm just sharing these tools with you, as they have been an important key on my journey in helping me to own my truth, to better understand myself and to heal to return to all that there is, which is love (i.e., if I'm carrying hurt around, this is the opposite of all that there is. When I can release this, I resonate more wholly and fully back into the truth of who I am, which is love).

Tools:

Once you've identified what's true for you with the above, if you do believe in past lives, and you want to begin to identify them, here are a few steps on how to do this. Keep in mind that, again, while I've seen a few people born with this gift, for many of us, getting very clear on this usually comes with a lot of personal growth work and clearing your old childhood patterns, which, many times, block us from seeing the truth clearly. As these are cleared, though, we are able to connect to our truths and, with this, other realms and dimensions, where identifying past lives is a lot more easily done and where past lives can be read much more accurately. Obviously, until you cross over, there is no way to guarantee that you're reading this 100% accurately, but I've found anything we can do to return to our truth is the key to higher and higher accuracy.

In the meantime, here's what I recommend:

1. Trust your sense of this.
Many times, even before I had done any of this work, I would have a sense that I had known someone before. Many times, especially when there's no attachment involved (for example, wanting to know that you've known the person you're dating before), this sense is accurate. Pay attention to this.

2. Ask questions.
The more I was able to read my yes, maybe and no, the more I could ask questions like, "Have I known this person before?" and get a clear answer. (I walk you through a brief exercise of this in Chapter 22. In my Connecting to Your Intuition Workshop, which you can purchase at deborahacker.com, I walk the class through a more in-depth exercise to begin to get connected to your yeses, maybes and nos, in addition to many awesome exercises to connect to your intuition.)

3. Keep clearing your childhood patterns.

I give a ton of tools in this book to clear childhood patterns, but this is definitely one of the biggest keys to getting connected to yourself and, with this, to be able to connect to the unconscious, subconscious and unseen.

How to Clear Past-Life Energy

Up until this point, I had never thought about clearing past-life energy. But, as this came into my field, I realized that this was a powerful way to heal myself and return to love.

Questions:

- Do you believe you can clear past-life energy, and if so, does this feel important to do on your journey? If so, use the below tool to start to do this.

Tools:

Again, this is a very advanced exercise, but we all have the ability to do this. When you are ready, here's an exercise to get you started:

1. After you have identified that you've known someone before and there's a feeling that there's some energy to clear, begin by closing your eyes, taking some nice deep breaths and getting present.

2. Once you feel present, feel this person's energy or role from this other lifetime. Then notice, do you feel mad, overwhelmed, angry, sad? Whatever it is, allow yourself to sit with it and feel it. Notice if any visions or anything you sense pops up, as this can be helpful in keying into the energy that

is there. Then, keep feeling it, until you feel the energy open, release and get lighter. Typically, if you choose to be super present with this, it doesn't have to take long, sometimes only a few minutes.

3. Once you've done this, check in and see if there's anything else you need to clear with this person, and if so, repeat this process again until everything that needs to be cleared is cleared or you are guided to stop until a later date.

Important to note: With many of these relationships, there were other ways I was guided to fully clear the energy. This exercise is a great starting point, though.

CHAPTER 43

Connection knows no time and space.

THANKFULLY, INTERMIXED WITH THESE PAST-LIFE EXPERIENCES HAVE ALSO BEEN SOME AMAZING CONNECTIONS.

One of these first ones also began a couple of years ago. I received an email with my mom's name in the subject line. Of course, that caught my attention!

In the email, there was a woman stating she was related to my great grandpa Max, my grandma Roz's father, on one of his brother's sides. Not too long before, I had realized Max was one of my Guides.

In any case, she was confirming if we were related, and at some point, mentioned their annual family reunion.

Behind her invitation, I could feel the magic that lay underneath. To me, I can feel all of the work that went into this synchronistic meeting, both in the physical world and with my Guides, especially Max, and one, if not more, of his brothers, too, on the other side.

It was cool, too, as when I went to my first family reunion, while

I had not met any of the 100-plus people that were there before in this lifetime, I absolutely felt like I was around my family and that I had known many of these people before.

It ended up being quite the enjoyable experience, and it was interesting as the family of another one of Max's brothers was there as well. They, too, hadn't met any of this side of the family's relatives.

It was on that side of the family where I found my closest connections, and I believe, too, that one of them was even my mother in another lifetime.

While I didn't make this connection at our first meeting, it did hit me, when we met for the second time, close to a year later. While there were several of my family members all spending time together that day, through much of our conversations, it may as well have only been the two of us. We even look alike, though she is closer to my mother's age. In talking with her, too, while she hadn't fully made the connection, she said that even in the first meeting that she knew "something was there" and confirmed, after we had spent a weekend together, with some of our other family members, that, while she didn't fully understand why, she had felt strong motherly feelings toward me, feelings that she had only felt for her daughter in this lifetime.

This was and has been pretty special, especially as our relationship continues to grow, and we are given the opportunity to pick up where we left off. For me, every time we talk, it feels like I'm home.

Either way, I know, as all of these relationships are unfolding on this side of my family, I can definitely see why I was destined to meet so many of these family members. For me, these relationships have been a beautiful combination of connection, support and synchronicity, all rolled into one.

LIFE LESSONS AND LEARNINGS

Opening to Possibilities and Leaning Into Magic, Miracles and Synchronicity

This experience of attending a family reunion with 100-plus "strangers" was a beautiful opportunity for me to trust and to see I'm always being guided.

When I first heard from my cousin, I knew forces from the other side had drawn us together. Then, when she invited me to our family reunion, I just knew I had to be there.

While this may have been intimidating for some, for me, I knew there was magic in it if I could lean in.

Of course, it turned out that there were so many gifts in it for me, gifts that continue to open and keep coming. I even recently spent my birthday at my cousin's lake house in Wisconsin.

This doesn't factor in one of the biggest gifts—reconnecting with my other cousin, whom I believe was my mother in a past life. It's amazing, as when we connect, I feel like we open a portal to another time and place. Our conversations can last for hours, and there's always more to talk about. I just know we were meant to meet and reconnect in this life.

QUESTIONS:

- Where do you shut yourself off from possibilities and connection, and with this, magic, miracles and synchronicity? Instead, how can you choose to stay open to what the Universe has in store for you?

Tools:

If you're desiring, here's how to invite more magic, miracles and synchronicity into your life:

1. Notice where you shut down.
In the example I shared, would you have shut down in any part of the process?

As part of this, would you have gone to a family reunion with over 100 people you didn't know? If not, this can be an area where we block opportunities.

In these situations, it's important to notice this, open your body by relaxing your shoulders, placing your hand on your heart and taking some deep breaths.

Also, as part of this, are you saying no because this is how you learned to show up or because it just doesn't feel right? This can be tricky to distinguish, but see if it feels light or heavy in your body, as again, lightness can be an indicator of truth as well as fun.

2. Choose anew.
If you have a history of shutting down and closing yourself to new possibilities, I recommend choosing anew and trying something different. With this, if you do choose this, it's important to go into whatever you're choosing with a positive attitude, knowing that if you go into it with negativity, that you will likely create a negative experience to be right.

3. Then, notice the magic, miracles and synchronicity.
I mentioned this in Chapter 24 with another perspective in Chapter 37, but it's important to reiterate. When something unique happens

as well as when you're going through everyday life, notice the magic, miracles and synchronicity that are occurring. We get more of what we put our focus on, so this last one is important.

CHAPTER 44

The magic lies in the unknown.

ANOTHER ONE OF THESE FUN PAST-LIFE CONNECTIONS OCCURRED ON MY TRAVELS. With the recent upswing of people opening their homes to stay in, I found myself staying in certain people's homes that I've felt drawn to. Typically, these were positive experiences.

It was on one such time that I found myself at a couple's house in the Denver area. During my stay there, while I felt connected to both of them, I was especially drawn to the woman.

During this trip, over the course of my stay, we had many late-night chats, and she was extremely generous with offering referrals for my business. On this first stay there, though, I didn't actually check in or make any past-life connections.

It was on my second stay there, right around the time this was coming more prevalently into my life, when I became very aware of our past-life connection. She was like family to me, and this feeling drew me to check in and ask.

While initially I thought she was my mom in a past life, as she had become more like a mother figure (as well as a friend) to me in this lifetime, I believe that I was her mom in one lifetime, and she was my dad or stepdad in another. (In the lifetime when I was her mom, we had one of those relationships where, even though she was the kid, she took care of me, which is why my strongest memory and feeling of her was that of a parent.)

Either way, I continue to stay at her and her husband's home, and each time we talk, we have a beautiful connection and our relationship and friendship grows.

On a side note, she recently sent me a message on Facebook that I didn't think was meant for me. When I wrote her back, asking about this, she said it was meant for her sister. This made me smile inside, as, reflecting on our past lives, I thought to myself, *"Of course it was!"*

LIFE LESSONS AND LEARNINGS

THE VALUE OF PAST-LIFE CONNECTIONS

For me, knowing of past-life connections with someone has helped to create a deeper closeness. I notice I feel safer and more connected to them. While, of course, I don't need this to cultivate that, it has helped me to forge stronger, more meaningful relationships quicker. Plus, I find it fun, as many times, I'm having a dual experience as we connect. This experience is the one that's happening in the present moment and the one that has already occurred.

QUESTIONS:

- Would you open to identifying past-life connections if they could help you in your life and business/work in addition to feeling safer and more taken care of? If not, why?

Tools:

In Chapter 42, I talked about how to begin to identify this, if this is something you're interested in. Another thing that could be a fun exercise to help you to identify these is to make a list of the people in your life that you feel closest to. Then, notice how they've supported and helped you, knowing that what we focus on, grows. From there, if you do want to identify your past-life connection(s), start to ask questions to get clarity on this. Was this person (insert full name here) my parent, sibling, friend, etc.? (It is important to be specific to get the clearest answer possible, again using the Yes/No/Maybe tool shared in Chapter 22, and if you get a sense of something, *trust that*.)

With this, note the answers you get. Have you previously been connected to the people you feel the closest to in this lifetime? How have these past relationships fostered richer, more positive and easier experiences for you? Write these down.

CHAPTER 45

With death comes the opportunity for new life.

ONE OTHER BEAUTIFUL PIECE THAT CAME FROM LEARNING HOW TO WORK WITH MY INTUITION AND THE MYSTICAL, AND REALLY, ENERGY, WAS MY EXPERIENCE OF FUNERALS. Earlier I shared with you how the experience of connecting with my mom on the other side changed as I opened to my innate ability to connect with energy. (We are all made up of energy, and while depending on how old a soul you are, this may or may not be easier for you, I believe we all have the ability to tune in if we do the work and practice.)

While the earlier part of my life had a lot of death in it, more recently, I hadn't been to a lot of funerals since I had developed my ability to connect with the other side.

So, it was an unexpected and interesting experience when recently I attended a funeral for a dear family friend. While I hadn't known him well in recent years, in years past, I had taught him and his wife Pilates at their home. (Yes, I used to teach all kinds of exercise classes, including this!) I remember what an adorable couple they were, and how they interacted with each other. You could just feel the love, and I always thought of both of them as family.

So, when I received the devastating news that the husband in this couple was sick, and then subsequently had passed away from pancreatic cancer, my heart broke. Death is always hard, and I think it can be awkward when you don't have a specific role in the family, and yet care deeply for the person who has passed.

So, it was important to me to attend his funeral and offer any support I could to his family and loved ones, especially his wife, whom I adore.

All this said, I did not expect the experience I ended up having at his funeral.

It was when I walked into the Chapel area, after I offered my condolences to his family and sat down, when I saw it, or really, *him*, through my third eye. I was a bit surprised, but after everything that I had experienced at this point, I guess I shouldn't have been.

As more and more people entered the chapel, I began watching him experiencing his own funeral! It was cute, as you could tell he was interested to see who had come out to say goodbye. To me, too, this was eye-opening and oddly comforting at the same time.

Then, as the funeral began, and as his loved ones began sharing their stories, I watched his response to each share, and the ways that many times, he would try to comfort his loved ones with a hand on the back or shoulder, when they would get choked up and the words struggled to come out.

This was such a different experience of death and being at a funeral, as if you had known me in previous years and decades, no matter who had passed, whether it was someone close to me or someone I barely knew, I was in tears. Many times, I was the most emotional person in the room.

Of course, while I didn't realize this at the time, a big part of this experience was due in part to being an Empath, but to shift from being a slobbering mess to feeling joy and connection, of course, mixed in with the sadness my human side felt along with deep compassion and understanding for the grieving and what they were experiencing, was huge.

For me, this experience was transforming, and I was really grateful to experience a funeral this way, given that so many funerals, especially funerals of loved ones I had barely known, had caused me so much pain.

It's important to note that having this experience did not negate the importance of feeling what was up for me.

When I had heard the news of his prognosis and then of his death, shortly after, I was devastated. I was reminded of the times I had spent with him and his family and also the little ways he would show he cared, especially how he would always ask about my sister and my work. I was also devastated for his family, especially his wife. I had written her a note to share my feelings of him, and really, spending time with them, the same morning he had passed away, before I had found out the news. It was as I wrote that note that I experienced my grief. I found myself sobbing, though I didn't fully understand why, until after I heard of his passing. (I think I was feeling his wife's grief mixed in with mine.)

For me, though, this experience at his funeral was really about having a dual experience. Given our relationship, and where I was on my journey, this felt right, but this may or may not feel right, depending on your relationship with the deceased and where you are on your path.

It was after his funeral, too, at their home, when I tried to comfort his wife, letting her know softly that he was with her and just wanted her to be okay. Of course, it was a message she wasn't ready to take in, but I did feel a gentle nudge to say it.

LIFE LESSONS AND LEARNINGS

FEELING OUR FEELINGS

Throughout this book, I've written about different elements of feeling our feelings. In this section, I want to emphasize the importance of feeling any pain you're going through, especially when a loved one has crossed over, and not doing what is commonly known as a spiritual bypass, where you go right to the higher awareness, saying things like "This happened for a reason or was meant to happen" and "He's not really dead."

This is not healthy and goes against everything that I believe we're meant to do when going through difficult experiences. During challenges, especially death, it's important we feel our pain, knowing that it comes in waves, and that both experiences, grieving and knowing they're still around us, can be held side by side. Also, when these can't be held side by side, it's important to choose your grief first. (There will be a time and place when you can really be open to their presence from the other side, but for me, for instance, with my mom, while I always knew she was around me, had I tried to go there before I had truly dealt with my grief, it wouldn't have been healthy.)

Also, again, if you are an Empath, know that you can use your emotions for good. For me, too, I wish I had known I was an Empath, as this would have explained many of my experiences at funerals where I wasn't super close to the loved one that had passed and yet I was super emotional.

QUESTIONS:

- Do you spiritually bypass? How so? Why do you do this and in what situations?

- How can you use your hypersensitivity for good? (In addition to using this gift in my work, I also use it to relate and express compassion in difficult times.)

Tools:

When spiritually bypassing:
If you find yourself spiritually bypassing, I recommend using one of the practices in this book to sit with your inner child and ask them why they are doing that and what they are scared to feel. Then, sit and be with it, until you are ready to feel it. Then, go there.

When feeling overwhelmed by emotions:
Know this doesn't have to be a bad thing. I know in our society we're taught that being emotional or too emotional, is wrong, but when you allow yourself to be all of you, which if you're an Empath like me, means feeling everything, this is when you actually feel in control of your life and your emotions because you're no longer trying to hold them back. You're just being the deep-feeling being that you are, and this is when they no longer overtake you and you're no longer making yourself wrong. When this happens, others around you reflect this.

For me, too, when I'm feeling, I'm living, and when I go *there*, it never fails that my emotions take me higher—*always*.

Connecting to the Other Side

Throughout this book, I've talked about our Guides and Angels and different ways to build a relationship with our loved ones on the other side. With what I've described, I want to add one more thing.

Before I started studying this work, often I might see or sense a loved one from the other side, but I would think this was just my imagination. As I starting studying this, and practicing connecting with the other side, though, I began to recognize what this looked like and that my experiences of my loved ones were actually my loved ones coming through. With this, I remember being at my friend's funeral years earlier, and distinctly feeling him next to me. Of course, at the time, I dismissed this, but looking back, had I been able to fully own and recognize this during that difficult time, it may have been more comforting.

As part of this, I started to realize when someone was talking about a loved one who had passed that I didn't know, and I got a vision, that, if it was someone whom I felt comfortable asking, they would confirm that my vision was accurate. This can be an important part in developing this gift.

Also, important to note: If you don't believe in this and this is weird or "out there" for you, that's okay, too. For me, I wish someone had walked me through what I was seeing and experiencing, as this would have helped bring more clarity and comfort in my life. If you're not ready for this, though, that's okay, and if you are ready for this, these tools and awarenesses will definitely help.

QUESTION:

- Do you want to connect with the other side? If so, use the below tools to help start to open to what this looks like for you. (It looks different for everyone.)

Tools:

If you are wanting to connect with the other side, when a loved one pops in, ask inside if this is your imagination or them coming through. You may hear or see a yes or a no or it might be more subtle, where you get a feeling or knowing about it. Whatever the case, it's important to tune in and trust your sense of what is coming through.

As part of this, too, when it feels right, if you have a friend or family member talking about a loved one on the other side, if you get a sense of something, ask them about it. This will help you to confirm what you're getting. I've done this before, and it can be very helpful in reinforcing your experience.

You'll notice, as you do this more and more, that you'll start to recognize when and how a loved one is coming through and that this is not just your "imagination."

Then, from there, when you're desiring guidance or connection, it will be easier to tune in and really feel the support that's always there for you, when we are connected.

CHAPTER 46

One of the greatest journeys our soul can take is the path to forgiveness. For it's on this path where we discover ourselves and what we are made of.

IT WASN'T TOO LONG AFTER THIS WHEN IT HIT ME. It was Father's Day weekend, just shy of six years from when I had started this journey, though it had really been a lifetime, and I was getting a card for my dad. As I stood in the drugstore picking out my card, it hit me.

For the first time ever, all I felt toward my dad was love. *No anger. No hurt. No resentment. Just love.*

As this feeling rushed through me, I felt my heart swell and tears flooding my eyes.

Holy crap. This was a big one.

Prior to this, no matter how much forgiveness work I had done on my dad, for as long as I can remember, I withheld love from him for the pain I had experienced when I was a kid, and up until now, no matter how much he reached out to me or how much love he showed, as he, too, had changed with me, this was always a part of my experience with him.

As I wrote the words, "I love you, Dad, and I'm grateful you're my dad," on his Father's Day card, though, I realized that this was complete. I felt all of this love filling my heart, love that I wanted to share with him and give to him fully and wholeheartedly.

So, this is what true forgiveness feels like?! Hell, yeah!!

I couldn't believe I had done it, and I felt overwhelmed with pride, joy and excitement. (If you had told me when I started this journey that this was even possible, and most importantly, that I would feel this free, I don't know that I would have believed you.)

With this realization, though, came the closing of this chapter, and really, this book, in my life.